Activism and

Activism and the Policy Process

edited by

Anna Yeatman

ALLEN & UNWIN

First published in 1998 by
Allen & Unwin
9 Atchison Street
St Leonards NSW 1590
Australia
Phone: (61 2) 8425 0100
Fax: (61 2) 9906 2218
E-mail: frontdesk@allen-unwin.com.au
Web: http://www.allen-unwin.com.au

National Library of Australia
Cataloguing-in-Publication entry:

Activism and the policy process.

  Bibliography.
  Includes index.
  ISBN 1 86448 704 6.

  1. Policy sciences. 2. Political planning—Citizen participation.
  I. Yeatman, Anna.

320.60994

Set in 10/13pt Sabon by DOCUPRO, Sydney
Printed by SRM Production Services SDN BHD, Malaysia

10 9 8 7 6 5 4 3 2 1

Contents

v

Acknowledgments

Thanks are due to all the contributors for their willingness to be rounded up into this collection, its conception, and for their good will in continuing to work on their chapters and to refine them. Special thanks are due to Elizabeth Morrow who has been the research assistant working with me on this collection. She has had most of the difficulty and tedium of sheepdogging contributor missing references, checking Allen & Unwin style guidelines, reading copy for consistency and sense, and generally ensuring that we finally got a manuscript together. Thanks are also due to John Iremonger for his view that a collection on policy activism sounded like a good idea.

Anna Yeatman
Editor

Contributors

Deborah Brennan is a senior lecturer in the Department of Government and Public Administration, University of Sydney. She was a founding member of the National Association of Community Based Children's Services and has been a long-term academic/activist in the area of Australian child care policy. The second edition of her book *The Politics of Australian Child Care* will be published by Cambridge University Press in 1998. She is also a member of the Board of the Australian Council of Social Services (ACOSS).

Glyn Davis is an Australian Research Council fellow at Griffith University, and writes about public policy, public management and Australian politics. He was previously Director-General of the Office of the Cabinet in Queensland and served on the Republic Advisory Committee. His most recent projects have been studies of participation in decision-making for the Organisation for Economic Co-operation and Development and the New South Wales Government.

Gary Dowsett is currently an associate professor and deputy director of the Centre for the Study of Sexually Transmissible Diseases, La Trobe University. Before that, he was a lecturer in Sociology at Macquarie University after having spent a number of years as the leading social researcher in the HIV/AIDS Centre for Social Research at Macquarie. He cut his queer teeth on Gay Liberation in Adelaide in the mid-1970s and has continued his close association with gay community activism since then in Sydney throughout the 1980s and early 1990s, before moving to Melbourne in 1997. His book *Practicing Desire: Homosexual Sex in the Era of AIDS* was published in 1996 by Stanford University Press.

Paul Dugdale is a medical practitioner and specialist in public health medicine. A member of the Doctors' Reform Society, he has worked in general practice, hospital administration, health service planning and health promotion. He was private secretary to the Commonwealth Minister for Health (Dr Neal Blewett) from 1988 to 1990. He holds masters degrees in sociology and public health, and is undertaking a PhD on health financing at the University of Sydney.

Gael Fraser runs her own consultancy business in social policy, planning and intergovernmental relations. Prior to this she worked in senior executive positions in the Department of Premier and Cabinet in the South Australian government. She was the project director for the governance review of the Adelaide City Council. 1997–98.

Andrew Gonzci is the Dean of the Faculty of Education at University of Technology Sydney. He began his working life in the legal profession and he has maintained an interest in the role of professions in society. Since he began his career in education he has been interested in the nature of professional education and the basis on which registration for practice is granted. The competency agenda provided an opportunity for him to consider the educational and especially the assessment issues associated with the professions and other occupations.

Paul Hager is presently an associate professor and the Research Co-ordinator of the Faculty of Education, University of Technology Sydney. His early career experiences as a TAFE teacher, coupled with his studies in philosophy, made him highly critical of the way vocational education is misperceived both in the academic world and in educational thought generally. The competencies agenda provided an opportunity to foreground the richness and complexity of sound vocational education. He is currently conducting further research in occupational competence, workplace learning and professional practice.

Gar Jones is Director of the Research Office at the University of Western Sydney, Nepean. He has been with UWS since 1990, and has overseen tremendous growth in research activity in a post-Dawkins university. Not unexpectedly, his research interests are focused on issues relating to the development of a research culture and analysis of factors influencing research productivity. Prior to his current appointment, he worked in the community sector, focusing especially on issues relating to income security for the aged. He is a published poet and has written a musical drama (*Absolutely Weill*) which was performed at the 1990 Adelaide Festival.

Alison Lee is a senior lecturer in the School of Adult Education at the University of Technology Sydney. Her research has been primarily concerned with literacy and the construction of knowledge in all education sectors. Most recently she has been researching questions of pedagogy and the formation of disciplines in the Australian PhD. Her concern with questions of methodology in discourse analysis has resulted in a collection, co-edited with Cate Poynton, *Culture and Text: Discourse and Methodology in Social Research and Cultural Studies*, forthcoming Allen & Unwin.

Julie Nyland is a consultant working as a partner in Bradfield/Nyland Group whose logo is 'breaking new ground'. Their consultancies tend to be oriented to community management, policy and programme development, and resource and training kits. For many years, Nyland was a lecturer in the School of Management, University of Technology, Sydney, and, prior to that, a policy activist working in the area of women's housing. She began her first employment experience in the community sector at Elsie Women's Refuge in 1975 whence she acquired the skills and identity as a policy activist.

Cate Poynton is Director of the Women's Research Centre of the University of Western Sydney, Nepean. Her expertise is in discourse analysis informed by both linguistics and broader Foucauldian conceptions of discourse. Her research focuses on language in the negotiation of social relations with special attention to gender. She has undertaken textual analyses of a range of material concerned with diverse sites such as the discursive construction of women's work skills, talk radio, communication curriculum in Australian management courses, and government policy documents.

Stephanie Short is senior lecturer in the School of Health Services Management, University of New South Wales. She has been a member of the editorial committee of *Health Forum*, the journal of the Consumers Health Forum of Australia since 1991. She is a health policy resource co-ordinator for the Australian Council of Social Services, and a member of the Social Justice Reference Group which is the major source of community advice to the New South Wales Labor government on social justice.

Anna Yeatman is the professor of Sociology at Macquarie University in Sydney. Her previous appointment was as foundation professor of Women's Studies, University of Waikato (1991–1993). She is the author of *Bureaucrats, Technocrats, Femocrats* (1994), and *Postmodern Revisionings of the Political* (1994); and a co-editor of *Feminism and the Politics of Difference* (1993), *Justice and Identity* (1995) and *The New Contractualism* (1997). She was a founding member of Women's Liberation in South Australia at the end of 1969 into 1970, and, more recently, conducted the review of the first Commonwealth/State Disability Agreement 1995–96.

Tables

Introduction

ANNA YEATMAN

Conceiving this collection

Over the period 1989–96 I undertook three major evaluations. These acquainted me further with a phenomenon I had come to know well through my friendship and acquaintance with a range of public servants, public institution builders and policy makers in the 1980s. Namely, what I have come to call policy activism. For the moment, let us just call this any kind of activism which is oriented to intervention within policy, as distinct from politics. Below we will see that there is some disagreement among the contributors to this collection as to the nature of policy activism.

The policy activists I encountered were people highly motivated by some conception of social justice and who sought to make a difference in their policy work. For some of these, this meant visionary policy formulation of a kind that developed policy in a particular area; for others, it meant undertaking internal governmental consultancy work in ways which facilitated good practice in other agencies; for others, it meant scrupulous care in getting to know individuals and groups who needed to use a particular government programme and who were willing to participate in the programme's development; for still others, it meant imaginative and innovative

1

service delivery of a kind that exemplified new directions for policy development.

My evaluation work deepened my impression that here is a type of activist work that has been relatively unrecognised: namely, a highly skilled, strategic and visionary commitment to public policy and public service. My first evaluation experience was the review of the Domiciliary Care Services in South Australia in 1989. This was a review undertaken on behalf of both Commonwealth and South Australian governments in a context where 'Dom Care' had become funded primarily by the still new Home and Community Care (HACC) programme. This review acquainted me with a range of policy activists, for example a Canberra-based senior bureaucrat in the programme who was promoting the then vision of HACC as a programme for the provision of home and community-based services for anyone whose disability was such that they needed assistance with the tasks of everyday living as well as of support for the carers involved. The conception of functional disability as the basis of service need and the growing awareness of carer needs combined to make HACC an innovative programme for its time. This bureaucrat could not possibly know that her promotion of the HACC vision, which was affirmed also in the first triennial review of the HACC programme (Home and Community Care Review Working Group 1989), would turn out to be occurring on the eve of an increasingly serious rationing of resources in this programme relative to growing need and that, over the next several years, HACC would be pulled back into its core fiscal rationale—essentially a programme targeted to keeping older people out of the more expensive option of nursing home support. In 1989, the same senior bureaucrat was doing a great deal of 'walking around' HACC-based services in Australia, and was promoting the use of targeted funds to produce experimental service development which could have demonstration or lighthouse effect for the rest of the HACC system. The regional head of the relevant Commonwealth government department in South Australia at this time was an eloquent promoter of the new idea which provided much of the conceptual shape of the first triennial review of the HACC programme: that services should be designed around the needs of individuals, not the other way around.

Other types of policy activist showed themselves in the course of the domiciliary care evaluation. For example, one of the most active members of the disability movement in South Australia in the 1980s, a man with severe physical disabilities, became an active contributor to the six month review of domiciliary care services. He was prepared to use the Dom Care review to publicise his experience of service from one of the regional Dom Care agencies which he found to be not particularly user responsive: an experience which included this agency's threat to withdraw services if he continued to complain even though, or indeed because, he was entirely dependent on such service for personal care. Another example was an experienced multicultural community development worker who was able to develop a highly strategic and imaginative process of needs-based planning around the needs of older Italians in consultation with the Italian community in the eastern suburbs. A further example was an extraordinary vision-ary in service development, the physiotherapist (Sue Burnell) who, with her husband, had been responsible for the conception and origins of South Australian Domiciliary Care Services, and who continued to provide leadership oriented especially to training and developing service staff as professionals who were committed to providing creative, resourceful and client-responsive service.

What all these policy activists demonstrated was guile and cun-ning, commitment and passion, imagination and vision, good management skills and a capacity for strategic networking in their pursuit of their own distinctive policy activist agenda. Theirs is not an heroic style of activism for its effectiveness depends upon either an often subtle and quiet facilitation of the work of others or, more latterly as public resources have become more tightly rationed, an attempt to make poorly designed policies work.

When I consider what it is that so deeply impressed me about these policy activists, and those that I have since encountered, is that it is the work of such people which builds the social capital on which the work of democratic state administration depends. Their deeply and reflectively held value commitments, vision, proactivity, strategic organisation and hard work combine to produce possibilities for, and instances of, a democratic state administration which works on behalf of and develops a citizen-based community.

Entirely contrary to the managerialist idea that good management is context-indifferent, and hardly surprisingly when we consider the impassioned motivation of these policy activists, their policy activism is generally tied to experience in either one particular policy context or to a cluster of policy contexts which share similar characteristics (for example, a regional Commonwealth government public servant who, in the 1980s, worked across disability, home and community care, and the Supported Assistance Accommodation Programme). This point is even truer of those professionals who pursue policy activism within their own professional domain, for instance reforming doctors who commit to public health agendas or, as in the case of the National Schools Network, the teachers who have led the policy agenda for school reform in Australia. Take these professionals out of the context of the professionalism which motivates their vision, and their vision loses its cogency because the specificity to which it is attached is lost.

There is also an evaluator type of policy activism which is not especially well documented although it is evident in the narratives of particular evaluators and their styles of evaluation offered in Shadish, Cook and Levitan (1995). Evaluators who approach their work with the intention of contributing to better policy-making, to more enlightened social problem-solving, to more reflective practitioners, or to better practice, are likely to be policy activists of one kind or another.

In the 1990s the macro agenda of Australian public policy has been reoriented within a neo-liberal contractualism. This is an agenda which repositions the work of public policy and public administration within a public sector entrepreneurialism designed to contract out as much of the work of government as possible. The Australian public services have been 'downsized' and remaining staff asked to do a good deal more with less. This is not a context which favours positive or creative policy activism, but it is astonishing how many dedicated public servants as well as publicly-funded non-government organisation staff are using their intelligence, wisdom, commitment and strategic management capacities to make the best of this situation for the clients of the programmes and services concerned. In this context, many very good and dedicated public servants have discovered that there is a limit to how far they are willing to make this adaptation to economic rationalism, and they have left the public service, often to set up their own consultancies, or to offer leadership to non-government organisations. In many instances, including that of Gael Fraser (one of the contributors to this collection), their policy activism will have shifted to a location outside the public service but still be connected with the work of government.

I discovered the idea of policy activist in a supervision session with Julie Nyland (another of the contributors to this collection, and see her chapter, p. 220) when we were talking about the nature of the people who contributed to the 1970s–1980s housing reform movement in New South Wales that she was investigating. It was the name we thought appropriate for these actors, and it was an idea that I had thought about before both in relation to femocrats and what Ivan Szelenyi many years ago, and following the title of a publication, called 'evangelical bureaucrats'. We discovered that policy activist as a concept was first used by Hugh Heclo. His idea of policy activist refers to professional policy advisers who are offering technically-based argumentation in order to develop a particular policy diagnosis, or issue. These activists are located in what Heclo calls issue networks. Heclo has in mind the sophisticated world of policy advice that surrounds the heart of government in Washington DC, a world that, for instance, encompasses the American Sociological Association's central office and the engagement of its professional officers with various policy issues. In this case, we encounter a policy engagement based in sociological expertise which is directed by the value orientation of this discipline to the social.

This was not exactly what Julie Nyland and I had in mind when we coined the term 'policy activist'. We were more interested in actors whose strength of value commitment could not be reduced to, even if it was located within, a professional disciplinary value orientation, and whose policy activism is not narrowly issue-based but oriented to the development of an entire policy agenda. For instance, Paul Hager and Andrew Gonczi (see chapter 3) are not simply technically sophisticated professionals whose background equips them to advance the idea of professional competencies, they are also committed to a conception, or more accurately an ethos, of professional education and training which develops reflective practitioners who can make a positive and creative contribution to the society in which they live. We also did not want to confine policy activism to the professionalised and centralised worlds of policy advising that constitute limpet-like attachments to the apparatus of central government. Instead we wanted to take in the varied and dispersed forms of policy activism that are implicated in the complex and extensive terrain of public sector work.

Commissioning the collection

I invited a range of people to contribute to the collection who I thought would be able to offer interesting case studies of policy activism in ways which could provoke useful further reflection about this concept. Inevitably, the collection which has eventuated is relatively arbitrary in that some important areas of policy activism have not been taken up. Four policy areas that are not covered here immediately come to mind: disability, Aboriginal and Torres Strait Islander affairs, environmentalism and education (schooling, higher education and technical and further education). It would be excellent if this collection stimulates work on policy activism in these and other areas.

The collection also inevitably assumed something of an elegiac air because all the instances of policy activism it encompasses belong to the reform era of an interventionist Australian state 1972–96 (although most of the contributions are focused more on the period 1993–96). This is the era which begins with the election of the reform federal Labor government led by Gough Whitlam and ends with the defeat of the federal Labor government led by Paul Keating in early 1996. From the May Economic Statement of 1987 until February 1996 (when a Coalition government under the leadership of John Howard was elected) what Australians call 'economic rationalism' came to dominate the macro policy agenda of the federal government which sustained a neo-Keynesian interventionist approach to the policy agenda. Such an approach fosters the development of *policy* as the most appropriate form of social problem-solving (see Yeatman 1994a, chapter 6, for some discussion of the presuppositions of this conception of policy as the most appropriate response to challenges for social problem-solving). In turn, a policy-oriented culture of social problem-solving invites all the different kinds of activism that are centred on the policy process. I shall say more of this shortly.

The contributions were workshopped over two days in November

1996. This had the dual value of pulling them more tightly into the idea for the collection and of enabling feedback to work in draft form.

Common themes and issues

There are two general and different conceptions of policy activism offered in this collection. First, Julie Nyland's conception of policy activism fits a situation where activists are engaged in strategic policy-oriented action to overturn the established policy agenda. Her particular emphasis is on how such activists network to do this, and she shows how such networks encompass both 'insiders', working within government, and those who are located outside government in a formal sense but who may be key proponents of the new policy framework. Nyland, in fact, argues that one of the strategic goals in getting a new policy agenda officially adopted is to move its advocates into the relevant government agency so that they become 'insiders' rather than 'outsiders'. Until the activists come 'inside' they are usually based in different kinds of community organisations and sometimes in academe. Nyland's conception of policy activism, then, is primarily focused on the value-oriented, ideational and strategic action that is required to disestablish an existing policy agenda and to replace it with a new one. It follows from this that once those whose activism has been central in establishing a new policy agenda succeed in this goal, they cease to be policy activists and become, instead, custodians of the newly established policy.

Second, my conception of policy activism is different because it responds to a different problematic. The problematic which concerns me is not the overturning of an established policy agenda and its replacement with a new one. I accept that this is a legitimate and important approach to policy activism which has the value of including the neo-liberal or economic rationalist instances of policy activism in the United Kingdom, New Zealand, Canada, Australia and elsewhere. The concerted effort to disestablish the Keynesian welfare state policy agenda by advocates of a libertarian neo-classical economics has been a remarkably important recent instance of policy activism that fits Nyland's approach. These policy activists have

7

replaced the Keynesian welfare state with a conception of 'small government' where, as far as possible, government is to cede place to the market as the central domain of action. The intellectual formation of this policy agenda comes from the new institutional economics as well as from the political–economic thinking of neo-classicist economists such as Milton Friedman and Friedrich Hayek. The organised influence of this policy agenda owes a great deal to the work of large corporations which have organised business roundtables or their equivalents in the United States, New Zealand and elsewhere, with the precise objective of disestablishing Keynesian welfare-statism and replacing it with a deregulatory policy agenda (for an account of this organised take-over of the policy agenda in Canada, see Clarke 1997). This is a policy agenda which frees up the sphere of market-based action and decreases the legitimate sphere of government intervention on behalf of the maintenance and development of a citizen community.

A policy agenda which favours the principle of the market over the principle of government delegitimises the work of the state as democratic public administration on behalf of a citizen community. Instead, the state's agency is defined in terms of what is required to facilitate and to stimulate the dynamics of market competition. Public service agencies find themselves redefined as the entrepreneurial managers of contracts with non-government organisations of various kinds (see Wanna, Forster and Graham 1996). Public forms of contractualist entrepreneurialism work on the assumption that each party to a contract—the government agency on one side, the contractor on the other—is oriented to maximising its own private advantage or utility. Accordingly, the relationship is designed so as to harness this kind of incentive as well as to ensure that this privately motivated form of action complies with the contractual requirements. Performance is controlled by means of contractualist techniques of setting and monitoring performance targets and standards. The work of state administration, then, is redefined primarily in terms of the logic of market-oriented action, and patterns of co-operation or collaboration are driven by the competitive dynamics of private utility maximisation. This is a very different conception of the work of government than that offered by the idea of a policy process which is located within a public sector oriented to public values and public goods.

The idea of policy activism that I have wanted to offer is one which is located within an interventionist and democratic state which provides both legitimacy and direction for a robust public sector. The administration of this public sector does not have to be undertaken entirely by the state. A good deal of it can be contracted out but it is contracted out as a public activity which is to be accountable to public values such as administrative law (on this, see Tang 1997) and to be driven by publicly-oriented motives such as the desire to provide the best possible service to others or the desire to educate others to become good and intelligent citizens. The public sector, on this conception, includes all action which is publicly-funded and which is undertaken on behalf of the maintenance, development and sustainability of a public or citizen community. Viewed from another angle, the sphere of this action constitutes the sphere of the policy process in this particular governmental jurisdiction. The policy process refers to all aspects of what is involved in providing policy direction for the work of the public sector. These include the ideas which inform policy conception, the talk and work which goes into providing the formulation of policy directions, and all the talk, work and collaboration which goes into translating these directions into practice.

I am arguing then that the idea of the policy process belongs to a cluster of values which include: an interventionist and democratic state, where such intervention is justified by reference to public goods, namely the shared interest of a citizen community; the public sector as the sphere of public action where both governmental and non-governmental agencies co-operate in the delivery of public goods; and public sector administration as driven by an ethos of responsiveness to citizen needs, including needs for information and participation. Policy does not have to become oriented in terms of this idea of the policy process, but when it is, policy activism becomes any kind of activism which is oriented to the challenges of any level or aspect of this policy process. It does not matter whether the activist agenda has become adopted as official policy or not. A policy activist remains one when he or she is responsible for the implementation of a policy agenda to which he or she is committed. The work of implementing policy is just as value-oriented and as demanding of pragmatic creativity and intelligence as the work of conceiving policy change.

Policy activism, by this account, is any and all instances of a strategic commitment to the policy process in the context of a democratic government on behalf of a citizen community. In chapter 1, I make it clear that this is a normative conception of policy activism. There I define a policy activist as anyone who champions in relatively consistent ways a value orientation and pragmatic commitment to a conception of policy which opens it up to the appropriate participation of all those who are involved in the policy process, all the way from points of policy conception to delivery on the ground.

Chapters in this collection by Short, Nyland, Brennan and Dugdale usefully develop the debate about what is a policy activist. Brennan's chapter is a particularly skilful exploration of how both Nyland's and my conceptions of policy activism can illuminate activism in the child care policy arena. Brennan especially picks up on the normative component of my conception as one which is tied to a participatory conception of state administration on behalf of a citizen community when she discusses the 1970s feminist agenda for child care: 'Feminists were seeking something truly radical and participatory—forms of child care which would be managed co-operatively by parents and workers, which would be based around respect for children'. Brennan also discusses the policy activism of the commercial child care sector which campaigned to have government subsidies extended to their services rather than be confined to the community child care sector, and sees this as an instance of Nyland's conception of policy activism. Brennan adds her own useful reflection on *resistance* to policy direction as a particular type of policy activism. She is thinking especially of ground level resistance where, for instance, child care providers in the community sector are attempting to resist current government policy and to keep alive the original ethos of community-based child care.

Activism in relation to the policy process can be represented schematically as in Table I.1.

The particular value of Hager and Gonczi's chapter (chapter 3) is that they bring out the different kinds of policy activism in the

Table I.1   Schematising activism in relation to the policy process

Setting the policy agenda	Activists who organise to change a policy agenda
Policy development	Activists who seek to affect policy development
Policy formulation	Activists who seek to affect how policy gets formulated
Policy implementation	Activists who seek to affect how policy gets implemented and who it involves
Policy delivery	Activists who seek to affect what policy is delivered at ground level and how
Policy evaluation	Activists who seek to improve policies/programmes and their responsiveness to citizen need or who may use policy/programme evaluation for 'enlightenment' and public learning
Policy monitoring	Activists who seek to ensure the administration of the public sector is accountable to administrative law, probity and sound management of public resources

area of professional competencies as these were called into being by the distinctive challenges of four stages or levels of the policy process: policy conception, policy implementation, policy delivery and policy evaluation. Short's chapter (chapter 6) makes the analytical point that the different stages in the health policy process interact with three structural interests in health (what she calls professional monopolists, corporate rationalisers and the community interest) so that each of these interests are positioned with different degrees of influence and power in this process.

Both Hager and Gonczi, and Fraser, make the point that usually, or perhaps mostly, policy change is an emergent strategy. That is, the strategic vision and direction for a new policy is not thought out in advance but emerges through the practices of conceiving, formulating, implementing, delivering and evaluating it. Olivia Golden's (1990) phrase 'innovation by groping along' offers a similar metaphor to this idea of 'policy as an emergent strategy'.

The story that Hager and Gonczi tell is a wonderful case study not only of policy as an emergent strategy but also of the importance of key actors pursuing a visionary opportunism at all points where the policy process seemed to invite it. They tell part of the story of NOOSR (National Office of Overseas Skills Recognition) officials who recognised the significance of the increasing pressure under a

Labor government federal administration to produce a more sensible and equitable national approach to the recognition of overseas professional qualifications. This pressure arose in a more general policy context where government was committed not only to an economistic multiculturalism but also to the pursuit of an extraordinarily systemic approach to the restructuring of higher education, training, union awards and the labour market. NOOSR was situated within the mega-department of Employment, Education and Training (DEET), and the NOOSR officials were oriented in terms of the integrated approach of this department to employment, education and training. They (and it is clear that their higher-ups in DEET encouraged or directed them to do this) saw the 'Trojan horse' value of a national policy for recognition of overseas professional qualifications as one which would legitimise the introduction of a competency-based approach to professional training and education. The visionary opportunism displayed by these officials at the level of policy formulation was sustained at other levels of this particular policy process: by the consultants (Hager and Gonczi) who were commissioned to formulate the policy, and by the professional associations who saw in a competency-based approach an opportunity to reform their own professionalism. The development of professional competencies in a number of professions is an important example to place alongside the very different case of the National Schools Network (see note 1, chapter 1). In both cases the federal government intelligently used policy to provoke and facilitate reform of professionalism.

Given the centrality of professionalism to important policy areas such as health, education and justice, if policy reform in these areas is to be effective it must harness this professionalism. This is a neglected topic of inquiry and it could be the subject of a collection of its own. It is noteworthy that professionalism, activism and the policy process come up as a central theme in chapters by Hager and Gonczi, Dugdale and Short.

Glyn Davis in his chapter (chapter 2) makes the important point that new policy ideas are not under anyone's control, and that one of the risks of policy activism is that we may find that our ideas are adopted by our opponents and made over to hostile agendas. He uses the idea of the post-bureaucratic organisational device of contracting out. Where Davis advocated an organisational model for public broadcasting in Australia which would break up a centralised bureaucratic monolith and open up space for a more pluralistic and decentralised approach, his advocacy for a more citizen-responsive type of public broadcasting system was all too easily co-opted by an economic rationalist advocacy of competitive tendering as a means of making public sector activity more contestable in relation to both non-commercial and commercial providers. Another example of a citizen-responsive value being co-opted by economic rationalism is that of 'choice'. For example, in areas such as home and community care, advocates of a participatory approach to state administration argued that both user choice and voice were important means of ensuring that service providers became more responsive to individual needs. This advocacy of individualised service delivery, which in Australia was elaborated in a number of policy discourses over the period 1986 to 1995, was co-opted by market models of consumer choice as offered in public or rational choice theory. Davis's reminder then is a salutary one:

> What if others take up our critique but not our policy recommendations? What if in proposing policy from the margins we unintentionally advance hostile agendas? Authorial intent, long suspect in literature, proves an equally doubtful concept in policy-making.

Good intentions, and good ideas, then, are no guarantee of success. Davis, however, is not suggesting that this provides an excuse for not engaging with the policy process. Rather, like Hunter (1994) in a different fashion, Davis is reminding us that the pragmatics of policy activism demand something quite different by way of intellectual, ethical and practical deportment than intellectuals who insist on the theoretical purity of ideas are willing to give. He puts it simply: if you want to engage in the policy process, you have to become a player—'by organising an interest group, joining the bureaucracy, entering politics or creating some influential public forum to promote a policy proposal'. Davis and Dugdale agree with Weber (1978) that the policy process demands what Weber called 'an ethics of responsibility'. This is an ethics of pragmatism that is *worldly* rather than *transcendental* in its orientation (Weber's

terminology was 'innerworldly' as distinct from 'otherworldly').
Hunter (1994), Dugdale and Davis agree that intellectuals who are
committed to a transcendental standard of critique do not have the
ethical disposition required for engagement with the policy process.

Davis' point that the force of policy ideas outruns their authorship
fits the emphasis of Jones, Lee and Poynton on policy *discourse*.
They make the important point with reference to higher education
research policy that the world of policy is a world of text-based
discourse among other things, and that intervention within the policy
process has to reckon with this kind of discursive materiality. In
other words, activists who want to change or affect policy, or at
least some of their number at some stage, have to grapple with the
discursive presence of policy, to reinterpret and to rewrite policy by
an activist engagement with policy discourse. Such engagement opens
up the multiple and contesting interpretations of what a particular
policy direction and even policy formulation seems to require. This
opening creates space for new kinds of opportunity for policy
activism. For instance, the Department of Employment, Education,
Training and Youth Affairs research quantum has given visibility to
a plurality of styles of university research which has helped to
counter, the mobilisation of bias in favour of 'scientific' research,
that is, research that is conducted in terms of epistemological models
associated with the natural sciences.

Several of the contributors (Dowsett, Fraser, Nyland, Short and
Dugdale) make the point that innovation *inside* the official policy
process often depends on the innovative, courageous and committed
work of community-based activists. Fraser and Nyland are especially
interested in networks which develop across both insider and outsider
policy activists, and in those activists who cross over from one point
to another. Dugdale, while acknowledging the significance of community-based, and also of professional association-based types of
policy activism, is particularly interested in the ethics and pragmatics
of insider policy activism. Bureaucratic work is by its nature discrete
and we do not have enough case studies of bureaucratic or insider
policy activism. In this context, Dugdale's insistence on the peculiar
ethical discipline and passion of insider activism with reference to
activists in the health policy bureaucracies is especially valuable.
Dowsett's equal insistence on the centrality of community-based gay

14

men's policy activism to the development of the innovative and highly effective national policy of containing the HIV/AIDS epidemic in Australia balances Dugdale's emphasis on insider activists, and offers an extended case study of just how the dynamics of the division of labour between insider and community-based activists can operate. Dowsett is arguing, I think, that if policy is to be responsive to the needs of a citizen community, then community-based activism has to be accorded precedence in these dynamics. This is also the thrust I think of Fraser's chapter about community-based activism in housing and urban renewal in an inner city suburb of Adelaide.

The point that innovative and citizen-responsive policy emerges out of community-based activism and its impact on both state and public officials is I think evident in a number of important areas: the well documented area of the women's movement and its inter- action with femocracy is an obvious example. A further example would be the impact on policy of an eloquent, experienced and visionary network of Aboriginal and Torres Strait Islander leaders over the period of the 1980s and 1990s. There is also a case study crying out to be done of the Commonwealth officials in the disability policy and programme area who undertook very innovative work over the period 1986–95, but whose legitimacy and vision in doing this was driven by the influence of the disability movement both on them and on government more generally. In acknowledging the centrality of community-based policy activism to citizen-responsive policy innovation and development, it is important not to lose sight of the critical role of dedicated government officials in making their own distinctive contribution to this policy innovation and develop- ment. Our focus should be on the division of labour between these two types of activism, not to emphasise one in a manner that occludes the significance and role of the other.

1

Activism and the policy process

ANNA YEATMAN

Activism and the policy process

This chapter is concerned with the particular kind of activism which comes into being when policy is understood to involve not only the decisions of policy makers and their directions to others for implementation but also to be a complex process which involves a host of different kinds of actors who are engaged in different stages of the policy process. These stages are: setting the policy agenda, policy development, policy formulation, policy implementation, policy delivery, policy evaluation and policy monitoring. The relationship of these stages to one another is more complex than that of a linear–circular sequence of feedback loops as it is often conceived. These stages can overlap in time and in ways which preclude any neat systemic view of the whole feedback loop.

Policy does not have to be viewed as a complex policy process. The alternative conception of policy is one that sees policy in terms of the policy *decisions* that are made by the executive government of the day. In the Westminster system, this refers to decisions made by Cabinet. The idea is that an executive government will equip itself so as to be able to make good decisions, and that it uses whatever mechanisms are needed to ensure that these decisions are carried out by those charged with doing this. This model of policy is not just a decisionistic one (see Majone 1991) but an *executive* one. The focus is on the quality of executive decision-making rather than on the talent, wisdom, skills and vision of all those who are affected by policy and which could be tracked into a more participative approach to policy. Emphasis on an executive conception of policy must privilege what is actually often only a relatively minor, though important, stage of policy-making: deciding what policy direction to adopt. When it is believed that sound policy emanates from strong executive leadership, this is an elitist conception of policy that must privilege the moment of policy-making that seems to exemplify strong leadership: decision-making.

The executive conception of policy is not one that can legitimately excite policy activism except of the kind which is oriented to changing the composition of the executive, either in individual membership or the nature of the party which is in power. However, when policy is conceived as a complex, multi-layered process involving a whole host of different actors, policy activism of various kinds is provoked into being. Thus, there is a phenomenological point to be made here. Policy activism is more or less legitimate, and more or less developed, depending on whether the government of the day favours an executive approach to policy or a participative approach to policy which turns it into a policy process. When the executive model is the one adopted by the government of the day, policy activism is less legitimate and developed even though policy activists of various kinds may resist the executive model. When the partici-pative approach is favoured by the government of the day, policy activism becomes both more legitimate and developed.

For the conception of policy as a policy process to be possible, the work of state administration has to be conceived democratically. What this means is that paternalistic and top-down conceptions of state administration have to be replaced by conceptions which require state administration to be open to public accountability and to public participation. When state administration becomes democratised in this way, the work of turning policy into operational practice can become visible both in its complexity *and* its dependency on the agency of those who are involved in this work. These agents include:

1   The public servants who are responsible for turning general policy directions into operational policy, plus those who are responsible for turning this operational policy into programme management, and those who co-ordinate the relationships between programme management and the non-government organisations on which government depends for the delivery of policy.
2   The different kinds of service provider who are responsible for delivering policy on the ground.
3   The users, both potential and actual, of policy.
4   All those who give evaluative feedback on the policy process whether these be professional evaluators, ordinary citizens, organised lobby groups or political party organisations.
5   Ombudsmen, administrative lawyers, and sometimes the wider judiciary, who determine whether principles of justice, due process and equity have been adequately responded to within particular instances of the policy process.
6   A number of agencies charged with monitoring and auditing the policy process—these include the Commonwealth and State Auditor-Generals.

The increasing subjection of social life to policy

The areas of social life which are subject to 'policy' have grown extraordinarily over the last two or three centuries. The development of the modern 'interventionist state' extends the scope of conventionalised phenomena, that is phenomena which are understood to be subject to the artful intervention of policy. For a phenomenon to become subject to policy intervention means that it is brought into the domain of political action where it is reconstructed in relation to contesting narratives about who we are as citizens, what it is we think we should do, and why (my debt to Weber 1948, and Arendt 1958, here is evident).

Social life becomes subject to policy to the degree that it is denaturalised, that is, no longer left to the implicit direction of customary practice. In all societies, social actors think about what they are doing and why. In many societies, the grounds of this reflection does not implicate 'policy' but, rather, refers to a body of customary law and practice which requires to be interpreted by those who are seen as closest to its divine source (elders, a priestly caste etc.). Policy occurs when social actors think about what they are doing and why in relation to different and alternative possible futures. To consider different possible futures means that social actors arrogate to themselves the power of determining their own fate. This is a project which requires them either as individuals or collectivities to weigh alternative courses of action in relation both to explicit statements of value or purpose and to consideration of the consequences of following one course of action rather than another. It also requires the collectivities to enter into dispute and contestation regarding alternative and contrary views of their shared future.

The state can be seen (Durkheim 1965) as the organised centre of social life. It is the sphere of action in which a society names itself to itself. This is why Durkheim was able to take law as the index of social solidarity. Law names and thereby constitutes particular ways of instituting social relationships, status and obligations. This constitutive role of the state (see also Franzway, Court and Connell 1989, p. 52) is expressed not only in how the state names social phenomena but in how it proceeds to regulate them and to subject them to policy. Viewed in this way, the history of the state is coterminous with the history of the subjection of social life to policy. The interventionist state, thus, is as old as the emergence of the modern state in the seventeenth and eighteenth centuries in the constitutional and absolutist monarchical regimes of Western and Middle Europe.

There are quite different types of policy regime which constitute the history of the state. For instance a patriarchal–absolutist monarchical state enjoins a different type of policy regime from that of a patriarchal–liberal democratic constitutional state, or that of a post-patriarchal and post-colonial liberal democratic constitutional state. In each case, how the culture of policy-making operates and who is constituted as being appropriately participant in, and/or influential with regard to, policy-making, varies. In addition, each type of policy regime has its own distinctive type of administration. From a top-down perspective, the business of administering, or as it has come to be called, managing, the state is the business of turning policy directives or decisions into authoritative operational guidelines, instructions and regulations for the conduct of all those (including a host of non-state organisations) which come under the jurisdiction of the state. This business extends also to the monitoring of the impact of the state's programmatic action on the conduct of those who are affected by it.

The issue of the democratic accountability of the administrative state and its impact on how policy is conceived

Policy, then, is inseparable from the state, and both the state and policy are dependent upon the apparatus of state administration or management. In a liberal democratic state–society, the question arises as to how the policy regime as the work of this administrative state is to be accountable to those whom government is meant to represent. As the work of the administrative state became, in the era after the Second World War, both more extensive and more complex, this question became a pressing one. There have been two responses to this question which work in different directions and, together, provide for a serious degree of incoherence in contemporary ideas of democratic accountability. The first response would have the elected executive level of government ('the government of the day' or, simply, GOD), with the assistance of its most senior officials, design and institute a series of controls over those who manage the work of the administrative state, including all the non-government agencies to whom the work of the state is contracted. These controls are intended to reduce the degree of slippage which occurs between the various stages of formulating and implementing a particular policy decision. This is the executive model of policy referred to above.

The second response to the problem of democratic accountability for the administrative state is to make the work of this state more open to the observation and participation of those who deliver and use its services and who are subject to its regulation. Where the first response is control-oriented and top-down in character, the second response is collaborative and bottom-up in character. The second response works in terms of metaphors of partnership and co-production. The policy process is seen as needing the input of *all* those who contribute to making it happen.

Different kinds of partnership and co-productive relationships are indicated at different levels. For example, policy *development* may need a partnership approach which involves senior government officials working with community-based groups and non-government providers to identify what needs to be done, and what kind of response to this need makes most sense. However, a different kind of partnership approach is indicated at the point of policy *delivery* when, for example, a domiciliary care physiotherapist makes a home visit to an individual whose bed needs adjustment for her to be more comfortable, to be as mobile as she can be, and to permit ease of her transfer from bed to wheelchair. In this instance, the physiotherapist may need to talk with someone from the domiciliary care workshop in dialogue and consultation with the client and her carer to undertake the problem-solving that will bring about an outcome that the client, carer and the professional find to be satisfactory or good enough. The partnership here may be four-way, and the outcome of the problem-solving process is one which depends on co-production.

The two responses to the problem of accountability of the administrative state are, then, respectively the *executive model* and the *partnership model*. To the extent that these two models coexist, they do so as an unexamined incoherence of the policy regime (what the left hand is doing is independent of what the right hand is doing). There is a current attempt to force coherence where control-oriented models of performance management, using performance targets, measures and monitoring, are synthesised with market-oriented models of competition for clients. Here, the service user or client does not get to participate in the policy process. Rather, the policy regime presents as a given to the citizen and instead, he or she is invited to 'choose' which particular service he or she wishes to use.

The difference between policy (the policy process) and politics (the political process)

The policy process is related to what is called 'politics' and 'the political process', but these also need to be kept distinct. As before, the policy process refers pre-eminently to the work of developing, formulating, implementing, delivering, monitoring and evaluating policy. To be sure, all of these aspects of policy—policy formulation, policy implementation and policy evaluation—are subject to politics. More accurately, they invite their own distinctive type of politics. This politics is one internal to the policy process and is shaped by it.

While the policy process intersects with official politics and the political process, they are not the same thing. Politics and the political process refer to the organised public theatre and private backrooms of party political contestation over governmental power and its distribution. When a Senate Estimates Committee, for example, calls before it senior public officials to explain and account for some aspect of policy, this process of accountability is likely to be driven by party political point-scoring and a zero-sum competitive game of wins and losses. In this case, the policy process is subordinated to the political process. However, when a politician becomes a minister with a particular portfolio, and discusses policy direction with the senior public officials managing this portfolio, party political concerns present a series of constraints on such exchange but they do not direct its substance. Something like the reverse of the former case occurs here: as long as those political constraints can be worked within, the political process is subordinated to the policy process.

Agenda-setting is the one aspect of the policy process which might appear to fall more into the party politics game than into the networks of the policy process which scoop up state bureaucratic agencies, non-government providers, advocacy organisations, professional associations and, often, professional educators. However, as Julie Nyland's (1998; and see her chapter in this volume) work shows, activism in agenda-setting is pre-eminently associated with such *policy networks*. While party political activists may be committed to particular policy positions, these are more like a framework for policy direction than a policy agenda. When political activism and policy activism converge in policy agenda-setting it is because the political activists are seeking and using the advice of policy activists who may be ministerial advisers, think-tank staff, or policy activist academics.

The policy process and the conditions of its emergence

There are older bodies of literature which refer to a science of statecraft (*staatswissenschaften*) intended for the instruction of an elite stratum of officialdom responsible for the work of administering the state (see Burke 1991; and Hunter 1994, chapter 5). The science of statecraft was never intended for the eyes or participation of those cast as the objects of state administration. Thus, whether the ethos of elite statecraft is that of advice to a prince (Machiavelli), the management of national wealth (Adam Smith) or the moral education of a national population (Durkheim), this conception of policy is not one that has to work with the problematic of democratic account-ability.

These older conceptions of policy tend to equate it with rational decision-making and the specific kinds of expert knowledge on which this particular type of reason depends. The decision maker in ques-tion can be a policy adviser to a king, an administrator of a particular bureau structured in terms of the classical bureaucratic model the-orised by Weber, the doctor in charge of a government department of health, an inspector of a public school system or a teacher in a public school classroom. The idea is that if the decision (diagnosis, judgment) is sound, that is, based in expert knowledge and good reasoning, then the action sequence the decision is to orient can be left to take care of itself. Where this action sequence implicates others, as it invariably does, we have to hand an authoritarian and, or, paternalistic set of presuppositions that these others can be effectively commanded, manipulated or induced to do what the decision requires them to do. In short, these others do not have to be positively engaged in the carrying out of the policy in question. There is no policy *process*, there is only policy.

It is when those others are drawn into the light, and are seen as others on whom the carrying out of a particular policy depends, that we begin to think about a policy *process*. This permits us also to think about the different aspects and stages of the policy process. There are three distinct sets of others who become progressively drawn into the policy process. They are: first, the public officials (sometimes called bureaucrats, public servants, public managers) charged with the transformation of a political decision (a piece of legislation, an executive decision, or a judgment of the judiciary) into an operational line of conduct for policy. This work falls in-between the operational formulation of a policy direction and its delivery on the ground. It includes what is nowadays called programme management.

Second, the on-the-ground deliverers of a policy or, what can be called, direct service deliverers. In the area of public schooling, these are all those who staff a school ranging from its principal through its teachers to its ancillary staff. In health, they include the various professionals and paraprofessionals engaged in the direct delivery of publicly funded and, or, publicly-regulated health services.

Third, the users of a particular policy as well as those who may not use it but who are subject to its regulation. Thus, users include citizens who receive public income support, citizens who need publicly-funded services for people with disabilities, citizens whose compliance is needed for effective public taxation collection and citizens who find themselves within publicly-funded institutions of detention.

How is it that these three distinct groups come to be seen as contributing to the carrying out of policy? It is because their agency becomes visible, and their agency becomes visible to the extent that it is problematised for purposes of carrying out a particular policy. The problematisation of their agency occurs in two modes: first, realist and pragmatic—this is an acceptance that top-down control models cannot work as they are intended to because human beings are not bureaucratically-oriented automatons, and it is best to reckon with, rather than to bracket out, their agency; second, democratic and anti-paternalistic—this is a normative commitment to the idea that policy will be the more democratic, intelligent and effective the more it depends on the active and informed participation of those who are affected by its processes and outcomes. A participative conception of policy permits it to be linked with what Lindblom and others call social problem-solving (Lindblom and Cohen 1979; Lindblom 1990), namely processes of public learning that allow problems to be publicly and dialogically probed, solved, attacked or, merely, better understood.

Paternalistic and control-oriented models of policy have by no means disappeared, but they have lost legitimacy. It is difficult for proponents of the executive model of policy to openly declare their attachment to an elitist and non-participative conception of policy. Instead, the executive model is reinstated by means of representing certain problems as not just pressing and urgent but as *technical* in character, thus requiring the advice of experts not the participation of citizens. This is the function of the recent take-over of the policy agenda by a libertarian neo-classical economics where the most important policy issues are represented as economic ones. This particular brand of economics is especially salient because it not only privileges the private power of business corporations who command enormous political influence but it seems to speak on behalf of the freedom of choice of the ordinary person. This is an executive model of the policy process which works in the direction of substituting market outcomes for government intervention, and status as an individual consumer for individualised participation as a member of a citizen community.

Neo-classical economics is committed to a scientistic and decisionistic view of policy: good policy is policy decisions which are appropriately informed by economic science. For the economic rationalist, there is no policy process, there are only policy decisions and consumer choices. In addition, the economic rationalist assumes that there is no such thing as a public or common interest. There are only private interests and privately-oriented choices. For this reason, and as far as possible, market action should substitute for government intervention. Government is far too prone to capture by government employees or groups seeking to make policy over to the pursuit of their own private interests. To this end, every effort to avoid such capture must be made. Such effort includes the conversion of tenured career positions with a stipend for public servants into time-limited contracts which offer performance pay and other kinds of incentive designed on the premise that a public servant is motivated by private utility rather than public interest. Where stipendiary support for a life-long career in public service guaranteed a professional independence of the public service in relation to the government of the day, the performance contract is designed to bring public servants into line with the executive model of policy.

The emergence of the policy process as a complex, multi-levelled and, to some degree at least, discontinuous process traversing very different spheres of agency and types of agent (politicians, public officials, service deliverers and service users) into the light of day is entirely contingent on struggles to democratise the policy process and to engage the agency of these very differently positioned players. It is worth elaborating a little on how public officials, direct deliverers and users have been brought into the policy process, although it is to be remembered that this is a contentious and non-establishment view of policy.

Public officials became positively situated as agents in their own right in the policy process within the so-called 'new public adminis-tration' movement of the 1970s (see Alaba 1994; Yeatman 1990, chapter 3; Wilenski 1986). This movement transported the rhetoric of 1970s 'new left' participatory democracy into the administration of the state. It not only espoused ideas of a more representative and democratically accountable public bureaucracy, but it insisted also that the 'implementation' of policy was not simply the technical translation into reality of decisions made by the government of the day. This was an insistence that the work of implementation of policy was itself a creative exercise demanding skill, judgment and value commitment. Thus, it was not that the discretion of public servants in undertaking this work of implementation should be curbed; rather their agency in this type of policy work was to be recognised and understood. Peter Wilenski (1986, p. 63) offers an eloquent statement of this conclusion, one that moves in an entirely different direction to the neo-classical economist's recommendations for the avoidance of bureaucratic capture. Where the latter seeks to harness the bureau-crat's desire for private gain and advancement to the work of the state and to minimise their policy activism, Wilenski seeks to harness the policy activism of the bureaucrat but to make it politically and socially accountable:

> We cannot continue to debate whether it is legitimate or not for the administrator's personal values to intrude into his or her decisions; the fact is that they do and, as our system of govern-ment operates, they must. Once this is accepted we can move to the far more important question which current public service ideology evades or ignores: what are the legitimate values in different circumstances and how are specific value choices to be justified?

The new public administration theorists offered a non-decisionistic model of the policy process. The formulation of a policy offers only a general framework for action. The work of making this framework operational all the way from the adoption of departmental policy, through its delivery as a programme, to the point of its delivery on the ground is itself a contribution to policy-*making*.

If the agency of public servants is to be recognised as a valid and important contribution to policy-making and understood in this way, then it has to be accorded legitimacy within this more complex conception of the policy process. As we know this is difficult to achieve under the Westminster model of representative democracy which centres democratic legitimacy on the sovereignty of an elected parliament and the executive government of the day. If public official agency is to be accorded its own place within the policy process, there are a number of ways of making it democratically accountable. These include: the new administrative law which develops the principle of public power as subject to administrative review (Tang 1997); a more representative bureaucracy where the merit principle is interpreted in terms of the principle of equal opportunity and anti-discrimination; access to government information, including freedom of information legal provisions; direct participation by citizens—including consumer and provider groups—in the policy process; the localisation of programme delivery in ways which make it more accountable to and informed by local ecologies of service users and providers in family and community context. In addition, the doctrine of separation of powers is an approach to democratic government which reconciles public official agency with the more established plurality of democratic decision-making authorities: the legislature, the executive and the judiciary.

The closer we move to the point of delivery of policy, the more policy becomes embedded in the pragmatics of delivery systems in both local and regional contexts. In the case of publicly-funded providers and direct service deliverers, what they understand to be their core or 'real' work is undertaken within the parameters and constraints supplied by the wider policy environment. At least this is how most service deliverers understand the relationship of their work to policy. Policy represents a set of parameters, requirements, constraints and regulations over which they see themselves as having little control. Their real work comprises the business of attending to the needs of students in a particular classroom, giving a university

27

lecture, co-ordinating services for an elderly woman in need of assistance at home, for example.

When the policy process is designed in terms of the executive model of policy, this service deliverer perception of the relationship of policy to their real work makes sense. The executive model of policy treats the service delivery level of the policy process as a given, as a variable to be manipulated and controlled, not as the agency of people who should be invited to get involved in the making of citizen-responsive, wise and intelligent policy. In these circumstances, it is hard for service deliverers to understand that how they interpret and implement policy in the classroom, lecture theatre, community service setting is contributing to the *making* of policy.

Service deliverers can make more or less creative 'adjustments' (Ball 1993, p. 13) with regard to the policy that is delivered from on high. For example, quality assurance imperatives can be understood as an external imposition which is oriented to the control orientation of an employer and/or funder, or, they can be understood as an opportunity for improvement, and made over to a creative process of action research where practices of service delivery are reviewed, experimentally improved, these improvements evaluated and their achievements incorporated into normal, ongoing practice.

However, there are some instances (for example, the Australian school reform movement as exemplified in the National Schools Network) where the providers and service deliverers are invited into the policy process. This occurs when these agents are seen as being vital to the improvement of what happens by way of delivery of policy on the ground. For example, the core assumption of the school reform movement might be that: the improvement of teaching and learning outcomes for students in schools depends on the effective improvement of teachers' work in both classrooms and on a whole school basis and, in turn, this improvement of teachers' work depends on their own learning and development in harness with that of the students.

When, in this way, the 'street-level' or the chalk-face (the level of direct service delivery) is seen as an inherent part of the policy process, policy-making encompasses all that occurs from the point of policy formulation to the point of its delivery. When the delivery of policy is seen to be contingent on the culture and practice of the

28

providers and service deliverers, it is possible also to see them as central to ensuring that policy gets delivered in ways which make sense to those who use it. Making sense, in this connection, means that the policy is delivered in ways which are creatively adapted to the ecology of users' needs and wants in a particular context. Given this conception of policy, it is impossible to design a policy process which leaves out the creative and dynamic role of those who work at the point of policy delivery. Moreover, this is a conception of policy which reconceives the ethos of the work of those who are positioned as the public officials who formulate, manage, and monitor operational policy. Instead of these being viewed in a relationship of control to the workers at the coalface, they are now viewed in a role of *facilitation* of creative, dynamic work and learning at the coalface. On this approach, an active and continuous feedback loop of dialogue is required between the officials and the providers or deliverers.

The National Schools Network has exemplified a more complex conception of feedback of this kind as it is linked to a more inclusive idea of partnership. At the national level, the network brought together participating schools, the two levels of federal (which up until 1997 was the principal funder of the network) and state government, academic associates, and the two national education unions (the Australian Education Union and the Independent Education Union).[1] This instance indicates how a participative and collaborative approach to the policy process might open up into a wider stakeholder partnership.

What of those who use services, or whose compliance is needed for the production of a particular public good (for example, traffic safety, taxation)? If policy is to make sense to those who use it, or whose compliance with particular rules and regulations is worth maximising, then policy needs to be designed in ways which take account of user or client views of what might enhance their use or compliance. The participation of the user or client in the policy process, then, is a necessary condition of good policy which makes sense to users and clients. This point can be taken further. If policy is also to be designed in ways which are creatively adapted to the needs of those who constitute particular and different communities of need, then it requires the active participation of these communities

29

in its design. Furthermore, if users or clients are to be responsible and realistic in what they can expect of policy, then they need to be engaged in an active and ongoing understanding of the policy process in both its systemic and point of delivery features.

In my experience arising out of the evaluation of major intergovernmental programmes in both home and community care and disability those who represent the actual or potential clients of the programme can be both responsible and resourceful if they are invited into a shared process of problem-setting and problem-solving with those who are responsible for managing the programme. More than anyone, it is the clients who understand the economies of good-enough service provision: what it is to combine reliance on services in kind with those which are professionalised and paid for; what it is to 'stretch' local resources and adapt them on a 'make do' and 'can do' basis. However, for this intelligence and co-operative creativity to emerge as a central asset of the programme in question, it has to be elicited, informed and resourced. To develop this kind of community-based asset for policy delivery, governmental systems not only have to invest much more in public learning of all kinds, but to promote designs for living which value and enhance what Eva Cox (1995) calls 'social capital'.

When the policy process is understood and designed so as to include users, or client participation, on an ongoing basis, we have to hand a coproduction model of the policy deliverer (user) relationship. That is, it is understood that the service, product or need for compliance cannot be 'customised' without the production of policy at the point of contact with the user or client being understood as a coproductive relationship. Schools which are supporting teachers in the development of negotiated curriculum and learning contracts with students are experimenting with a coproduction model. These schools are presupposing that an individual student's capacity to learn cannot be enhanced and developed without this individual participating in determining the what, why and when of his or her learning process. It may seem obvious that the quality and outcomes of services such as teaching and learning strongly depend on their coproduced features. However, until there are models of service delivery which explicitly emphasise and resource this relationship of co-production, it cannot be turned into an asset of the relationship (see Yeatman 1994b, p. 292).

Policy, then, is reconceived as the *policy process* when the distinctive contributions to policy of public officials, direct deliverers and clients are accorded visibility and valued. This is a conception which is emergent in public policy and management discourse but which still has to vie with establishment models of policy which are oriented in terms of the efforts of rational decision makers to control those who do the work of carrying out those decisions (for the idea of the policy process as a new 'post-bureaucratic' paradigm of public management, see Yeatman 1994b).

It is also a democratic conception, one that values the participation of all those who are positioned as subjects within the work of conceiving, implementing and evaluating policy. To see policy as a policy *process* emphasises the need to develop mechanisms of using and valuing this participation so that these differently positioned subjects within the policy process enter into dialogue with one another. It is this which constitutes the intersubjective character of the policy process.

Elsewhere (Yeatman 1994b), I have argued that it is not just the democratisation of our social relationships which underlies this conception of policy as a policy process. It is also the dynamics of increased complexity and uncertainty in our lives. When attention is paid to these two dynamics, it becomes clear that rationalistic and intellectualistic models of policy that are predicated on some idea of rational mastery engage those who follow them in a rather dangerous kind of fantasy. We cannot predict or plan for our futures in ways which enable us to subject our lives to rational direction and control. Rather, we have to learn to live in ways which enable us to adapt to ongoing change, complexity and uncertainty.

To be sure, we can attempt to push the burden of uncertainty, as Marris (1996) calls it, onto the shoulders of those who are too weak to protect themselves from it. This is how a competitive rather than a co-operative management of uncertainty works. For example, we can turn the business of managing uncertainty over to the dynamics of how privately-oriented 'choice' operates in a market of competitively priced goods. By doing so, we create incentives for actors to operate in self-regarding ways, and to work to enhance their own market power in competition with each other. On these dynamics, those who have relatively more market power to start with tend to accumulate such power at the expense and relative impoverishment of their fellows. This impoverishment extends to the environment because these same dynamics encourage asset-stripping of anything that can be converted into a commodity and, thus, into private market power for somebody. Since actors are social beings dependent in multitudinous ways on their social connectedness, this competitive strategy of managing uncertainty is self-defeating. It risks undermining the social capital on which this connectedness, if it is to be well-functioning, depends, as well as undermining the ecological capital on which species wellbeing depends. Co-operative strategies of managing uncertainty on the one hand, and responding to complexity on the other, demand that we begin to think in terms of a policy process which is informed by a culture and infrastructure of public learning.

Policy activists

Activism is a category of political action which is wed to the participatory conceptions of democracy that have come to displace paternalistic models of democracy in the last several decades. Paternalistic models of democracy are those that cast the vast majority of the subjects of democratic government in whatever jurisdiction is considered (nation, organisation or school) as those in whose interests a professional elite of some kind rules. This elite may or may not be elected. Sometimes, the scientific expertise of the elite is used as a surrogate for election as a basis for authority, as in the case of Lenin's conception of the professional revolutionary. In the paternalistic models, it is the professionalism of the politician, mandarin-bureaucrat and service deliverer (archetypically, the priest or doctor) which is to underpin their work in making decisions on behalf of all those who are subject to their authority.

As mentioned previously, when paternalistic models of democracy prevail, activism is neither legitimate nor effective. This is not to say that these paternalistic models are not challenged by activist movements, for example, the workers' movements of the nineteenth and twentieth centuries; they are. Rather it is to underline the fact that in order to be effective these movements had to be organised in ways which matched the structures of paternalistic democracy. Typically, then, movements of this kind were directed by a professional elite of unionists, Labor politicians or professional revolutionaries and, depending on how open or clandestine their organising could be, the mass base of the organisation was structured either bureaucratically or as a series of cells. An activist who is required to act in ways which are secretive, unaccountable, and not open to dialogical engagement with others is an activist who is displacing activism in favour of professional elitism.

Activism, I am suggesting, by its nature is a publicly declared and open contribution to political life. It is a commitment, statement of vision, declaration of values, and offering of strategic action, all of which are publicly declared. The activist is an actor who is prepared to stand for and by his or her vision and values within what is an openly contested territory concerning which and whose values are to prevail in setting the culture and orienting the structures of a particular governmental jurisdiction (again bearing in mind, this may be a nation, province, agency, school, hospital, for example). The activist does not stop being an activist if and when he or she succeeds in having this vision adopted as policy. Until the contest itself subsides, those who are prepared to publicly stand for particular value commitments and visions are required to be activists on their behalf.

To be sure, when the policy process is defined in terms of an executive model of policy, activists who are positioned in strategic organisational and, or, policy roles may find that they cannot be open about their vision and commitments, or, at least, that this openness has to be disciplined within a professionalised discourse of intrabureaucratic or intraprofessional talk. For example, a senior public official who chairs a committee of senior officials from both federal and provincial levels of government in a particular policy area undertakes this task in ways which cannot help but betray how he or she prioritises closed-bureaucratic relative to open-stakeholder types of politics in relation to policy discussion. If this public official consistently champions an open-stakeholder conception of policy (policy as a policy process), no doubt in ways which deploy management discourse of the kinds that support such an orientation, then he or she has declared himself to be a policy activist.

I am offering a normative definition of *policy activist*, then, as anyone who champions in relatively consistent ways a value orientation and pragmatic commitment to what I have called the policy process, namely a conception of policy which opens it up to the appropriate participation of all those who are involved in policy all the way through points of conception, operational formulation, implementation, delivery on the ground, consumption and evaluation. Within this conception we may want to distinguish between bureaucratic, professional, practitioner and consumer types of policy activist. It would make sense to do this.

To define policy activist in this way means that we can enter into some interesting debates concerning the extent to which particular types of policy actor were or are policy activist. For example, are policy actors who are willing to offer accounts of their policy action in relation to vision, ideas and values within the public domain policy activists: Hugh Stretton, H.C. Coombs, for example? Are femocrats policy activists? Each of these in qualified ways might be termed a policy activist. Policy actors who are also policy intellectuals like Hugh Stretton are prepared to be publicly accountable for their ideas, and to locate those ideas within processes of public learning. However, this does not necessarily carry over into a conception of policy as the policy process. It may still sustain a professional elitist view of policy. Femocrats, on the other hand, can be seen as partial champions of policy as the policy process to the extent to which they believe policy should be open to the participation of women. However, when femocrats champion the cause of women in ways which de-authorise the participation of men in policy (as some femocrats have done), this is surely a shift away from policy activism toward cadre activity (or, professional revolutionary type action).

On this approach, we may want to introduce a number of distinctions between different types of policy agency, those which are more open and participatory in relation to those which are more closed and top-down. The idea of policy entrepreneur, as discussed by Roberts and King (1991), is a conception of policy agency which is non-participatory and top-down. Much the same might be said of Heclo's (1978, p. 100) idea of policy professional.[2]

34

The normative definition of policy activist that I am offering is contestable, of course. Its virtue is that it draws attention to a particular model of policy that legitimises as it invites different kinds of policy activism from different kinds of policy actor. It is a definition located within a democratic participatory conception of policy as an open policy process. As I have argued, a conception of policy as a policy process is located within a complex of value commitments. These include: a positive evaluation of government as a public authority working on behalf of public values and public interests; a belief that these public interests include the governmental provision of infrastructure of public learning and social problem-solving; and, a fundamental belief in the capacities of citizens in their various roles (public servants, professionals, clients, carers, neighbours, volunteers) to wisely explore how problems need to be defined and, then, addressed.

2

Policy from the margins: reshaping the Australian Broadcasting Corporation

GLYN DAVIS

Policy activists have ideas, hopes and aspirations. Activists want a policy process which is permeable, open to new ways of seeing a problem and willing to imagine better solutions. Yet for those outside the policy process—those on the margin—influence is a haphazard affair. We throw conceits at our targets, hoping to move them through force of argument. That this can be an effective technique was demonstrated by feminist authors from the late 1960s. Indeed, as Max Weber argued, new ideas help create new world images which 'fundamentally reshape the terms of struggle among interests' (Weir 1992, p. 188). For most policy activists, though, disappointment beckons. Ideas are either ignored or contending voices carry the argument. Sometimes new world images return in unwelcome ways, opening up policy possibilities which silence the original activist.

This chapter tells such a story, of no import but perhaps of some interest. Accepting an invitation from the editor to reflect on personal experience, the chapter describes how an academic argued for a reshaping of the Australian Broadcasting Corporation (ABC), based on then novel management techniques. These ideas failed to find sufficient policy sponsors. Yet in subsequent years I watched others take up the same techniques, and use them to suggest very different futures for the ABC. Where I spoke from the irrelevancy of a university, the new activists are government advisers, people of

36

apparent influence. Their application of our shared management model fills me with profound unease. Ideas can reshape the struggle, but not perhaps always in desired ways.

The experience illustrates something of the difficulties of arguing from the margins. It also acknowledges the potential for advocating ideas with major but unforeseen consequences. There are risks in policy activism. What if others take up our critique but not our policy recommendations? What if in proposing policy from the margins we unintentionally advance hostile agendas? Authorial intent, long suspect in literature, proves an equally doubtful concept in policy-making.

Policy emerges from a process with many steps and players. Ideas are the key input, but they languish without sponsors to shepherd the idea onto the agenda of decision makers. The work of proposing new ideas—such as the material described in this chapter—is at best 'policy thinking'. To be a policy activist requires more than dreaming up programmes for others. It means becoming a player, by organising an interest group, joining the bureaucracy, entering politics or creating some influential public forum from which to promote a policy proposal. Academic work can be the first step to policy activism, but ideas matter little until they find an audience.

Proposing policy in an Australian context

Anyone trained in American notions of public policy expects to find a Heraclitean flux, the constant making and remaking of choices, in a system where change can embrace everything: the policy, the policy makers and the institutions they inhabit. Since no decision is final, ideas can circulate through the various policy arenas, competing with conventional wisdom, forever undermining the settled and the ordered. It is a world captured in Yogi Berra's observation that 'it's not over until it's over, and even then it is not over' (Davis 1990).

In this literature the key instruments of change, ideas, are marshalled through 'issue networks'. These networks have no solid shape or character. They are informal links between politicians, bureaucrats, academics and journalists with a mutual interest in some policy field. Issue networks provide the raw material; policy brokers ensure their production. Policy brokers are entrepreneurs who, through conviction or ambition, pull together a coalition of support aiming to put an idea onto the agenda of a senator or president. They have a solution and are looking for someone with the right problem. Since members of Congress make their reputation through the bills they sponsor, there is competition not just of, but for, ideas. Policy proposals course through the system, attracting patrons, hinting at career opportunities, making or threatening public institutions.

Even on the dry pages of textbooks this vibrant policy world, with its endless pitch and roll, seems remote from Australian experience. We know a more sedate process, with less chance for influence by issue network members, or by independent policy entrepreneurs. Two key institutions, both missing in America, ensure that stability in Australia: disciplined political parties and a professional bureaucracy. Strong and machine-based political parties severely restrict scope for policy brokerage. Since parties, rather than individual representatives, make the decisions, only one winning coalition is possible—that of government support. A private member's bill has little chance of even being heard in parliament unless it is taken up by the leadership; party priorities prevail. This provides greater consistency in government, but at the cost of those local victories possible for shifting coalitions in a more fragmented, open system.

Further, Australia does not experience the turnover of a presidentially appointed federal bureaucracy. American participants in an issue network can move suddenly from the periphery to the centre, joining the traffic each four years between think-tanks, universities and the White House. The American electoral system, with its tradition of patronage appointments, regularly disperses and reforms the senior levels of the public service; people, carrying their ideas, circulate. If the President is not hiring then a senator may be; many on Capital Hill have large staffs and specialised advisers, or can deliver jobs in the many research institutes which dot Washington. In Australia, by contrast, there is not such constant movement. Those bureaucracies which provide advice on broadcasting policy or arts funding are small, permanent and avowedly non-partisan. A tiny cadre of ministerial staff and senior officials may change, but the regular divisions of the Australian Public Service, and the wider universe of government-funded commissions and agencies, are less

POLICY FROM THE MARGINS

moved by shifting political fortune. Consistency, rather than rotation, is the hallmark of Australia's system of responsible government.

Which is not to suggest that the Australian policy process is entirely closed. There are lobbyists aplenty in Canberra, interest groups seeking influence, and newspaper columnists competing to dictate government choices. Ideas matter, as much here as in any other nation. Politicians care about good policy and hire advisers to critically evaluate proposals. Australians even participate in issue networks, though often without the elevations to power and influence which are available to their American counterparts. But ours is a more formal, structured system, in which a would-be policy broker faces a formidable task moving not just individuals, but the institutions of parliamentary government. There are fewer points of entry, so agitating from the outside can be an uncertain business. Since opportunities for influence are more constrained, proposals not taken up by key players vanish without trace.

Potential policy activists must find other ways into the discussion. Some join industry associations or petition under letterhead. Others attach themselves to a shadow minister, hoping for prominence when opposition turns to government. Repetition can be an alternative, promoting the same basic idea, in forum after forum, as Hew Evans did on the future of the Special Broadcasting Service (SBS). His argument, that SBS should be restructured along the Channel 4 model, has not been taken up in its entirety. Yet through unremitting promotion, the Evans line permeated policy considerations. It was conceded in government position papers as an option, albeit an unwelcome one, and can now be seen, in muted form, in SBS commissioning decisions. As SBS has come to rely on commercial sponsorship, so the logic presented by Evans became more appealing. Still, the Evans strategy requires patience and humility, repeating an idea until authorship is lost and it has become part of the disembodied common sense of conversation, a voice in the air heard so often it begins to sound reasonable.

Writing on the ABC

Writing a book is one way to seek entrance to a policy debate. Talking about the ABC from the outside, however, confronts a familiar problem: how to get people interested in new ideas about an old, and apparently, settled, issue. The policy field is largely confined to established players including the Corporation itself and its many public figures, the Minister and Department of Communications, SBS and commercial competitors speaking through newspaper and industry associations. Together these players have worked through innumerable reports touching on the ABC, many recommending substantial changes to the organisation but few questioning the validity of its basic form and function. Getting alternatives discussed from outside this policy network is difficult, since those with no institutional base inside the policy community lack legitimacy. Public advocacy is the main tactic available—books, articles, letters to the editor, submissions to inquiries and the Evans technique of posing ideas and hoping the refrain might achieve currency.

My book, *Breaking Up the ABC*, published in 1988, sought to present new ideas about an old institution. It offered an alternative vision to the (excellent) institutional history of the ABC prepared by Ken Inglis (1983) for the half century anniversary of the organisation, and to the very traditional endorsements of public service broadcasting which attended that celebration.

The central theme running through *Breaking Up the ABC* is that the Corporation's problems are not of its own making. ABC influence in public life has declined because of external factors—a budget squeeze which afflicts most public sector organisations, an aggressive commercial broadcasting industry moving into territory once the preserve of the national broadcaster, the diversification of government support for the arts with the corresponding eclipse of flagship enterprises such as the ABC and the Australian Opera, and new technology which in multiplying choices reduces the audience for any individual service.

Faced with such challenges, the Corporation's ability to respond is limited by its inherited institutional form, that of a single public service broadcaster expected to speak to, and for, the nation. This model, developed for a monopoly British Broadcasting Corporation (BBC) in the 1920s and 1930s, imposes on the ABC an unworkable, because contradictory, mandate. Legislation requires the organisation to be comprehensive yet fit into the wider broadcasting system. The

Corporation must 'contribute to a sense of national identity' but also 'reflect the cultural diversity of the Australian community'. The ABC must broadcast programmes of 'wide appeal' and also include 'specialised' services. At a time when an unfriendly environment demands more tightly defined purposes and objectives, the ABC is trapped by anachronistic legislative provisions which demand that it be national yet regional, popular yet focused, comprehensive yet complementary.

In Britain, the BBC is able to meet similar responsibilities through a range of channels. Two television networks, numerous national and regional radio stations and greatly restricted commercial competition enable the BBC to sustain a variety of audiences. ABC radio shares similar good fortune, with three national networks and a pastiche of local and syndicated programming. Australian governments have yet to be persuaded, however, that ABC television is worth funding twice; it remains a single national service, with scope only for occasional regional 'windows'. With just one service ABC television must meet the entire range of ABC objectives, an impossible task. If ABC television confines itself to cultural and educational programmes, the Corporation can be certain of low ratings, accusations of elitism and questions as to why compulsory taxation should support a privileged minority of regular ABC viewers. If, on the other hand, ABC television seeks legitimacy through popularity, then it simply repeats the programming of commercial stations and becomes a threat to the private sector. Government intervention is likely to follow. A mix of approaches looks like vacillation but is the Corporation's only option, thus ensuring that it satisfies no one.

The predicament posed for ABC directors—and it is a problem primarily of television programming—is knowing which audiences to pursue. Since politicians provide the budgets, they are the final arbiters of success. But ABC legislation sends only confused signals. Performance indicators used by the private sector are inappropriate, yet no credible alternative exists. The ABC may be a 'public broadcaster', but its charter demands that it eschew a purely market-based assessment of what the public wants in favour of normative judgments about what the public needs. Necessarily then, it is a guess as to what the Corporation should be broadcasting. The ABC can always be accused of failure but has no criterion for proving success.

It is caught in an organisational form which assumes a single national audience, yet expects the Corporation to flourish in a diverse and competitive system.

Since these problems are imposed on the ABC they cannot be solved by reform within. Tinkering with ABC structures and schedules will not halt the relative decline in audiences, which is the result of greater commercial reach, new technologies and a shortage of funds. Since the environment does not accommodate the ABC, the Corporation must adapt itself to its surroundings. Hence *Breaking Up the ABC* (a title suggested by Henry Mayer) concludes that disaggregating the Corporation might allow smaller units to achieve what a large bureaucracy cannot: a genuine multiplicity of services, each focused on a particular audience, supplying services in sum which one organisation is now expected to provide in total.

The idea of disbanding a large corporation has a curious resonance across political views. Those attracted to market solutions usually assume that public bureaucracies are wasteful, consuming resources in administration which could be employed in production. The argument used in the take-over of giant combinations, which are then broken down and sold as separate businesses, has been that dispersement improves responsiveness. British tycoon Sir James Goldsmith once spoke of 'liberating' small enterprises trapped in large conglomerates.

The same suspicion that size begets inefficiency or worse is found in non-market accounts of organisational structure. Tim Rowse (1985, p. 167) has warned of the risks in centralising public subsidy for the arts. The emphasis instead should be on pluralism, what Rowse labels 'decentralised patronage'. Rowse builds on this concern to question the need for a consolidated Australia Council. Implicit is a preference for multiple and perhaps overlapping small centres over a single large state institution. Similarly, Hew Evan's suggestion for rewriting the SBS charter is premised on buying programmes from independent production houses rather than concentrating the manufacture of public radio and television products in a few public sector bureaucracies.

Breaking Up the ABC pursues a similar line. An argument for continued public sector broadcasting, it suggests, is not necessarily a case for retaining the present ABC. There may be better forms for delivering the required services of independent news, access for alternative voices and unconventional programmes. We should compare the known returns of a single public service broadcasting agency with the possibilities inherent in a cluster of separate organisations. There might be more effective ways of achieving public broadcasting objectives.

The central idea

In 1990 Toby Miller, then a colleague at Griffith University, asked for an article reflecting on my *Breaking Up the ABC*. Surprised, but delighted, I subjected the readers of *Culture and Policy* to an account of my failed attempt to influence policy about public broadcasting in Australia. For the book, I concluded, made negligible impact; policy advice 'from the margins' had swayed neither public nor political opinion.

Six years later Jock Given, Director of the Communications Law Centre at the University of New South Wales, requested an urgent review of the National Commission of Audit (NCA), established by the Howard government after the 1996 federal election. The Commission, it seemed, had picked up ideas at least similar to those in *Breaking Up the ABC*, and was proposing radical surgery for the national broadcaster. Could I provide a commentary for *Communications Update* on the Audit Commission Report and its implications?

It would be flattering to conclude that I underestimated the influence of my ideas, but mistaken. It was not that the National Commission of Audit had appropriated the logic of *Breaking Up the ABC*. Rather, people who make policy reach for new ideas, scanning the horizon for alternative ways of achieving their objectives. In the mid-1980s, I glimpsed a new way of organising national broadcasting which I hoped might preserve virtues but remove inefficiencies. There were few clues in the literature, but some emerging discussion among those interested in the arts about this very different funding model.

A decade later, this inchoate schema had been worked through, and found expression as the principal/agent or purchaser/provider model. In its scan for ideas, the Commission of Audit could call upon a now well developed economic theory, and point to its implementation in many Australian jurisdictions. The technology of contracting, which once seemed to offer radical possibilities, had become a standard tool of conservative governments wishing to reduce the size and scope of the state.

Even the kindest reviewers commented on the abbreviated nature of the policy proposal at the core of *Breaking Up the ABC*. They were right to do so, for the final chapter did not have the analytic detail readers might reasonably expect, a point which holds for other parts of the book. In condensing a 100 000 word doctorate into a 40 000 word book pitched at a general audience, too much was lost. Even so the publisher's fears proved well-founded, with *Breaking Up the ABC* barely selling its modest, first and only, print run.

Yet there was a more fundamental reason for the brevity of the central idea. Promoting disaggregation was a tactical judgment about expanding the debate. In the mid-1980s, right-wing commentaries were proposing other, worrying, fates for the organisation. The spectre of sponsorship or even advertising had hovered during the Fraser years and seemed likely to return under Treasurer Keating. Economic ministers were among the fiercest critics of a Corporation which appeared to have lost its way under a new board and senior management. Meanwhile the Coalition, and its allies in various think-tanks, were talking about major cuts to the Corporation—an idea which endured through two further election defeats to be implemented by Prime Minister Howard. Those hostile to the national broadcaster appeared to hold the field, opposed only by 'ABC staff in denial' responses. Concerned that economic criteria would overwhelm the case for public broadcasting, I sought to shift the debate by offering a distinctive, and radically different, future.

Breaking up the ABC—liberating its constituent parts—seemed a plausible candidate. The analysis offered in the book made clear my biases—a commitment to maintaining real funding for public service broadcasting, a search for greater diversity of content and artistic control given goal displacement in such a large bureaucracy and, above all, a viable and long-term structure which could provide a counterweight to commercial media. The principal/agent model (though few had heard that name in 1988) appeared to offer a mechanism which could achieve those political objectives. It was relatively easy to work through the details—separate funding and boards for each radio network, contracting out of production for television, directors who would manage the Corporation's channels as a forum for access and debate—and set down a vision for a new type of institution. 'If the new broadcasters which result from deconstructing the ABC had multiple sources of funding and different boards of control, then the ideal of public service broadcasting— diverse viewpoints, services and experiences—would be realised' (Davis 1988, p. 134).

Underpinning these multiple, overlapping and federal post-ABC organisations would be a separate ABC news service, its independence and funding protected by statute, providing impartial and authoritative news to public broadcasters and beyond.

The problem—and hence the brevity—was the then lack of real information about such a model. There were few if any examples anywhere in the public sector world. New Zealand had briefly flirted with breaking up its public broadcasting organisation in the 1970s, but abandoned the experiment following a change of government. There were clues too in the emerging private sector 'network enterprises', but these would not enter the literature for some time yet.

The principal/agent model arose from private sector problems with joint-stock companies (Pratt and Zeckhauser 1985). How could owners, working from a distance, control managers? After all, managers can operate a company to appropriate profits for themselves, hiding rents which should follow property rights. The model posits a legal answer, with each side specifying their expectations and obligations in a binding contract. Principals can then use market discipline to restrain agents, by testing prices through competitive tenders. If one group of managers charge too much, another group can be hired in their place.

A principal/agent model makes possible new forms of organisation. A small core of agents can operate extended networks of suppliers, using contracts to regulate exchange. Those at the centre need no longer maintain capital facilities. They carry few employees or typical business overheads. Much of their attention is focused on writing contracts and monitoring performance. A contract organisation must be able to specify with some precision the product it wants to buy, and co-ordinate the activities of a large range of diverse suppliers. It must be strong on policy and skilled in contract management.

This separation of funding from production—usually known as the purchaser/provider model—has become well established in some Australian States. It usually applies to easily quantifiable and measurable goods, such as construction and computers, but in places has been extended to human services such as health and domiciliary care. The purchaser—the government—specifies services it wishes to buy, and seeks expressions of interest. The assumption is that competition among suppliers will deliver efficiencies.

One can imagine public service broadcasting delivered through such a model. Using a legislative charter as its guide, a board of ABC directors could set out objectives for their organisation. Suppliers would tender to provide programmes, leaving the national broadcaster expert, lean and focused on output rather than the mechanics of production. If the ABC were, in turn, broken down into its various components, and each contracted out its production, then the purchaser/provider model could offer a plethora of virtual organisations, each with a competing vision of public sector broadcasting, collectively expanding choice through more cost-effective delivery.

Yet such descriptions assume that the principal/agent model would, if implemented, complement public service broadcasting values. Such are the risks of promoting new ideas—for what if those who take up the technology do not share the policy thinker's values? What are the consequences if policy makers accept the logic of the suggestion but not its objective? The principal/agent model can be promoted as a progressive instrument for better outcomes. But it may open other, more ominous, possibilities.

Applying a contract logic

By 1996 it seemed that demons were to be set loose. Despite specific election promises about maintaining ABC funding, the incoming Coalition government under John Howard had announced significant cuts to the Corporation. From 1997 the ABC would lose $55 million, a figure Managing Director Brian Johns warned must have a 'savage impact on ABC services' (Davis 1996a). The Corporation would also be subject to an external review by former Optus and Fairfax chief executive Bob Mansfield.

Though the cuts were perhaps predictable, few anticipated more radical suggestions for Corporation change. Following the established pattern of conservative governments, the Howard administration established an audit commission, designed both to quantify the state of the budget and to legitimise subsequent cuts. Chaired by Bob Officer, a University of Chicago trained Professor of Finance at the Melbourne Business School, the National Commission of Audit (NCA) reported in June 1996. It recommended savings of between 10 and 20 per cent over the following three years for Commonwealth instrumentalities—consistent with cuts subsequently announced for the national broadcaster.

More surprisingly, in a passing reference, the National Commission of Audit advocated major structural change to the ABC. To quote the relevant passage in full:

> Under existing arrangements, the ABC receives over $500m of taxpayers' funds each year. As a mechanism to ensure that editorial independence is guaranteed, the allocation of these funds is largely a matter for the ABC.
>
> The arrangements allow the ABC Board to determine how money will be spent and how the community will be served, without direct accountability to government for the outcomes of its activity. The ABC's recent failed venture into pay TV is a case where the ABC Board spent public moneys to expand into peripheral activities without a clear benefit to the general public.
>
> A purchaser-provider funding model could provide a basis for funding public broadcasting in a way that ensures community needs are satisfied while editorial independence over programme material is preserved. Funding of specific categories of public interest broadcasting could be allocated to broadcasters on a contestable basis or tied to the ABC. The performance of the programme deliverers could be assessed by the funding authority against legislated criteria or other principles that are available to the public. (NAC 1996, pp. 102–3)

The ABC has long purchased programmes from independent production companies. It is not difficult to imagine extending this practice, until the organisation would commission programmes from independent producers but not make the product itself. Instead of a large ABC with producers, studios and production units, the Corporation would become small and focused, comprising only commissioning agents and transmission staff. Most of the ABC budget would flow through to those companies awarded contracts to make programmes.

Yet the National Commission of Audit contemplates a very different model. Taking the purchaser/provider model literally, government becomes the principal for public broadcasting. Ministers and public servants would specify the required programme outputs and allow a range of players, or perhaps just the ABC, to tender. Clearly such a model breaks all existing rules about public service broadcasting. It removes the 'arms length' relationship between content and government, making programming explicitly a political choice, purchased by the government on behalf of the community. Unacceptable content could simply be removed from the tender list, along with intransigent broadcasters.

To avoid this trap, the National Commission of Audit briefly mentions a 'funding authority', presumably as insurance against overt political control over content. Yet this is simply to restate the existing arrangement—a statutory body making independent programme decisions on behalf of the community—and seems pointless duplication of the ABC Board.

What, then, does the Audit Commission have in mind? Perhaps the more recent New Zealand experiment with disaggregating public broadcasting. A public agency now collects licence fees and disperses the money to broadcasters, private and public, following competition to fulfil programme contracts. With government funding dispersed across public and private sectors, the remaining public broadcasting stations have insufficient government income. They must seek substantial commercial sponsorship, and endure scepticism about their independence.

In a contestable model substitution can take place, as commercial networks attract funds for news or current affairs programming once reserved for the public broadcaster. Instead of competition and a range of offerings, choice is narrowed as funding once reserved for the ABC becomes a subsidy for existing commercial programmes.

This is a serious, if non-economic, consequence of cost cutting through a purchaser/provider model.

As Brian Johns pointed out in a speech to the Communications and Media Law Association in July 1996, the National Commission of Audit appears to have confused independence and accountability. To make the ABC accountable, the National Commission of Audit would make the ABC 'an agency of government'. Alternatively, to ensure independence, it would duplicate the ABC with another funding body. In either case, concluded Johns, a purchaser/provider model is a borrowed foreign concept which has 'proved to be highly flawed'.

These views were shared by Bob Mansfield, the person selected by Communications Minister Senator Richard Alston to review the ABC from June 1996. The Mansfield Report dismisses the NCA model out of hand. As Mansfield notes:

> One option put forward as a means of generating efficiency savings was the so-called 'purchaser/provider' model. The National Commission of Audit (NCA) has suggested that the Government could fund specific categories of public interest broadcasting on a contestable basis . . . This was supported by the Department of Finance submission to the review.
>
> The NCA suggested that the performance of programne deliverers could be assessed by a funding authority against legislated criteria or other principles made available to the public.
>
> Such a model has been implemented in New Zealand where a statutory body, New Zealand on Air, collects licence fees (known as the Public Broadcasting Fee) and allocates resulting funds to New Zealand radio and television public broadcasting authorities and to other commercial and community broadcasters. (Mansfield Report, vol. 1, p. 16)

Mansfield (1997, vol. 1, p. 16) rejects a purchaser/provider model for overall public broadcasting on a range of grounds. He believes it wrong in principle that government decides which programmes to fund. He does not wish the ABC to rely on advertising, or to surrender its traditional public broadcasting role in the search for markets. He fears an overall purchaser/provider model would require an additional layer of bureaucracy within the public service to distribute and monitor programming money, and is worried about the long-term prospects for an ABC living from contract to contract.

Yet Mansfield is not adverse to some purchasing within the ABC. Recommendation 15 of his report requires the ABC to 'outsource the majority of non-news and current affairs television production over the next three years' (Mansfield 1997, vol. 1, p. 37). The ABC was already planning to contract out some 30 per cent of non-news and current affairs television production, but Mansfield seeks to quicken the pace. Thus far it seems the ABC has escaped the widest application of the model only to be forced into a local implementation of this now standard management tool.

Who is responsible for ideas?

A powerful idea such as the principal/agent model is open to many interpretations. When policy makers pay attention to issues such as information and capacity, a principal/agent approach can empower clients, providing choice and accountability (Yeatman 1995, 1996a). If those in the community requiring domiciliary care, for example, can purchase services from a range of providers, then diversity in service, and product tailored to the individual customer, become possible. The consumer is spared the pathologies of a bureaucratic monopoly.

In this spirit Tim Rowse (1985) proposed disaggregating the Australia Council: a range of funding providers might better serve the individual artist and, through them, the nation's cultural interests. An artist unhappy with either the criteria of judgment or the funding priorities of one body could search for others. More and different viewpoints could inform funding decisions, with the maintenance costs of a large and permanent institution instead dedicated to the core business of supporting cultural works.

Yet other readings of the model are available. The Coalition, for example, used a principal/agent split as the basis for *Jobsback!*, a 1993 industrial relations policy statement. Once again the model focused on individuals, promising contracts between employers and each employee. Here the bureaucracy being removed was that of unions and arbitration commissions. Instead of collective bargaining protected by law, a principal/agent model would restrict negotiations to single workers, entrenching an asymmetry which favoured the employer (Davis and Gardner 1995). This model subsequently informed the Commonwealth's 1996 industrial relations legislation.

The principal/agent model, in short, is a skilfully contrived machine designed to favour a specified customer—artists in one case, employers in another. It does so by removing all extraneous social or political complications from the equation. That unions and awards—or an arts bureaucracy—serve other important functions becomes irrelevant to the issue at hand. If not parties to the deal they have no place at the table. Such broader interests become victims of the need to clarify and document a direct relationship between principal and agent, patron and artist, employer and worker.

Once grasped, the model is easy to apply, yet its consequences are open to question. Take the hypothetical example of a university. The traditional notion of a place of higher learning bundles together a range of functions, from research and teaching to community participation and, in much of Australia, regional development. Applying a principal/agent model, it should be possible to separate each of these functions and to identify the relevant customer. A 'virtual university' would then buy required outputs from independent suppliers. Teachers would be hired on a casual basis and research commissioned as funds become available. As in some European settings, whole courses could be contracted out, with teams of academics tendering to deliver the same course at a range of different institutions. Buildings could be sold, and venues hired on an 'as-needed' basis, so reducing capital costs. The university need no longer be confined to a geographic region, since its services could be delivered by contractors at any place.

Such an institution could be cost-effective and efficient. It might achieve most functions now expected of a university, and abandon those, such as community participation, not considered as 'core business'. Contracts would ensure flexibility, with labour supply matched to student demand. A virtual university would become the hub for networks of academics and researchers, an institution only lightly sketched onto the page, changing form as markets expand and contract.

Yet most people—and almost all academics—recoil at the suggestion. Why not embrace a virtual university when such efficiencies are possible? Partially, no doubt, we are inherently conservative about the familiar, preferring the certainties of the present to the unsure returns of an alternative, parallel, world. When pressed, we might also argue the benefits of such radical change do not clearly outweigh the price. The transaction costs of operating through networks and markets are significant, and vertical integration in the form of traditional universities may still be preferable (following Williamson 1975, 1985). This defence may not survive close scrutiny; the success of distance education in regional Australia is an important counter example of how tertiary education can be organised and delivered without the need for either campus or permanent staff.

The hostility to a virtual university resides not in opposition to contracting out individual activities (casual tutoring is already endemic), but to a belief that the sum of a traditional university exceeds its parts. Students benefit from sustained interaction with people and ideas. Teaching is improved by peer review and discussion. Professional values are acquired through socialisation in tutorials, lectures and the social life which radiates from the campus. A community of scholars can be more productive if settled in the one place. A society benefits from dissident ideas nurtured in a supportive institution.

These are the overtones, not the substance, of the university. Yet they are valued as much as the ordinary functional objectives of teaching and research. A single institution, with its own identity, location and culture, is a way of organising and experiencing the academic craft. It lifts the collectivity above its individual elements or printed objectives, providing a sustained internal life. We defend universities *because* they bundle together the necessary with a broader, if sometimes extraneous, set of social and political outcomes, suspecting that networks could deliver the parts but not the whole.

The objections to breaking up the ABC followed a similar pattern. The book received some kind notices, but the most hostile responses came—and still do—from those who work for the ABC. (This is more than reasonable—I am touchy about others' writing about universities, and share a belief that those 'outside' cannot really understand my institution or sector.) Whatever the merits of different forms of organisation, those inside the ABC saw the collectivity as too valuable to risk. ABC virtues rely on its large, bureaucratic, form and even its inefficiencies. A leaner Corporation might lose that sense of indulgence and experimentation essential to a creative undertaking. More radical surgery could destroy the spirit of public broadcasting entirely. Scattering ABC staff to competing production houses would dissipate a critical mass of ideas and experience, an irreplaceable intellectual capital. As Edward Tenner (1994) argues, a virtual society gains breadth but risks losing 'deep' organisations, those with vision, resources and institutional memory broader than the immediate task.

Hence the reluctance of the policy community to accept policy from the margins probably reflected a calculus of comfort with the status quo and reasoned scepticism about the alternative. A failure to work through the consequences of the principal/agent model proposed for the ABC justified such reservations. Policy thinking must aim to persuade, since the only test of a good policy idea is whether it wins the support of significant others (Lindblom 1959).[1] It can be hard for academics to win a policy audience—particularly for non-economists, who lack the apparent rigour and certainty of decimal point proposals. Often it requires provocative statements to attract attention, and political agitation to secure serious consideration of an issue (if not necessarily a preferred solution) (Kingdom 1995). Yet, if the policy world is not moved, the problem may be the proposal on offer. When persuasion falters, intellectual honesty demands that we examine our own ideas and motives.

And what of the intellectual responsibility for propagating ideas with unforeseen consequences? We should not flail ourselves because others use the same evidence to arrive at different and unwelcome conclusions. Any new idea, though, risks giving comfort to strangers, so the imperative to avoid ambiguity or misunderstanding is strong. Proposing a principal/agent model may contribute to a climate of opinion which justifies radical but unwanted change. That the original propositions are couched in terms of objectives and values is irrelevant; the ideas become part of the invisible chorus expressing doubt and hostility about a public institution, inviting harsh intervention. There is no escape from this dilemma for the policy thinker, just a practical and ethical requirement for good faith and political judgment when throwing ideas at public targets.

Still, the contrast with policy-making in the United States is instructive. In the 1950s and 1960s a small chorus—some academics, some bureaucrats—called for the expansion of publicly funded educational radio and television stations. Their case was taken up by a private philanthropic trust, the Carnegie Corporation, which, in 1967, submitted a detailed report to the then Johnson administration. Carnegie investigators examined, but rejected as inappropriate, the organisational model underlying the BBC and ABC, before settling on an indigenous structure for American public broadcasting. It was argued that public broadcasting should be a microcosm of American society, a federation of stations sharing some common programmes but also emphasising local production. Finance would depend on a partnership of Congress, subscribers and corporate sponsorship. Above all the system should not be controlled from the centre, and not be allowed to become overly bureaucratic. President Johnson was impressed and, in the same year he received the report, authorised creation of a Corporation for Public Broadcasting (CPB).

In short a group of outsiders—well placed and influential perhaps, but outside the White House nevertheless—persuaded the administration to rethink its entire broadcasting policy. An idea worked through the system managed to attract supporters, find legislative voice and call up a new set of structures (Davis 1991).

Such a swift and definitive outcome is less likely in the Australian context. If ideas do not persuade—as the Australian public broadcasting policy community was not persuaded about disaggregating their Corporation—then a policy process which moves only when the chorus grows loud and insistent ensures some distance and judgment about proposals for change. Bureaucrats, ministers and parties must all be convinced, public opinion tested and governments persuaded that the issue has salience so that benefits will outweigh costs. Since policy networks are restricted, policy brokers rare and coalitions for change difficult to establish, policy is more likely to be durable than experimental, cautious rather than risk-taking, continuous rather than irregular. These are the attributes which sustain viable long-term policy, ensure stability and pressure governments toward coherent and consistent choices. And they are the very attributes which make it difficult for policy thinkers to persuade from the margins.

Politics is a fascinating brew of interests, structures, ideas and chance. Policy thinkers must look for openings—for sponsors, for opportunities to become activists. There are ethical responsibilities about the arguments we advance. But there is also a duty to create those new world images, to reshape the struggle around new goals. If we could do so through words alone, policy activism would be of little significance.

Acknowledgments

I would like to thank Anna Yeatman for the invitation to participate, and acknowledge helpful comments from Margaret Gardner, Pat Weller and Howard Whitton. The permission of Dr Jennifer Craik, editor of *Culture and Politics*, and Jock Given, editor of *Communications Update*, to draw on some earlier work is much appreciated.

3

Development of professional competencies—a case study in the complexities of corporatist policy implementation

ANDREW GONCZI AND PAUL HAGER

Introduction

The concept of a policy activist is an emerging one. Various themes and features have been proposed tentatively as characteristics of policy activism. Yeatman suggests that a policy activist is 'anyone who champions in relatively consistent ways a value orientation and pragmatic commitment to . . . the policy process' based on it being open 'to the appropriate participation of all those who are involved in policy . . .' (Yeatman, chapter 1, p. 34). This chapter uses the development of professional competencies in Australia as a case study to illustrate these emerging characteristics of policy activism. However, the case study itself will turn out to be so complex that it appears that further distinctions within the notion of policy activist would be needed to even begin to account for this complexity.

As will become evident in subsequent sections of this chapter, the authors were heavily involved in the development of professional competencies in Australia in the period 1990 to 1994. However, it should be noted at the outset that this involvement was not a consciously planned strategy stemming from prior policy activism. Rather, our involvement was more a result of good fortune than design.[1] Thus, we have viewed the writing of this chapter as an opportunity to reflect back on our own policy activism in this case and the way that it evolved over time.

This case study is an example of corporatist policy implementation, that is a partnership between the state, professional bodies and employers of professionals acting together to achieve some agreed objectives. It represents the professions being brought into the policy arena via the lever of recognition of overseas qualifications. This is a major challenge to many professions who have for so long relied on 'the implicit direction of customary practice' (Yeatman, chapter 1, pp. 18–19). It is argued on the basis of this case study of policy process that an adequate model of policy activism will need to take account of complexity on at least three dimensions. These dimensions include:

The diversity of ends that a policy initiative might serve In the case of the development of professional competency standards in Australia there were very many proposed uses for the competencies and individual professions were free to select their own uses.

The diversity of motivations of activists involved in the policy process The development of professional competencies in Australia showed that the motivations of those most instrumental in effecting the change are typically multiple and various. Not only did different key people have significantly different motivations, but the motivations of a particular person involved in the change were likely to be very mixed. As well, there were different key people who were influential in the different stages of the policy process. Finally, the motivations of key individuals changed or evolved over the different stages of the policy process. Cutting across the diversity of motivations were distinctively different policy activist roles: bureaucratic policy activists; professional policy activists; and consultant policy activists.

The non-unitary character of the policy process itself The development of professional competency standards in Australia, in common with most other examples of policy process, involved at least four relatively independent stages, namely policy conception, policy implementation, policy delivery and policy evaluation.

The complexity of the present case study was largely due to the fact that, within each of these stages of the policy process, there was multiple causation at work in that diverse activists, favouring diverse uses of the competencies, were influential. This chapter will examine each of these three dimensions in some detail, but first some more general background information needs to be sketched.

The development of professional competencies in Australia

In the last decade, a competency-based approach to education, training and assessment has emerged as a key educational policy in the English speaking countries. In Australia, governments of quite different political persuasions have joined with business groups and the trade unions to promote the competency agenda. In Britain, similar developments are occurring, though, in England at least, without the same degree of involvement and consensus from the social partners. In the United States there have been recent initiatives in developing national competency standards for the teaching profession, and for certain craft occupations. In addition, organisations such as the American Society of Orthopaedic Surgeons have been developing a competency-based approach to curriculum (Green *et al.* 1990). In Canada, similar approaches have been used in social work training in a number of provinces for some time and are being tried currently in a number of middle level occupations.

What is unique about the Australian version of the competency movement, however, is the widespread involvement of the professions. Encouraged by the Commonwealth government, most of the professions have developed competency-based standards and are currently developing competency-based assessment strategies. Obviously this will affect higher education teaching and assessment practices as well as those of a variety of providers of continuing professional education.

About twenty professions undertook the development of competency standards and assessment strategies with funding provided by the National Office of Overseas Skills Recognition (NOOSR). Most of these standards were pitched at entry level to the various professions. Funding for these initiatives was available in the period from 1990 to 1994, after which it ceased. The principle was that the NOOSR funding would largely cover start-up costs, after which the professions themselves would carry ongoing costs, usually from their own resources as well as by charging some categories of assessees. In addition to these government funded projects there have been, and continue to be, self-supported competency projects in a variety of other professions or groups of professions. The specialist accreditation scheme of the New South Wales (NSW) Law Society, which is now spreading to some other States, is one such example. Other examples include professions which, following successful implementation of entry level competency standards, chose to proceed to the development of higher level or specialist standards. These include nursing and engineering (NOOSR 1995, p. 62).

It needs to be stressed that the development of competency standards and their implementation by professions was entirely voluntary. The government strategy was to respect the traditional autonomy of the professions, but to fund the development of the standards for those professions who, recognising the benefits, chose to co-operate. In the event, some traditional and powerful professions, such as medicine and dentistry, elected not to develop competency standards. This freedom of choice for the professions was different from the situation applying to other occupational groups covered by Australia's national training reform agenda[2] for whom development of competency standards was mandatory. Although funding had ceased by 1995, NOOSR was satisfied with the ongoing momentum generated by the competency standards projects and was not ruling out the funding of further developmental projects in the future (NOOSR 1995, p. 55). However, the tight budgetary policies of the Howard government, elected in 1996, probably makes further funding unlikely in the short term.

The professional competency standards developed in Australia were based on an 'integrated approach'. According to the integrated conception, competence is conceptualised in terms of knowledge, abilities, skills and attitudes displayed in the context of a carefully chosen set of realistic professional tasks ('intentional actions') which are of an appropriate level of generality. A feature of this integrated approach is that it avoids the problem of a myriad of tasks by selecting key tasks ('intentional actions') that are central to the practice of the profession. The main attributes that are required for the competent performance of these key tasks ('intentional actions') are then identified. Experience has shown that when both of these are integrated to produce competency standards, the results do capture the holistic richness of professional practice. We will not describe here the processes (see Gonczi, Hager and Oliver 1990; Ash, Gonczi and Hager 1992; and Heywood, Gonczi and Hager 1992 for details), but the focus is on applying a suitable combination of applied social science research methods to arrive at a logically structured set of action categories. The performance criteria are 'described' standards which are not expressed as long checklists, but in ordinary prose which is meant to suggest the holism of the nature of competence.

The diversity of reasons for developing professional competency standards

There are many reasons that have been advanced in favour of the professions using competency standards.

- It will help governments to devise means to fairly assess and grant professional status to overseas-trained professionals. This will be important in a world for the most part committed to the internationalisation of trade and services.
- It is desirable to have public statements about what the qualified members of a profession are competent to do and what the public can reasonably expect of them. This will help the professions to monitor more effectively the quality of their members' services. For the community it will lead to an enhanced capacity to choose between professionals and to judge the quality of service received. Additionally, it serves the democratic purpose of demystifying the specialised knowledge of the professions and potentially enabling more non-professionals to engage in debate about complex political issues such as health, education, justice and social welfare.
- It will facilitate mutual recognition of professional qualifications across States and Territories. This is important in federations such as Australia where achieving such mutual recognition has been a problem.
- It will provide the basis for assessing the competence of people re-entering a profession after a lengthy absence. It will also assist

in devising appropriate refresher courses for the various categories of absentee.

- The provision of clearer goals than currently exist for providers of professional education and training can be expected. This potentially will lead to much more coherent, integrated courses of professional preparation. Currently there is not much thought given to the relationship between on and off-the-job education (training) of professionals or to the respective roles of the universities and the professions in initial and continuing professional education.

- More effective continuing professional education programmes could be developed, particularly in those professions where various levels of competency standards have been established (see Hager and Gonczi 1991).

- Professional associations and registration authorities will be assisted in the accreditation of educational programmes.

- It will assist educational providers who wish to incorporate some competency-based assessment into their programmes.

- It will provide the basis for people with competencies in similar occupational areas to move more easily into the professions by making it clearer what is expected of a beginning professional. Likewise, in those professions where various levels of the competency standards have been established, it will be much clearer what is required of those seeking specialist or advanced status.

- It provides the opportunity for professionals to reflect on the nature of their work within a broader framework than has been previously possible. In fact, in Australia it has resulted in the incorporation of a far wider range of attributes into the description of competent performance in many professions than has existed previously. It amounts to a rejection of the narrow model of technocratic professionalisation that has characterised the professions in North America at least (Collins 1991).

- Improvement in the rather weak assessment procedures which lead to professional qualification in most professions, at least in Australia, can be expected.

Given the large number of possible uses of professional competency standards, it is unsurprising that different uses might appeal to different professions. This diversity was realised in practice, since, given that the development of professional competency standards was voluntary, individual professions were completely free to choose what uses they made of the standards once they had been developed. Hence, significant diversity in matters of implementation and delivery was virtually guaranteed in the case of the professions. However, the wide range of possible uses of professional competency standards also ensured that the standards development projects attracted many different kinds of activists. This was because the project methodologies ensured that there was wide representation from all parts of the particular professions. Thus activists of all kinds who were prepared to give freely of their time were able to participate in the standards development processes.[3]

The diversity of types of activists

A very diverse range of types of activists participated in the policy process for professional competency standards. As noted earlier, the diversity of types of activists stems from diversity in both motivations and roles. Policy activist roles that should be distinguished in this case study include bureaucrat policy activists, for example NOOSR officials, professional policy activists, such as active members of professional bodies, and consultant policy activists, for example the authors. The importance of the different activist roles will become apparent in a later discussion of the stages of the policy process.

The importance of the diverse motivations of policy activists can be appreciated by considering the sources of the diverse motivations of the professional policy activists involved in this case study. The sense in which these people were 'activists' is well captured in Yeatman's characterisation (see chapter 1, p. 33) as someone who is making 'a publicly declared and open contribution to political life', in this case mainly within a professional association. Such an activist was 'prepared to stand for and by his or her vision or values within what is openly contested territory concerning which and whose values are to prevail in setting the culture and orienting the structures' within the professional association.

The reason for this diversity of types of activists is that within professional associations there are many varied issues to engage the attention of activists. Based on our experiences in the development of professional competency standards, the typical professional association features just such a diversity of activists. The varied issues that attract these many types of activists include the following.

A commitment to excellence of practice

Despite the current widespread community suspicion and even disenchantment with many of the professions, our own experience in working with a variety of professions has been that there are substantial numbers of activists in the professional associations who are committed to the improvement of practice. This has always been the case and, indeed, the definition of a profession often includes the requirement that there must be such a commitment. For the activists within the professions, their professional association has been the vehicle through which their activism has been expressed. The development of competency standards and the assessment procedures that accompanied them was seen by activists in a number of professions as an opportunity to systematically review and improve practice.

One of the most interesing examples is the influence of activists in the NSW Law Society. Despite the popular view that the legal profession is one of the most conservative and self-interested of the professions, the work of the Law Society in the development of a specialist accreditation scheme based on standards and a rigorous assessment process illustrates how activists can bring about changes in a profession. The aims of this scheme are stated as:

> . . . offering the public and the professions a reliable means of identifying solicitors as having special competency in an area of practice; encouraging improvement in the quality, speed, and cost of legal services; providing practitioners with an incentive and opportunity to improve their competency. (Armitage, Roper and Vignaendra 1996, p. 219)

The scheme involved the authors working with groups of experienced lawyers in a variety of fields (criminal law, family law, commercial litigation) to develop a set of standards for each specialism and an assessment strategy which provided the accreditation mechanism.

(For more details see Gonczi, Hager and Palmer 1994.) This process gave the authors, as activists, the opportunity to put into practice their theoretical framework developed for NOOSR. The activists from the profession gave freely of their time to develop the standards (developed over three or four weekend or evening sessions, with 'homework' in between the sessions), to design the assessment tasks, and to mark candidates' assessments. As will be shown later the development and marking were substantial tasks, as the assessment of performance is far more complex and time consuming than traditional pen and paper assessment.

The quest for recognition

There are various related facets to this phenomenon. One is the emergence of groups seeking to better establish their credentials as professions. There are numerous examples of this. In the nursing profession many activists saw the development of competency standards as an opportunity to define the work of the profession and to gain recognition in the eyes of a community who still tended to equate nursing with mundane practical activities. With the preparation of nurses moving from workplace-based training to universities, competency standards, it was thought, would provide a guide for the design of nursing degree courses. This proved to be so particularly in nursing degrees based on a problem-based learning approach.

Related to this are the newly emerging professions (formerly known as 'paraprofessions') such as podiatry. In the last few years, podiatry courses were located in universities in all States except NSW, where it was still a TAFE course. In a clear bid for full professional status, the professional body threatened non-recognition of NSW graduates thereby effecting the desired change in arrangements in that State. Also, the influence of recent feminist thought on the activism of some newly emerging professions should not be underestimated. It is no accident that a number of these professions, such as nursing, occupational therapy and dietetics, are predominantly female in their membership.

A further facet of the quest for recognition is the tension created when two or more bodies, sometimes having different status, exist in a single profession or in closely related professions. In accountancy there is the traditional stand-off between the Institute of Chartered Accountants and the Australian Society of Certified Practising Accountants. A related case is the uneasy relationship between welfare work and social work. Situations such as these create at least two kinds of activists: those who wish to join the smaller groups into a bigger united organisation and those who wish to keep them apart at all costs.

Clearly these various, sometimes overlapping, facets of the quest for recognition offer scope for a wide variety of activisms.

Consequences of rapid change

The current era is characterised by an historically unprecedented kind of rapid and accelerating change that is affecting all areas of our lives including work. The main impacts on work include drastic labour market changes, evolving technology, reskilling and deskilling of workers. While all professions are experiencing some effects of this change, some are affected more than others. In extreme cases, the very existence of the profession is under threat, a situation bound to engage the attention of activists. For instance, evolving technology has meant that optometrists are under pressure both from above (by ophthalmologists who offer new corrective eye operations) and from below (by optical technicians who use sophisticated dispensing equipment). Architects being displaced by project managers is a further instance of this phenomenon.

A further current effect of rapid and accelerating change is to create doubts about the efficacy of the 'front end' approach to professional education. More and more, a three to five-year course at the start of a professional career is seen merely as the necessary foundation for the early years of practice, rather than as sufficient basis for a lifetime of practice. Thus there is increasing interest in the notion of lifelong learning as a guiding principle for professional education (Candy, Crebert and O'Leary 1994). As a result of this, there is a growing focus on the development of more effective continuing professional education (CPE). This is evident in such things as: a marked trend towards mandatory CPE (in law and accountancy); compulsory refresher courses for returners following a significant absence from the practice of the profession (in nursing);

and the placing of expiry dates on initial qualifications with periodic 'topping up' components being required in order to maintain currency (this has become common in the USA).

Public dissatisfaction with the professions

Another issue that has engaged the attention of activists within professions has been the growing dissatisfaction of the public everywhere in the liberal democratic world with the professions and with the performance of particular professionals. This has been fuelled by an increased willingness of the media to expose professional incompetence and malpractice, by the increasing knowledge and sophistication of consumers together with increased willingness to turn to the legal system, and by general demands in society for greater accountability. Professional bodies have reacted to these developments in various ways, including making the scrutiny of their processes for assessment and certification of professionals more stringent, by increasing CPE requirements, and by reforming assessment procedures in tertiary professional preparation courses. One major reason for Australian professions establishing competency standards was a desire to deal effectively with these issues. For example, the specialist accreditation programme of the NSW Law Society, discussed earlier, is one such case.

Autonomy of the professions

The traditional autonomy of the professions is arguably in some decline (compared with the traditional autonomy of universities). This decline in professional autonomy is linked to some of the previously listed factors and provides a focus for some activists within professional bodies. The major importance of professional autonomy in this case study is reflected in the fact that, as explained earlier, the development of competency standards by the professions in Australia was voluntary. This is a main basis of the complexity of the case study, since individual professions, motivated by a complex of considerations of the kind outlined earlier, were free to choose whether or not to establish competency standards, and, if they did so, what use, if any, they would make of them.

These various factors are enough in themselves to ensure that within professional bodies there would be activists with many kinds of motivations and a wide variety of issues on which to focus their activism. Certainly, this case study involved a very diverse range of activists. Most of them had 'commitment, vision, and strategy which are sustained over time'. These activists were also typically involved in influencing policy agendas. However, they were not all working to influence the same policy agendas. The competencies agenda was a major vehicle for furthering various sub-agendas. Is this an unusual situation? If so, this case study may be of limited interest. If not, this case study may point to the need for an understanding of policy activism to better take account of complexity. However, the variety of uses for professional competency standards and the diversity of types of professional activists were far from being the only contributors to the complexity of this case study.

The multi-stage policy process

As already noted, four relatively independent stages, namely policy conception, implementation, delivery and evaluation, can be identified in the policy process. These four relatively independent stages, when combined with the large number of uses of professional competency standards and the participation of the diversity of types of activists, as outlined in the last two sections, ensured the complexity of the present case study. The complexity was further underlined by the participation of a variety of other activists, such as bureaucrat policy activists (government officials) and consultant policy activists (the authors), who were not directly connected with the professions but who were acting with a variety of aims of their own. Briefly, this is how the four stages looked:

Policy conception

The main activities here were decisions taken by politicians and senior bureaucrats about the role of the professions in the national training reform agenda, followed by the commissioning of two research papers to present and critically evaluate the various options for the use of competency standards by professions. Although we have, at best, a shadowy notion of what occurred in the first of these activities, as authors of one of the two research papers, we were close observers of the later activities.

Policy implementation

This centred on the process by which various professions went about establishing their competency standards. Basically this involved the use of a suitable combination of applied social science research methods to which a widely representative group of professionals and other interested parties contributed their knowledge and understanding of high quality performance in the particular profession. We were closely involved in this process for a number of the professions for whom we acted as consultants and facilitators in the establishment of the competency standards. We also provided feedback and advice to other professions where we were less directly involved in the establishment of the competency standards. However, in all cases our commissioned research paper (Gonczi, Hager and Oliver 1990) guided the establishment of the competency standards, since it provided the generic definitional basis by which professional competence could be conceptualised.

Policy delivery

This centred on the uses that the various professions made of their competency standards. A major issue here was assessment, since nearly all of the uses of competency standards involve some form of performance assessment. Since performance assessment is in many ways different from familiar and traditional forms of assessment, this stage typically involved significant amounts of learning on the part of participants. We were closely involved in this process for a number of the professions, with our own understanding of performance assessment and its relation to more traditional approaches to assessment being both enriched and enhanced by the experience.

Policy evaluation

While the use of competency standards by Australian professions is still relatively new, individual professions have been monitoring their own activities and refining the processes on a regular basis. In addition, the National Office of Overseas Skills Recognition (NOOSR) conducted an interim evaluation of the impact of professional competency standards in Australia (NOOSR 1995). Our involvement in this stage has been more remote consisting mainly of informal discussion and feedback with key players on the progress of the uses of competency standards by various professions.

Each of these four stages in the professional competencies case study will now be outlined and discussed in more detail.

Policy conception

While we cannot pretend to have had access to all of the details of the process of policy conception, it is fairly clear that the main influences on the process were the following:

1 Government, unions, and big business as the joint proponents of Australia's ongoing national training reform agenda centred on the adoption of competency standards as a basis for advancing the skill levels of the workforce and for the reform of training for occupations. This occurred during the late 1980s and early 1990s, a time when the federal Labor government was an experienced champion and broker of corporatist approaches to power.

2 Officials in the then Department of Employment, Education and Training. Those who were most visible were officials of the National Office of Overseas Skills Recognition (NOOSR) who commissioned the two research papers that stimulated the national debate on competency standards in the professions and guided the early work in the establishment of such standards.

3 Academic consultants engaged to produce documents and advice. These consisted of two consultants from the Australian Council for Educational Research with expertise in assessment and three consultants from the University of Technology, Sydney, with expertise in vocational education.

4 The existing literature. A small, but well-argued, body of work that pointed towards the directions that the research papers

would take had been identified by the NOOSR officials who commissioned the two research papers.

From the time that the consultants became involved in the process, it was very clear that the NOOSR officials who commissioned the research papers had well formed ideas about what was needed. Their vision went well beyond considerations of equity in recognition processes for overseas qualifications, to the wider ramifications of the professions being significantly involved in the national training reform agenda. It was also clear that their views were grounded in acquaintance with relevant literature and overseas trends. Thus their influence in the commissioning and the writing of the discussion papers was significant. It was noticeable to us on many occasions that the NOOSR officials had a more sophisticated understanding of the issues than most other participants including academics. The latter, in particular, often made the mistake of assuming that, because the NOOSR officials were public servants, they could not possess sophisticated theoretical understanding of the issues. Because of the effects of the traditional academic–vocational divide discussed below, it was, in fact, usually the academics who needed to do some fast learning. This strong influence of the NOOSR officials illustrates Yeatman's plausible view that policy 'is inseparable from the state, and both . . . are dependent upon the apparatus of state administration or management' (Yeatman chapter 1, p. 20).

The main component of the policy conception process was the commissioning and the writing of the discussion papers 'Establishing Competency-Based Standards in the Professions' (Gonczi, Hager and Oliver 1990) and 'Competency-Based Assessment in the Professions' (Masters and McCurry 1990). These were launched at a national conference which included representatives of the various professions as well as key figures from the universities. It is worth noting that these research papers were consciously designed to start a national discussion. This meant that though they needed to be strongly grounded in research literature, they also had to be written in an approachable, non-technical style since most readers would have little or no familiarity with the literature from which they were derived.

As authors of one of the research papers, our prime activism at that stage concerned the need to combat the denigration of the vocational that has been typical in the academic world and in educational circles generally. This denigration is captured in such dubious dichotomies as education–training, mind–body, head–hand, general–vocational, and has been a guiding theme of western education. Yet, in our view, it is grossly mistaken (see Hager 1994). The competencies agenda represented a chance for us to pursue further a somewhat broader agenda that we had been pushing for some time, that is, to make the richness and complexity of sound vocational education a matter of serious theoretical interest in the field of education. We also had an ongoing interest in issues about professionalism and the education of professionals based on our own careers and those of the diverse professionals that we had worked with over many years as a result of designing and teaching a graduate diploma course for vocational teachers.

During the writing of the research papers, which took about three months, matters moved quickly. There were four main drafts, during which the commissioners moved from their initial position of requiring an emphasis on equity in recognition of the qualifications of overseas trained professionals, to the broader position focused on the Australian professions that is evident in the published papers. During the various drafts a number of 'side issues' were also deleted, for example an early concern with 'paraprofessions' as well as professions was dropped. Thus this later phase of the writing was the outcome of the interplay of the activism of the authors (consultant-policy activists) and the activism of the NOOSR officials (bureaucrat-policy activists).

The shift in emphasis during the writing of the research papers from equity in recognition of overseas qualifications to a broader focus on professional standards calls for more comment. As the name 'National Office of Overseas Skills Recognition' suggests, the main work of NOOSR is the equitable evaluation of skills gained overseas against qualifications required for entry into occupations in Australia. Even in the days when Australia's immigration intake was mostly European, and hence most immigrants had gained their formal qualifications from institutions that had similar traditions to Australian educational institutions, comparing qualifications was not always easy. For instance, one of the authors once had the experience of provisionally admitting a student to a graduate diploma course pending confirmation of the equivalence of a degree in Spanish from a Spanish university. NOOSR's ruling in that case was that the 'degree' was only equivalent to the completion of high school in Australia.

As Australia's more recent immigration intake has increasingly come from non-European countries, and as the emphasis has shifted more towards skilled immigrants, NOOSR's work has grown considerably. It is very common for immigrants with trade, technician, paraprofessional or professional qualifications in their own country to find that their qualifications are not fully recognised in Australia. Not only is NOOSR charged with ensuring that such judgments are equitable, it has also been active in facilitating bridging arrangements to enable overseas trained immigrants to raise their qualifications to the level needed for practice in Australia. Thus the initial emphasis in the draft research papers on competency standards as a way of increasing equity in recognition of overseas professional qualifications was unsurprising.

We can only speculate on the reasons for the shift to a broader focus on professional competency standards that was required in the published research papers. Our impression was that the decision was taken by officials at higher levels in the Department of Employment, Education and Training than any NOOSR official occupied. Perhaps there was a recognition that bringing the professions into the national training reform agenda made sense in a climate of increasing globalisation, pressure for portability of qualifications, reductions of barriers to free trade, etc. Or, possibly, it was a strategic decision that, given the hostility towards competency standards in influential parts of the professions, a more general approach might be more effective in achieving desired changes.

Policy implementation

This phase was more complicated in that there were more kinds of activists involved in shaping the outcomes. The main types of activists involved in the development of the professional competency standards were:

- NOOSR officials (bureaucrat policy activists) responsible for commissioning and overseeing the various competency standards projects, that is, NOOSR entered into contracts with individual professions.

- Academics and consultants (consultant policy activists). We and others employed by the individual professions to facilitate the processes of competency standards establishment.
- Activists in the various professions (professional policy activists) with a variety of agendas who played a major part in the establishment of the competency standards.
- Activists responsible for the various professional courses at universities (a different, but usually influential, group of professional policy activists) who played a significant part in the establishment of the competency standards.

This phase centred on the processes by which various professions went about establishing their competency standards. Basically this involved the use of a suitable combination of applied social science research methods (modified functional analysis, focus groups, critical incident interviews, etc.) to which a widely representative group of professionals and other interested parties (employers, unions, Australian Vice-Chancellors Committee, registration authorities, etc.) contributed their knowledge and understanding of high quality performance in the particular profession. We were closely involved in this process for various of the professions for whom we acted as consultants and facilitators. We also provided feedback and advice to a number of other professions where we were less directly involved in the competency standards establishment process. We were further involved in the overall process in that NOOSR officials commissioned us and others to write two 'how to' documents describing and explaining the process of establishing competency standards (Ash, Gonczi and Hager 1992; Heywood, Gonczi and Hager 1992).

Our main interest at this stage, flowing from our concern to combat denigration of the vocational, was to show that holistic competency standards could provide a rich representation of practice as well as have educationally sophisticated implications. For us, this stage was about making it work, whereas the earlier one was about showing that it was theoretically possible.

The overall process of the establishment of competency standards was one in which many parties had an input with the final product representing a broad consensus of those involved. In most cases, the professional body was influenced more or less by the NOOSR documents and by us as facilitators (where we were retained as consultants). There was diverse input from the wider representation: university providers, registration boards, unions, NOOSR, consumer groups, etc. As well there were the diverse motivations and agendas of the activists from the various professional bodies (as discussed earlier). Though the role of other participants was significant, it was inevitable that activists from within the profession had the most influential voices when it came to developing a rich representation of good practice in that profession.

Policy delivery

At the heart of a competency-based approach to professional accred-itation and registration is assessment. How courses which prepare professionals for practice and how registration authorities (registra-tion boards, professional associations, etc.) actually undertake the accreditation procedures was a vital part of the process of policy activism. The importance of assessment, however, was not clear at the earlier stages of the policy process. Certainly when the authors were asked to develop their theoretical framework for a competency-based approach based on standards (the conception phase) we were not fully aware of the assessment implications of such an approach. However, during the implementation phase, when, along with the activists in the professions, we first began to develop actual compe-tency standards with various professional associations, assessment issues began to emerge. The government officials (bureaucrat policy activists) who had been involved at the conception of the policy also saw the need to analyse the assessment issues and again commis-sioned us (consultant policy activists) to write a research paper to try to unpack the issues (Gonczi, Hager and Athanasou 1993).

In undertaking the research for this paper, the opportunity to make a contribution to another long-standing problem emerged for the authors. This problem was the questionable validity of much assessment in professional education, based as it was (and to some extent remains) on the exclusive testing of theoretical knowledge through the use of pen and paper tests. Of course this is a subset of the point made earlier about the dichotomy between applied and theoretical knowledge, between vocational and general education. The opportunity to challenge these dichotomies was the major motivating force for the authors' involvement in the policy process in this case.

It became clear during the writing of the paper not only that assessment procedures in universities and professional associations were not well understood, but that the assessment of performance and the relationship between this and the assessment of knowledge was not well understood even by assessment experts (see Hager and Butler 1996). While the authors lacked the confidence to develop such a framework directly, they worked from first principles and created a framework for developing strategies for assessing competence.

This framework was used to help a number of professional associations develop their own assessment and accreditation instruments. The example of the NSW Law Society is again instructive here. Working with the various specialist groups, ways of assessing whether individuals could meet the competency standards were created. Traditionally, law examinations in universities have been time-honoured tests of knowledge and it is not surprising that a number of the specialist groups wanted to (and some did) retain a traditional three hour written test of knowledge of the law. However, the activists in the various groups were keen to move beyond such assessment and in all cases new forms of assessment were developed. Typical were simulations which tested knowledge alongside communication skills and dispositions of various kinds (care in recording facts), mock files which tested research and drafting skills, moots which tested presentation skills, and so on.

Activists in the other professions seized on the framework which enabled them to develop alternate assessments since they too were highly critical of traditional tests. They were highly skilful in designing these performance tests and were confident that they would be a much better way of assessing competence to practice than were traditional tests. The next section on evaluation demonstrates that this confidence was justified.

Before moving on to the fourth stage, it is worth pointing out another factor that contributed to the overall complexity of the policy process for professional competency standards. The relative independence of the stages was enhanced by the major differences in the personnel involved in the various stages. Even where the same people were involved in more than one stage (in most cases stages two and three), their thinking was likely to have evolved and, or, their main concerns were likely to differ between stages. So, for example, our own activism moved from a focus in the second stage on showing that holistic competency standards could simultaneously capture the vocational, yet be rich from an educational perspective, to a related, but different, focus in the third stage on proving the worth of performance assessment as against more traditional alternatives.

We have found somewhat similar changes in personnel in the four stages of the policy process in a project that we are currently completing on the Australian key competencies (DEETYA 1996a). The Finn Committee formulated the policy. The Mayer Committee was charged with implementing it. A series of people were then commissioned to conduct projects on the delivery of the key competencies. Finally, many people are doing evaluations of various kinds. These four stages are relatively independent and there is little overlap of personnel between the stages.

Policy evaluation

As noted above, a major element in the complexity of the professional competencies case study was the freedom of each profession to decide the uses, if any, that it would make of its competency standards. The results of this freedom are evident in a National Office of Overseas Skills Recognition survey (NOOSR 1995) of the professions that had established competency standards which, among other things, investigated what uses were being made of these standards. Given the various main possible uses of competency standards outlined above, it is interesting to see the definite ways in which the Australian professions are employing their competency standards. Table 3.1 (NOOSR 1995, pp. 14–15) shows the percentage of survey

Table 3.1 Uses of competency standards by Australian professions

Uses of competency standards 'yes' responses	%
Assessing competence of overseas trained professionals	73
Providing public information on professional roles/responsibilities	50
Facilitating mutual recognition within Australia	47
Assisting in accreditation of education programmes	43
Assessing eligibility for professional registration	42
Developing continuing professional education courses	38
Assessing competence of lengthy absentees from practice	37
Assisting in development of university curriculum	34
Developing competency-based assessment	31
Assessing eligibility for membership of a professional body	29
Facilitating articulation between levels within a profession	26
Assessing competence of people with no formal qualification	21
Determining individual continuing professional education needs	17
Facilitating articulation from paraprofession to profession	16
Defending professionals against legal action	13
Assisting employers to evaluate performance	12
Assisting employers in recruitment and promotion of staff	11

respondents[4] who asserted that their profession had adopted the respective uses of competency standards.

These figures reflect the fact that there are not just one or two main uses of competency standards that have been adopted by virtually all professions. Rather, there is great diversity between the individual professions in the ways that they are employing their competency standards. This in turn supports claims made for the multipurpose nature of competency standards. This diversity of uses points to the fact that each profession has its own unique features and needs so that the implementation of competency standards is viewed somewhat differently in each case.

Overall the development of professional competency standards has stimulated an unprecedented amount of research, development and internal professional debate within the Australian professions. In relation to policy activism, these figures represent further support for the complexity that is, by now, evident in the professional competencies case study.

Interestingly, the National Office of Overseas Skills Recognition survey found significant positive support for the use of holistic, integrated competency standards among university staff who have been involved in their implementation. This contrasts with findings by other research that academics in general, most of whom have had no experience with these sorts of competency standards, are opposed to their use.

At the level of the individual profession, it is instructive to examine further the impact of the policy implementation and delivery on professional practice. The example of law specialist accreditation in NSW is instructive once again, as the policy and its impact on the profession have been systematically evaluated.

The reviewers (Armitage, Roper and Vignaendra 1995) used focus groups and a survey to assess the perceptions of clients. While they caution readers to be careful in interpreting their results, they conclude that there has been an increase in expectations of clients as a result of the scheme and that there are high levels of satisfaction among clients:

> Overall the data reveal an increasingly discerning clientele whose expectations of service have consistently risen and have almost universally been satisfied or exceeded by their specialists. These findings reflect the *ultimate performance indicator* [their italics] for the accreditation programme which is client satisfaction with specialists' service: and more specifically they demonstrate the overall effectiveness of the assessment process in providing a mechanism for the identification of solicitors as having special competence in an area of practice. (p. 17)

When asked whether the assessment had influenced their practices, 62 per cent of the successful candidates felt that it had. In the area of wills and estates the proportion was as high as 79 per cent. They identified a range of areas such as: review of office procedures; increased awareness of precedents; heightened awareness of time limits in practice; increased knowledge of law and legal principles. This is strong evidence of the consequential validity of this particular competency-based assessment.

What these evaluations also show is that those accreditation methods which concentrate on the *performance* of 'real' tasks meet with strong satisfaction while traditional written tests meet with relatively low approval. In 1994 for example, in the personal injury speciality, the mock file (a task which asks solicitors to undertake research, draft pleadings for court, organise a brief for barristers, etc.) was rated by 53 per cent as likely 'to a great extent' to give them an opportunity to demonstrate their ability—this was the top of a five point scale. Taking the fourth and fifth points together, the satisfaction rates were 91 per cent for the mock file. The same level of satisfaction for the written test of knowledge was 13 per cent for the fifth point of the scale and 41 per cent for the fourth and fifth points combined. In the same year in the family law speciality, satisfaction rates were 19 per cent and 1.6 per cent for the top of the scale for the mock file and written knowledge test respectively. For the fourth and fifth points of the scale combined, satisfaction levels were 81 per cent for the mock file and 37 per cent for the written test of knowledge. Similar results are available for the other specialities.

Significantly, 100 per cent of candidates felt that the assessment experience was educational in the sense that it gave them the opportunity to exchange ideas with colleagues, to revise and to get up to date.

Conclusion

This chapter has used the development of professional competencies in Australia as a case study to illustrate emerging characteristics of policy activism. The case study has broadly supported the emerging conception of 'policy activist'. However, the case study itself has been so complex across many dimensions that it seems that further distinctions within the notion of policy activist would be necessary to account for this complexity, for example bureaucrat policy activists, professional policy activists, and consultant policy activists.

The case study involved a very diverse range of activists. Most of them had 'commitment, vision, and strategy which are sustained over time'. These activists were also typically involved in influencing policy agendas. However, they were not all working to influence the same policy agendas. The competencies agenda was a major vehicle for furthering various subagendas. If such complexity is typical, then it needs to be accounted for in any satisfactory theory of policy activism by identifying the main policy activists roles that apply in a given situation and also the relative power of the different roles in that situation.

The traditional autonomy of the professions, which is arguably in some decline, was a key factor in this case study. It was reflected in the fact that the development of competency standards by the professions was voluntary. Perhaps this is a main basis of the complexity of the case study. However, such complexity should not be unusual given the important role of democratic participation in policy activism (see Yeatman, chapter 1, especially pp. 30–5).

Illustrating the complexity of this case study, definite phases, which were not preplanned, were evident in our own consultant policy activism. Our initial major concern was the promotion of a rich conception of competence and competencies in opposition to more limited perceptions of vocational education. Once the establishment of competency standards was underway, however, our focus was more on the production of standards that were themselves holistic and educationally rich. Then, when the uses of the competency standards began to be piloted by the professions, our attention shifted to assessment, since most of the uses involve some form of assessment. For the pilot phases to be successful, it turned out that there was an urgent need for participants to understand performance assessment and its vital differences from traditional norm-referenced assessment. These three phases correspond broadly to policy conception, implementation and delivery. We were not significantly involved in the fourth stage, policy evaluation.

4

Children's services and policy activism

DEBORAH BRENNAN

Government involvement in the provision of services for young children provides fertile ground for the exploration of policy activism. There have been major swings in the direction of government policy in this area over the last two and a half decades, and a range of players with a diversity of interests have been policy activists. Not all lobbying or pressure group activity is policy activism, however, and this chapter seeks to distinguish between different types of lobbying behaviour and to illuminate the nature of policy activism.

Although the Commonwealth became involved in this area only in the early 1970s, child care is now a significant area of government policy and a major industry. The Commonwealth and State governments together spend more than $1.5 billion dollars each year on children's services; over 70 000 people are employed in the industry and almost 600 000 children use Commonwealth funded services (Economic Planning and Advisory Council 1996, p. 23). Given that government funding for child care commenced only in 1972, this appears to be a straightforward 'success story'. Yet, almost every aspect of child care provision has been fiercely contested—from the very existence of government policy in this area, to the fine detail of policy implementation. Should governments be making policy in this area or should the care of children be a private family matter?

If government provision is to exist, should the focus be on preschool education or a broader range of services? Should commercial operators have access to the same subsidies as non-profit providers?

This chapter will focus on three episodes in the development of child care policy and will explore the types of policy activism which were exhibited in each. The three episodes are, first, the late 1960s to early 1970s when groups associated with the women's liberation movement began the process of getting community-based child care onto the national agenda and shaping government policy to give effect to feminist demands. Second, the extension of government subsidies to commercial child care centres (a policy change which was first explored under the Fraser Coalition government but which later came into effect under the Hawke Labor government). Third, attempts by governments in the 1990s to restrict child care provision to the children of workforce participants.

Historical background

A notable feature of the child care policy arena is the long history which preceded contemporary 'policy activism'. Philanthropists and progressive educationists (mainly women) established the first kindergartens and day nurseries in the inner suburbs of the major cities in the early 1890s (Spearritt 1974). These reformers, however, could not be described as 'policy activists'. In the early decades, the services they provided were entirely private (in the sense that they were conducted outside the realm of state activity); they were staffed by volunteers and received no government assistance. Later, most State governments provided grants which matched the fundraising efforts of volunteer committees. Even then, however, efforts were piecemeal and there was no systematic government 'policy'. Significantly, there was no contest about the authority of professional early childhood educators over matters concerning the care and education of young children. Until the late 1960s, they were the unchallenged source of advice to governments on such matters. The philosophy of these early reformers was distinctly elitist. They regarded themselves as uniquely positioned to advise on the needs of young children because of their specialised knowledge (in some cases gained through study in

England or the United States) and because they were not tainted by commercial interests. Early on, they became the acknowledged stand-ard-setters in matters relating to young children. One matter on which they held clear views was the distinction between services deemed educational and those which simply provided 'care'. Kinder-gartens and preschools, which catered mainly for children in the year or two before school, belonged in the former category. Most children attended such services for only a few hours each week, which meant that they could not be said to threaten the bond between mother and child. Day nurseries, on the other hand, provided long hours of care for the children of needy working mothers and were seen as far less desirable. Effectively, these were seen as welfare services—not the type of service that people would actively desire for their children, but an unfortunate necessity (Brennan 1994, pp. 13–31).

Activists in search of policy

With the resurgence of the women's movement at the end of the 1960s feminists began to articulate a new approach to child care. They argued that services for children should not be regarded in a narrow way as either an educational service or a workplace facility. Rather, children's services were a fundamental social requirement for any serious challenge to be made to the sexual division of labour either in the workplace or in the home. Feminists insisted that the idealisation of intense and exclusive mother–child relationships oppressed not only women but children as well. They argued that child care could be undertaken outside the family and that it need not necessarily be done by other women; men could share this work whether it occurred inside or outside the home.

One of the earliest statements of the feminist position on child care was made by community activist Winsome McCaughey:

> In our society, the nuclear family (read 'mother') has been held
> to be fully responsible for the development and socialisation of
> the child under school age. Women's Liberation holds this to be
> an unreasonable and unsatisfactory method of childrearing.
>
> Children are in a very real sense, the children of the whole
> community and [Community Controlled Child Care] believe it to

be the responsibility of the government to make 'educational' facilities available to children under five years of age, in the form of good child care centres. (McCaughey 1972, pp. 3–6)

The philosophy of Community Child Care and similar groups was firmly grounded in a variant of feminism which placed a high value on self-help activities and opposed the 'professionalisation' of child care. It was thus positioned in opposition to the dominant discourse of the professional early childhood educators. As an early manifesto explained: child care '[does] not have to mean simply handing your child over to professionals' (McCaughey and Sebastian 1977, pp. 9–10).

Community Child Care called for the provision of free child care, available to all parents, regardless of their reasons for seeking it. Its members cautioned that child care services should not be provided simply to free women to work outside the home at dreary, exhausting labour that left them with the housework to do at night. 'To only want day care on the grounds that it will give us a chance to prove we are as good as men in a man's world is to entirely miss the point of the new feminism' (McCaughey 1972, p. 7). Rather, child care was seen as part of a struggle towards less rigid sex role and generational stereotypes, and towards providing opportunities for individuals to maximise their choices concerning work, leisure and child-rearing, depending upon individual temperament and ability.

The Australian Pre-School Association (the peak body representing early childhood educators) vigorously opposed Community Child Care and appeared to resent the intrusion of this new group into its area of expertise. Winsome McCaughey met 'a furious response' from professional preschool educators when she attempted to speak at a seminar on child care. Sara Dowse, later to head the Office of the Status of Women, remembered the Australian Pre-School Association (APA) 'sending home leaflets pinned to children's jumpers exhorting mothers not to go out to work' (Dowse 1988, p. 210).

In October 1972, almost at the end of its twenty-three year ascendancy, the Coalition government introduced legislation relating to child care matters. Tellingly, the Minister who guided the *Child Care Act* through the parliament was the Minister for Labour and

National Service. The *Child Care Act* made it possible for the Commonwealth to provide subsidies for non-profit, centre-based care for the children of working parents. The Minister's speech introducing the legislation and the statements made by government members during its passage through parliament made it clear that the legislation was a labour force measure, motivated by the needs of industry for female labour. Although some provisions of the legislation, such as its emphasis upon trained staff, indicated that the Australian Pre-School Association had had an influence on the final shape of the legislation, it was apparent that the dominant considerations had been those of the labour market. Behind the scenes, public servants employed in the Women's Bureau (established in the Department of Labour in 1963) had worked very hard for the introduction of such legislation.

The groups who contended in the public arena for dominance of the early childhood field in the late 1960s—both the early childhood educators represented in the Australian Pre-School Association and the women's liberationists involved in groups such as Community Child Care—were obviously attempting to influence the direction of government policy. However, at this time *they were not policy activists*. Both groups were positioned as pressure groups working *outside* the key forums of government policy-making. While each acted as a powerful advocate for their particular approach to child care, and sought to influence public perceptions of the need for child care services, their engagement was with the broad outline and general philosophical direction of government policies; neither group had any kind of insider status and neither was involved in the actual *policy process* surrounding child care.

Setting the Australian Labor Party policy agenda

After the election of the Whitlam government, groups with different interests and values (early childhood educators, philanthropic organisations and feminists) continued to vie with one another to influence the broad outlines of government policy. However, some of the activists (most particularly members of women's liberation organisations) began to engage directly in detailed, policy-focused activities.

A significant episode in this process was a successful attempt by members of the Labor Women's Committee[1] to change the wording of the new government's early childhood policy. Labor had come to office with a policy supporting preschool education for every Australian child—a position which was an extension of its general commitment to education. The most significant influence on the formation of Labor's early childhood policy had been the Australian Pre-School Association; the emerging women's movement had not had any impact. Labor's education minister, Kim Beazley (senior), was very sympathetic to the preschool lobby. As a devout Christian, Beazley endorsed the traditional family values which the Association promoted.

On coming to office, the new government moved rapidly to commence implementation of its early childhood policy. It established the Australian Pre-Schools Committee and charged it with reporting on the measures that government would need to take in order to provide all Australian children with one year of preschool education. A secondary issue for the Committee to consider was how to provide care services for the children of working parents and underprivileged families.

The policy, however, was entirely inadequate—indeed reactionary—from the point of view of feminists. They did not want to see an extension of the traditional model of a professionally run preschool, rather they aspired to the development of a network of community-based, parent-managed child care centres. Further, they were incensed at the idea that child care should be provided only for working parents and 'underprivileged' families. Their vision was the establishment of a totally new approach to children's services; one which would not pigeon-hole children on the basis of their parents' workforce status or financial situation.

During the early years of the Whitlam government, feminist activists in the Labor party and within organisations such as Community Child Care repositioned themselves as *insiders* in the debate about the needs of children and the rights of parents. Policy activism in child care began when these women put down their banners calling for 'free, twenty-four hour child care' and began the more tedious and mundane task of bringing about change in the Labor party platform and in government and public service thinking on this issue. Many groups were involved in attempting to reshape government policy on this issue, but one in particular—the NSW Labor Women's Committee—was directly responsible for the rewording of Labor policy.

In April 1973, just four months after the election of the new government, the Federal Labor Women's Conference passed a resolution calling on the party to change its policy. In particular, it sought to change the emphasis of existing policy on preschool education. Preschools, it was pointed out, had very limited hours and were accessible mainly to those families who could afford to have one parent out of the workforce; they were of little assistance to two-parent or two-earner households. The Labor Women sought:

> . . . a comprehensive child care services [to be] established throughout Australia on a priority needs basis. This service should be Government sponsored and community based. The aim of the service would be to provide community support for women to participate more fully in society. (Federal Labor Women's Conference 1973, p. 4)

A small group of women from the New South Wales (NSW) branch of the Labor Women's Committee (Ann Symonds, Jeannette McHugh and Anne Gorman) took on the task of persuading the Australian Labor Party (ALP) conference to adopt the women's resolution as its new policy. Conference is the supreme policy-making body of the ALP. It comprises parliamentary leaders, delegates from each State and Territory and delegates from trade unions affiliated with the party. Such conferences were (and still are) heavily male-dominated. There were no female delegates to the 1973 conference. Elizabeth Reid, the Prime Minister's Adviser on Women's Affairs, had sought permission to attend as an observer but had not been allowed (Brennan 1990, p. 104). The New South Wales group of Labor Women thus faced a formidable task: they were not delegates to the conference; they had no obvious allies there; and they were attempting to raise an issue which was not even on the agenda.

The women travelled to the conference venue, Surfers Paradise, at their own expense, bringing with them bundles of documents to distribute. Each delegate was provided with the text of the Labor Women's resolution, a statement explaining the background to the resolution with statistics and commentary concerning the need for a policy on early childhood which covered child care services as well as preschool education. The women spoke personally to every delegate at conference.

In addition to changes to the content of the child care policy, the New South Wales women also sought to have responsibility for its implementation transferred from the Department of Education to the Department of Social Security. This, they claimed, would be an appropriate recognition of the wider goals that the new policy espoused. The resolution to change the government's policy was moved and seconded by sympathetic male delegates and, despite the strong opposition of the relevant Minister, Kim Beazley (senior), it was passed. The attempt to have responsibility for the implementation of the new policy moved to the Department of Social Security was, however, defeated. In an 'emotional and dramatic' speech Beazley described the attempt to relocate responsibility for child care as a 'gross indecency' perpetrated behind his back 'on the vague grounds that a lot of women want it' (*Australian Financial Review*, 11 July 1973).

The Labor women who engineered this change were undoubtedly 'policy activists' (in the sense defined by Yeatman, chapter 1). They were engaged in an open contest about the content of party policy, they worked from a clearly articulated value position which had been arrived at through the democratic processes of the National Labor Women's Conference and they were prepared to argue for, and defend, their ideas in a challenging and potentially hostile environment. They were part of a broader movement of activists who were not prepared to accept the decisions of a well-intentioned elite (in this case early childhood professionals) about what was best for children and families. Crucially, they were engaged in strategic action inside the relevant policy-making process (in this case the Labor Party Conference) even though officially positioned as outsiders.

Simultaneously, a complementary form of policy activism was occurring within the federal bureaucracy. The Prime Minister's Adviser on Women's Affairs, Elizabeth Reid, worked tirelessly to persuade key ministers and officials of the importance of broadening

Labor's policy beyond its focus on preschool education as the major service for children below school age. Other feminists working within the government included Lyndall Ryan who was employed in a central policy review body called the Priorities Review Staff and Marie Coleman who headed the Government's Social Welfare Commission (Ryan 1990; Dowse 1988). These women formed strategic alliances with activists who operated inside the Labor party as well as those in lobby groups such as Community Child Care and the Women's Electoral Lobby.

Feminists were seeking something truly radical and participatory—forms of child care which would be managed co-operatively by parents and workers, which would be based around respect for children and for the different values of parents. This was not a conception of child care based on the premise that members of women's liberation knew better than the traditional early childhood educators who preceded them about what was good for children. Rather, it was a new departure in thinking about the relationship between parents, children, professionals and the state.

Entrepreneurs as policy activists

The second instance of policy activism I wish to discuss is the campaign by commercial child care operators to have government subsidies extended to their services. This is an unusual instance of policy activism, in that the activists (owners of private 'for profit' child care centres and their representative organisations) were motivated by commercial interests rather than the ideas of a progressive lobby group or social movement. Nevertheless, their activities fit comfortably within the framework of policy activism set out in Nyland's chapter in this collection: they were actively engaged in seeking to reshape the basic assumptions of government policy; they operated not as outsiders but *inside* the policy-making process (in particular they formed alliances with key bureaucrats); and they were involved in seeking to overturn the dominant agenda (i.e. the dominance of non-profit, community-based child care).

The context of this chain of events was very different from that which surrounded the policy activism of Labor party women in 1973.

By the early 1980s, Commonwealth child care was an established, although still controversial area of public policy. The level of funding and service provision had grown considerably since the programme began, and an Office of Child Care had been established to administer the Children's Services Programme in accordance with the relevant legislation—the Commonwealth *Child Care Act*. Under the Act, government support could be directed only to non-profit child care centres. This provision reflected the dominance of the Australian Preschool Association (APA) as a source of advice to government at the time the legislation was introduced. Community child care advocates were also fully in support of restricting subsidies to the non-profit sector. While on some issues—such as their preference for parent-managed, co-operatively run services—they were in opposition to the APA, they were completely in accord with it and other traditional early childhood groups in opposing government child care subsidies being extended to the private, for-profit sector.

The restrictive nature of the *Child Care Act* was of great concern to owners of private child care centres. The fact that users of their services could not gain access to subsidies which were available to families in identical circumstances using community-based, non-profit child care, represented a considerable limitation to their businesses. When the Coalition came to power in 1975 the commercial operators anticipated that the new government would be sympathetic to their cause. After all, Coalition philosophy was supportive of private enterprise and distrustful of government-based solutions and the new government had made much of its desire to reduce Commonwealth expenditure (Elliott 1982).

In 1981, in the context of a series of inquiries into government expenditure, the Fraser government established a Review of the Children's Services Programme, under the chairmanship of back-bencher John Spender. The brief given to this committee was to examine the policies and administration of the Children's Services Programme and to make recommendations with a view to achieving greater consistency between the Programme and the principles of family responsibility, restricting government subsidies to the needy, avoiding overlap with State governments and the private sector, and containing government expenditure (Review of the Children's Services Programme 1981, Annexure 1).

Private child care operators worked hard to influence the recommendations of the Spender inquiry. Through their national peak organisation, the Australian Federation of Child Care Associations, they presented a submission to the inquiry in which they characterised community-based, non-profit care as 'unfair competition' and claimed that since the introduction of government funding for child care, 'there [had] been considerable erosion of the market available to the independent area' (Australian Federation of Child Care Associations 1981, p. 25). They also encouraged parents using their centres to make direct representations to their local members and the Prime Minister.

The New South Wales branch of the Association of Child Care Centres also made a submission to the inquiry, appealing to the government's cost cutting objectives rather than to arguments about social equity. It stated that:

> . . . extending government subsidies to needy parents whose children were enrolled in commercial centres would allow the Government to make full use of existing services, before having to provide expensive capital and recurrent funding. It would stop discrimination against Private Centres and therefore may encourage expansion of private capital into this field . . . (Association of Child Care Centres of NSW 1981, p. 5)

The goals of the commercial centre lobbyists were to eliminate subsidies enjoyed by the non-profit sector that were not available to private operators (such as the capital and operational subsidies paid to community-based centres) and to extend fee relief to users of private centres. In short, they were early proponents of the 'level playing field'.

Opposition to the commercial child care proposal came from a range of quarters. As a basic principle, advocates of parent-managed, non-profit services regarded the profit motive as incompatible with the provision of a high quality service to children. They also claimed that standards of care were lower in for-profit services, despite the fact that these were subject to the same State government licensing requirements as community-based services. Some of the practices of the commercial operators suggested that they were keen to avoid certain relatively costly measures (such as employing trained staff) even when the importance of these was widely recognised. In New South Wales, for example, where State regulations required trained staff to be employed only if thirty or more children were being cared for, a large number of commercial centres had taken licences for precisely twenty-nine children. Another criticism of commercial centres was their lack of commitment to parent involvement. Whereas all community-based services receiving federal funding were required to provide opportunities for parents to become involved in the management of the services, commercial centres did not operate under any such strictures. Parents who had had experience of commercial child care frequently complained about this. Not only did commercial centres fail to provide avenues through which parents could influence the management of services, but quite often parents were not allowed to accompany their children inside the centre or to visit them during the day. Such practices obviously conflicted with the most fundamental principles of the community child care movement. In addition, private centres tended to be located in relatively affluent areas and opponents of their campaign were able to argue that subsidising users in these areas would do very little to help the government's target of the 'truly needy' (Brennan 1994, p. 111).

In the event, the Spender Report made the cautious recommendation that a pilot study of providing subsidies to users of commercial centres should be initiated. However, while the pilot project featured in the 1982 budget proposals, it did not get off the ground before the defeat of the Coalition early in 1983.

Following the election of the Hawke government, the level of interest in child care policy and provision intensified. Steps were taken towards integrating child care with key areas of government policy, notably labour market strategies and social security reform. Even more significantly, under the Accord negotiated between the government and the trade union movement, child care was defined as part of the social wage. The Children's Services Programme became of interest to far more community groups, trade unions, government ministers and departments than ever before.

The issue of extending fee relief subsidies to users of commercial services proved an extremely difficult issue for Labor—but ultimately it was Labor which changed Commonwealth policy in the direction advocated by commercial providers. In its first few years in office, the expansion of community-based child care was a high priority for Labor and party policy remained firmly based on the expansion of non-profit, community controlled services. But there were strong countervailing forces. Labor party backbenchers in marginal electorates were sensitive to representations from constituents whose incomes would qualify them for fee relief in a community-based centre but who could not get assistance because their children attended a private centre. Economic pressures were also having an impact and the government was looking for ways to reduce public expenditure.

Finance Minister Peter Walsh was the key player in bringing Labor's policy in line with the wishes of the commercial child care lobby. His arguments were based on the economic rationalism of the time together with old style Labor hostility to 'middle class welfare'. Government fee relief was directed to families on low and middle incomes, but, since families who need child care are almost always two-income families, this seems to have been enough to mark most of them as 'middle class' in Walsh's opinion. In a supposedly off-the-record post-budget speech to the Australian Society of Labor Lawyers in 1987, Walsh claimed, 'I can give you . . . a list of 200 bloody programmes off the top of my head that can't be justified by social justice, equity, or economic efficiency grounds, and the reason we haven't abandoned them is because we don't have the political courage to do so' (*Sydney Morning Herald*, 22 September 1987). Publicly subsidised child care and free tertiary education were high on Walsh's list. Such services, he claimed, had resulted from a 'middle class push' in the 1970s and had become far too costly for the country to afford. He argued that money was not available for further increases in public child care provision and that, in any case, on equity grounds the continuation of the programme could not be justified. Instead, Walsh suggested, the establishment of new child care services should be left to the private sector with government providing assistance to low-income users: 'The money could be found for a means-tested voucher system which would then remove child care from the public sector and send it back to the private sector from whence, I believe, it should never have been enticed away' (*Sydney Morning Herald*, 22 September 1987).

It was several years before Senator Walsh was able to convince his colleagues that the private sector should be brought within the ambit of the Children's Services Programme by extending subsidies to users of commercial child care. Significantly, senior Canberra based public servants seem to have accepted the arguments of the private sector even before they were adopted by the government. At a number of public meetings and small consultations, senior bureaucrats made clear to community-based child care supporters that they supported a shift towards private, for-profit provision. The agenda of the commercial operators fitted well with prevailing ideas about reducing public expenditure and the size of government and promoting small business. Hence it is not possible to say that the lobby groups representing commercial child care had been responsible for convincing public servants that their preferred policy direction was correct. It may well have been more the case that the two sets of ideas coincided by the late 1980s. In any case, it was apparent from statements made in public forums by senior public servants from this period on, that many of them supported the agenda of the commercial operators and that the latter had gained insider status in terms of developing ideas about future policy direction.

The extension of subsidies to users of such services was announced by Prime Minister Hawke in the context of the 1990 election campaign and was justified as necessary in order to achieve equity between families using public and private services. At the time, ALP policy stated unequivocally: 'There should be no subsidies for private child care' (ALP 1988, p. 225). While some sections of the community child care lobby regarded this step as a bitter blow to their aspirations for a nationwide system of publicly subsidised, parent-controlled services (Community Child Care Victoria described it as 'disastrous' in their July *News Sheet*), many others had softened their views on the issue by the time the announcement was made. The Australian Council of Trade Unions (ACTU), once staunchly opposed to the extension of subsidies to users of commercial centres, had changed its position in the run-up to the 1990 election and become a strong advocate of the move.

The policy activism of commercial child care operators in the 1980s had a great deal in common with that of feminist and community child care activists a decade earlier. While diametrically opposed in the content of their policy aspirations, the two groups used similar techniques including making direct representations to local members and ministers, developing alliances with sympathetic 'insiders' (both bureaucratic and political) and orchestrating grass-roots support from parents. The concept of policy activism allows us to think beyond the normative content of policy to see the common threads in terms of the modes and sites of activism.

Resistance to Commonwealth policy at the service delivery level

The third illustration of policy activism centres around the resistance of a range of groups to attempts by the Labor governments of Hawke and Keating to restructure Australia's child care programme, placing the emphasis on child care as an adjunct to workforce participation, rather than making it available as a broadly-based community service. In this instance, policy activism was more diffused than in the previous examples. It is more difficult to track because it was not played out in the 'high politics' of national party conferences or representation to Ministers; nor did it always involve public activities such as demonstrations and orchestrated letter writing campaigns. Much of it took place quietly, without display, at two key sites: the bureaucratic arena and the level of service delivery.

The questions of *why* and *for whom* child care is provided have been contentious throughout the history of the programme. As discussed earlier, feminists both inside and outside the structures of government worked hard in the 1970s to ensure that the focus of Commonwealth children's services policy went beyond preschool education and incorporated the needs of children with parents in paid employment.

During the 1980s, however, the Labor government came increasingly to favour workforce participation as the primary goal of the Children's Services Programme. Concerned about the rising cost of child care, the Commonwealth sought to distinguish its own role in the children's services realm from the role of the States. It did this by attempting to sharpen the focus of the programme on workforce participation, anticipating that the States would continue their support of preschool education and hoping that they would provide

95

support for families who needed child care for reasons other than labour force participation. This was a large gamble since the latter group included children at risk of abuse and neglect as well as children whose parents were suffering high levels of stress and anxiety due to poverty and unemployment. Families in these situations often do not have even one parent in paid employment, much less two.

What kinds of policy activism (if any) lay behind this change in the direction of children's services policy? The conduct of particular kinds of research and the dissemination and interpretation of research findings was one important feature. Of particular note was the 'active society' ethos which gained popularity during and after the review of social security initiated by the Minister for Social Security in 1986 and carried out under the leadership of feminist sociologist and policy analyst Bettina Cass. The review stimulated debate and policy change in a number of areas. With its emphasis upon supporting and facilitating the entry of welfare recipients into the labour force, the review almost certainly contributed to the Commonwealth's determination to re-focus its child care policy. It would be misleading, however, to suggest that Cass herself actively sought to reshape child care policy in this way. In fact, as Chair of the Commonwealth government's National Children's Services Advisory Council (1991–93) and later as Chair of the International Year of the Family (1994) Cass fought strenuously for children's services to be available regardless of parental workforce status. Nonetheless, the general thrust of the review undoubtedly fed into the Commonwealth's determination to focus its own child care strategy upon the needs of families in paid employment.

From the mid-1970s to the mid-1980s Australia's sole parent population had increased by 73 per cent, from 183 000 to 316 400, while the number of two-parent families with dependent children rose by only 4 per cent to 1 884 400. Over the same period there was a sharp increase in the proportion of sole parents reliant on Commonwealth income support and a corresponding decline in the labour force participation rates of both male and female sole parents. From 1975 to 1983 the proportion of female sole parents in the labour force declined from 48 per cent to 39 per cent; for male sole parents the decline was from 93 per cent to 80 per cent (Raymond 1987, p. 31).

Research studies surveyed in the context of the review indicated that these trends did not reflect the choices of sole parent pensioners: a high proportion of sole parents wished to have a job. The barriers to their workforce participation ranged from low self-esteem and lack of self-confidence to the costs of working, including the poverty traps which reduce the overall benefit of undertaking paid work. Research also showed that the lack of appropriate, affordable child care was one of the most important workforce barriers confronting sole parents. According to Australian Bureau of Statistics data, 56 per cent of sole mothers who wanted work and could start within four weeks were not actively seeking jobs because their children were too young or they could not find suitable child care (Raymond 1987, p. 86). A study commissioned by the Department of Social Security from Australian Market Research also showed that more than half of those not currently working saw child care as the main factor inhibiting them from seeking employment (Australian Market Research 1986). A smaller study carried out for the Social Security Review showed that 60 per cent of sole parents saw child care as the major barrier to workforce participation. According to the author of this report child care was unequivocally 'the most commonly cited workforce barrier' (Frey 1986, p. 86).

In May 1987, following the Social Security Review, the criteria for supporting parents' benefit were changed so that recipients would lose eligibility once their youngest child reached sixteen years of age. Previously, the cut-off point was twenty-four years of age if the young person was a full-time student. This increased the pressure on parents of younger children to maintain, or initiate, contact with the workforce. Parallel changes were made to Widows' Pensions.

The Social Security Review was, of course, not the only source of new ideas about the relationship between paid work and family life. In 1990 the Commonwealth government ratified International Labor Organisation Convention 156 'Equal Opportunities and Equal Treatment for Men and Women Workers: Workers with Family Responsibilities'. Ratification of this Convention brought with it a commitment to developing services which would enable workers (and prospective workers) with family responsibilities to undertake training and educational programmes as well as to take part in employment. Countries which ratify the Convention commit themselves to working towards the provision of parental leave, to introducing laws which prohibit direct or indirect discrimination on the basis of marital status or family responsibilities and to providing a range of community services such as home help and child care.

All these developments—moves to encourage and facilitate the labour force participation of women, the review of social security and other measures to secure the equal treatment of workers with family responsibilities—contributed to the government's desire to focus on child care in relation to employment.

To achieve its end—and perhaps to reduce criticism about public funds being used for supposedly frivolous ends such as enabling mothers to play tennis—Labor announced 'priority of access' guidelines which were to be applied by centre directors and co-ordinators of family day care schemes. The guidelines (which were issued without any consultation with the major children's services groups) stated that preference should be given to:

- children in families in which the sole parent is, or both parents are, employed, looking for employment or studying or training for future employment (Priority 1);
- children who have, or children of parents who have, a continuing disability (Priority 2);
- children at risk of serious abuse or neglect (Priority 3);
- children of parents at home with more than one child below school age and sole parents at home (Priority 4).

Within each priority group there was a further hierarchy. Services were required to consider 'the particular benefits or restricted alternatives affecting' families on lower incomes; Aboriginal and Torres Strait Islander families; parents or children with a disability; families of non-English speaking backgrounds; sole parents and isolated families (Australian Law Reform Commission 1994).

From this time onwards, the provision of child care for reasons other than parents' workforce participation—to enhance the social development of children or to provide respite for home-based mothers, for example—assumed a much lower priority. Also, the language of the debate about child care changed. Child care was described as being about 'facilitating workforce participation', 'enhancing productivity' and 'assisting the welfare to work transition'. The rhetoric of the 1970s feminist movement which promoted child care as enhancing women's autonomy, providing alternatives to traditional nuclear family care arrangements, and encouraging independence and sociability among young children all but disappeared from public debates about child care.

Further intensification of the focus on work-related care took place in 1987. In response to Senator Peter Walsh's attack on subsidised child care as 'middle class welfare' and a drain on the public purse, Neal Blewett, the Minister for Community Services and Health, whose department covered the child care programme, commissioned a study on the economics of publicly funded child care (Anstie *et al.* 1988). The commissioning of this report can, in itself, be considered as an interesting form of 'policy activism'—in this instance, activism engaged in by a Minister. It bears all the hallmarks of policy activism previously referred to: it represented a challenge to the dominant ideas in the policy field (in this case, the argument of Treasury and Finance officials that expenditure on child care was unsustainable); it offered a fundamental reframing of policy assumptions (as discussed below, the report was designed to show an entirely new way of conceptualising the costs and benefits of child care); and its site of agency was indisputably inside the policy process.

The report, conducted by the Centre for Economic Policy Research at the Australian National University, presented a strong challenge to the views of Senator Walsh. It argued that publicly funded child care resulted in major economic and social benefits and that these outweighed the costs of the direct expenditure (Anstie *et al.* 1988). According to the authors of the report, the non-taxation of child care provided in the home, plus the high costs of purchasing child care outside the home, combined to create strong disincentives to women's participation in the workforce and thus distorted their choice. This had consequences for the economic wellbeing of families since women's participation in the labour force was one of the chief ways for low-income families to avoid poverty. It also had implications for the economy as a whole since high employment rates for able-bodied adults contributed to economic and industrial development and aided governments in providing for those outside the labour force because of age, poor health or disability.

According to this study, publicly funded child care (particularly schemes such as the Children's Services Programme where the major beneficiaries were low and middle-income families) also contributed to social equity and income redistribution. In the absence of public subsidies, the cost of child care would represent a significant workforce disincentive for women with low-income earning potential. The existence of such a programme, therefore contributed to a fairer distribution of jobs and income by helping to facilitate entry to the labour market by single parents and second earners in low-income families.

The most influential and widely quoted aspect of the report was its assessment of the net fiscal impact of publicly funded child care. Against direct expenditure on the Children's Services Programme it set the gains to the Commonwealth which accrued from increased taxation revenue, savings on the dependent spouse rebate and savings on social security pensions and benefits. The report estimated that net gains from the programme could have been as high as $296 million in 1987–88, compared with expenditure of $190 million. Hence, publicly funded child care may have resulted in a net addition to the budget as high as $106 million (Anstie et al. 1988, p. 27).

The report received extensive publicity. It was a crucial weapon in countering the arguments of Senator Walsh and the Department of Finance who would have handed child care over to the private sector entirely. Dr Blewett used it to argue both publicly and in Cabinet that there were 'sound arguments for the programme's expansion' (Sydney Morning Herald, 1 June 1988). At a time when economic considerations were paramount, it was extremely important politically that the case in favour of publicly funded child care had been produced by a group of mainstream economists.

However, the success of this report and the persuasiveness of the arguments about the positive link between publicly funded child care, workforce participation and economic benefits, paved the way for the tightening of the link between child care and workforce participation. Cabinet was prepared to accept an expansion of child care, so long as there were economic benefits. Many community-based lobby groups, by drawing extensively on the Anstie report, unwittingly deepened the government's opposition to non-work-related child care. As Glyn Davis suggests (chapter 2, this volume), we sometimes disseminate ideas with implications we do not grasp, preparing the ground for results we might not desire.

In mid-1991, again without prior consultation, Labor announced its intention to introduce major changes to the fee relief system. It proposed the introduction of a 'two-tier' system in which work-related and non-work-related care would attract different rates of fee relief. This proposal was intended to discourage non-employed parents from using long day care, family day care and out-of-school hours care. Almost all users in this category would have been, by definition, one-income households, and the suggestion that they could afford to pay more for their child care than two-parent households provoked a strong reaction. Particular concern was expressed about the possibility that children at risk of abuse might lose their access to child care. Another problem concerned families with unemployed adults. With the national rate of unemployment hovering around 9 per cent, Labor's two-tiered fee relief was regarded by many as an implicit attack on unemployed families.

The two-tier fee relief proposal was withdrawn by the government after intensive campaigning by a range of organisations—including strong representations from the Ministerial Advisory Council on Children's Services (of which I was a member). However, the government continued to make statements emphasising the importance of child care as an adjunct of workforce policy. Ironically, it was precisely the success of Senator Walsh and the private sector in having subsidies extended to users of commercial centres, which was at the heart of the problem. Commercial centres have far higher rates of non-work-related care than do community-based centres. In 1993 the level of such care in centres was 39 per cent; in community-based care, 24 per cent and in family day care 12 per cent (Department of Health and Family Services 1993). Far from leading to expenditure savings (as the commercial lobby had always indicated) the new policy had led to a cost explosion.

The Commonwealth's guidelines concerning priority of access have encountered considerable resistance. An inquiry into the Children's Services Programme by the Australian Law Reform Commission (ALRC 1994) provided the opportunity for many groups to express their dissatisfaction with the perceived unfairness of the guidelines. Submissions to the ALRC from a wide range of groups including the major early childhood organisations, feminist groups, conservative organisations and child care centre directors shared a number of concerns. One submission, said by the ALRC to be 'typical' of many responses, stated that: 'Priority of access guidelines as they now stand are based on a fallacious judgment which values the economics of paid employment above all else' (1994, p. 43). Other criticisms were that the priority listing seemed incompatible with Labor's avowed commitment to social justice and that it 'implied that some families have less right to support from the Commonwealth . . . than others'. Many submissions implied that the government's commitment to social justice was violated by the child care guidelines. A submission from Townsville City Council, for example, claimed that Labor's policy 'discriminated against children from disadvantaged groups, for example, children from Aboriginal and Torres Strait Islander or non-English speaking backgrounds and children with a disability, because their parents are not well represented in the workforce' (ALRC 1994, p. 31).

It is not possible to document actual instances of child care staff disregarding the priority of access guidelines—adherence to the guidelines is a condition of receiving Commonwealth funding. Anecdotal evidence, however, combined with the figures on the extent of non-work-related usage, suggest that the practice is widespread, especially in commercial centres. Can such behaviour be interpreted as 'policy activism' or is it simply a form of passive resistance? Disregard of the priority of access guidelines, in my view, was intended to bring about a change in the policy embedded in the guidelines by showing them up as absurd and unworkable. The practice was also intended to embarrass the Labor government by pointing to an apparent conflict between its professed support for low-income and disadvantaged families, and a policy which excluded the most vulnerable. The ultimate aim of such action was to bring about a change in policy and in the basic assumptions underlying the policy.

Conclusion

Applied to the history of the Commonwealth Children's Services Programme the concept of policy activism enables useful distinctions to be drawn between different types of political mobilisation and engagement. This chapter has focused on three episodes in the history of child care: feminist and Labor party activism in the early 1970s; policy change generated by commercial child care owners in the 1980s; and resistance to Commonwealth government 'priority of access' guidelines by both public and private child care services in the 1990s. I have argued that policy activism in this particular domain was preceded by many decades of traditional lobbying and pressure group activity. The early activists in this arena were clearly positioned as outsiders: they did not contribute to the making and shaping of policy, but rather towards getting 'their' issue onto the government agenda. Policy activism is distinguished by the 'insider' status attained by those who engage in it and by their efforts to transform fundamental assumptions and practices of the dominant policy agenda.

I have also argued that policy activism is not the preserve of social movements or other self-identified 'progressive' groups. The activities of commercial child care operators in seeking to change the policy of the Labor government to their own benefit were as much an instance of policy activism as the activities of feminists seeking to change Labor party policy in the early 1970s—and for just the same reasons. In each case, activists engaged in the policy process as 'insiders' involved in a collaborative exercise with bureaucrats, ministers and ministerial advisers. In each case, they presented and sustained a substantial challenge to the dominant agenda.

In my third example, I have suggested that policy activism can be built around *resistance* to change as well as around the promotion of new ideas. This example is the most problematic, but in some ways the most interesting. Resistance to the transformation of the Children's Services Programme into a workforce-related programme did not depend upon alliances between activists and bureaucrats or senior government officials. It was played out largely at the level of service delivery. Recognising it as an instance of policy activism requires accepting the implementation phase as a crucial part of the policy process and acknowledging that decision-making at this level can also be construed as policy activism when it challenges the dominant assumptions of the policy makers.

5

The art of insider activism: policy activism and the governance of health

PAUL DUGDALE

> Use political practice as an intensifier of thought and analysis as a multiplier of the forms and domains for the intervention of political action. (Foucault 1983, p. xiv)

This chapter explores the policy activism of people who work in government agencies, using empirical material that traverses a range of agencies and policy matters in the health sector. I am interested in the ethics of policy activism inside government. I contrast transcendent and immanent activism, and argue that the latter is more helpful for understanding the activism of the insider. This is illustrated with reference to the ethics of a public health professional working inside a government agency. Out of the different constraints, privileges, powers and concerns associated with activists in different institutional and community locations, a division of activist labour emerges: insider activists become oriented to different deployments of their activism than community-based activists.

The following sections suggest two activist technologies or 'power tools' that can be wielded by insider activists in the analysis of the policy discourse. These focus on showing what there is to be done and how to do it; and in this way open up opportunities to use policy to produce social change. These two sections explore the way insider activists are concerned with how the historical permutations

104

of policy debates produce opportunities for the identification of activist goals, and also the possibilities that arise out of the enunciation of policy statements for the pursuit of those goals. These matters are illustrated by considering some of the major features of Australia's Medicare health system.

The chapter concludes with an examination of the relationship between insider activists and the institutions they work within, and reflects on the impact of the institutional environment on the subjective experience of insider activism. Each portrayal of activism is based on a particular person whom I consider to be a policy activist inside the health system. They are, by force of circumstance, shy about their activism so I have ensured that they cannot be identified.

Policy activists inside the health system

In considering what the term 'policy activist' might mean, different issues arise depending on whether these policy activists are working inside the government or are based in community organisations and networks. For community-based activists the major issue concerns the integrity of their role in the policy process, whereas for the policy insider the issue resides in deciding whether or not they are an activist. What would make them an activist? Weber (1978) identifies the following characteristics of those who follow politics as a vocation: an urge for power, an attitude of detachment to facilitate good judgment, and a passion for a realistic cause. The characteristics that suit a person for the vocation of public service are markedly different: an eye for detail, respect for authority, a sense of fairness. Nevertheless, the bureaucracy may attract the activist, and it may nurture activism among those working within it. Much of what Weber discusses in 'Politics as a Vocation' is applicable to a career in public service with an activist orientation. In this chapter I have adapted two of Weber's (1978, pp. 216–18) themes, specifically his concern with the ethics of deploying state power for the good of the people, and an insistence that the capacity to sustain a reasonable cause is central to policy activism as a vocation.

As an undergraduate, I was involved in student politics. During a reflective discussion in the campus tavern on what the future would hold, a colleague declared that when he left the political nursery of the university he wanted to become a faceless bureaucrat with multi-million dollar budgets to play with. The attraction was the realistic chance of achieving something worthwhile. He had no hankering after fame or recognition, having had a small taste of it on campus. Looking to the bureaucracy, he saw its hierarchical organisation and cross-linking to the policies of the elected government as potential means to be worked with for activist ends, a counter-intuitive perception for most young outsider activists. My friend became a career bureaucrat with a policy orientation. Over the last decade as an insider activist he has been intimately involved in the struggle to produce progressive health policy in both Commonwealth and State departments, under both Labor and Coalition governments.

Alternatively, rather than bringing their activism with them, people may develop an activist orientation through working in government agencies. Health professionals working in service delivery may take up the cause of their client group, and try to influence policy on their behalf (social workers have even defined such advocacy as one of their professional competencies). People working in health policy development may develop a commitment to particular issues. Public health professionals providing technical input to policy development may become passionate about the policy outcome and broaden their engagement in the policy process well beyond the role of expert. For these transformations to count as orientations to activism, the primary motivation must be compassionately directed towards the people the policy governs, not towards furthering the career of the insider.

It may be more or less easy to be an insider activist at different times and in different agencies. While one's activism may often be at odds with the policy orientation and operational style of a particular agency, there are occasions where there is considerable affinity between the two. For example, the government of the day may adopt policies advocated by community-based activists, and then ask for these to be implemented by specific government agencies. Community-based activists may be appointed to senior positions within the bureaucracy because of this government support (for further discussion of this point, see Nyland, this volume).

Insiders with an orientation to policy activism may demonstrate their activism in many ways. They may build networks of relationships across government agencies and with outsiders who share their cause or activist leanings. They may go beyond the brief of their allocated work and push for their cause. They may prioritise their activist interests at the expense of other work. They may argue their cause passionately with their superiors against the latter's expressed preferences. These ways of working risk the sacrifice of bureaucratic career advancement to activist commitments. This brings us to a discussion of the practical ethics of insider activism.

The ethics of insider activism

Bureaucratic insider activism has much in common with the ethical positioning of professionals within government agencies. Professionalism supplies a basis for the formation of policy priorities external to government. The professional owes a primary allegiance to the profession that is not easily supplanted. Both the professional and the activist who work inside government have loyalties to something other than the requirements of bureaucratic office. Each is compelled by a substantive ethical attachment to the pursuit of their work as bringing about some good.

The basis of the professional's ethical attachment resides in the ethos of the profession concerned, and in this sense is immanent to this professionalism. This is in a different way true of policy activists. Unlike political revolutionaries who are motivated by a transcendent view of 'what is to be done', policy activists find their cause in the situation at hand. From this immanent perspective, it is not possible to know what to do until you are in a position to do it (Deleuze 1988, p. 125). It is only through immersion in the circumstances of the field that the policy activist recognises the possibilities for action and achievement available from this position. In what follows, I am interested in the case of policy activism which is driven by *both* an autonomous professional ethos *and* the immanent ethical perspective of an actor located within a government agency.

Consider two examples. First, the female medical practitioner who stands for election to her Australian Medical Association branch council and gets elected on a vote relating to the need for new blood. Once in position she has to determine what is to be done. She will no doubt be aware of the cultural tensions within the profession as it drags its feet towards the next century, but until actually elected to a position of authority she cannot know what are the possibilities that would allow her to make a difference. Second, what of the public service bureaucrat, who after a restructure finds him or herself in a new branch that did not exist previously? Initially, she or he may not know what the branch's role is or could be. But as the work programme of the branch develops s/he sets about working out the possibilities of what can be done from an activist perspective.

The contemporary environment of government agencies in the health arena lends itself to an immanent activist engagement. In support of this consider the public health professional working in the public health system. This is a case where professionalism and policy activism often intersect. Public health replete with multidisciplinary diversity has always been central to health policy. The influence of public health doctors on the development of government departments of health from 1910 to 1960 has been documented by James Gillespie (1991). During the 1970s, the influence of public health professionals on government health agencies declined. This was partly due to a decline in the perceived importance of traditional core activities of public health such as communicable disease surveillance and control, partly due to a purge of medically qualified people from management positions in Commonwealth and State government health departments, and partly because of the lack of an external professional base for public health professionals outside government agencies at this time.

During the 1980s, public health experienced a considerable renaissance related to a number of developments: the 'new public health' movement that developed under the auspices of the World Health Organisation (WHO 1986), the expansion of the Public Health Association, the creation of the Australian Faculty of Public Health Medicine within the Royal Australasian College of Physicians, the development of popular Masters of Public Health courses in many universities, and the expansion of public health and related units within the major health bureaucracies. The improved professional organisation of public health and the growth in numbers of public health professionals within government agencies have greatly expanded the conditions of possibility for an engagement by these people in the policy process. Let us now tease out how this can occur, and examine the differences and overlaps between professional conduct and activism in the policy process.

The involvement of public health professionals in the policy process is based on the relevance of their technical skills and expert knowledge. Technical skills include a facility with statistical methods, information technology, field surveillance and disease prevention or control. Expert knowledge is of historical and contemporary patterns of disease development and medical response at the population level. These skills and knowledges are based on a strong interdisciplinary academic structure encompassing public health, biostatistics, demography and epidemiology together with the more recent emergence within public health of the sub-disciplines of health promotion, public administration and health economics.

Public health professionals have an interest in policy because of the potential for the policy process to bring about a greater level of health or wellbeing in the community. Public health professionals are often brought into the policy process solely for their skills. Many have had the experience of being used in a piecemeal fashion, being asked to extract statistics on this or that topic, with no clear idea of how the information will be used.

As I have said, the policy activist–professional is a hybrid creature. Activist–professionals strive to actively join in policy processes, and may seek to stimulate debate and policy development in line with their activist motivations. They seek to gain access to the key policy decision-making forums of interest to them, with the aim of realising substantive goals. In the pursuit of their influence in the policy process, activists–professionals have to determine the relevance of public health knowledges and techniques to the debate at hand, with a view to maximising their own involvement and that of sympathetic professional colleagues. They also need to develop an understanding of the various agencies, relationships and perspectives involved, and to reflect on whether it would be helpful to involve other agencies or seek representation from those who will be receiving the services under discussion. This pragmatic approach distinguishes the activist–professional and marks him or her off as different from fellow professionals within the policy process. Professionals are captured by their own profession's perspective and interests, unwilling to venture beyond the bounds of their professional expertise, and uninterested in the concerns and perspectives of other policy actors, particularly non-professional ones.

Professional and activist orientations converge in a synergistic way when the policy activist–professional pursues a rational, empirically informed approach, takes the trouble to understand diverging interests in the policy process, and attempts to keep the focus on the optimum structure, co-ordination and operation of the health system in its efforts to improve the health of the public. These efforts may be restricted to a single issue, such as the provision of services to people with HIV/AIDS, or increasing support for relatives who care for the chronically ill. In my experience, however, single issue insider policy activist–professionals are rare: most are committed to the pursuit of broadly focused change in the health system. For policy activist–professionals who entered the bureaucracy with a transcendent single-issue fixation, over time this gives way to a broad and opportunistic immanent orientation.

A division of activist labour

A preliminary specification of the components of policy activist work might include: identification of causes for activists in a form that can be taken up in the policy discourse; the placement of issues on governmental policy agendas; provoking community debate on issues; involving political parties in the cause; determining policy processes through which the cause can be pursued; and using the policy process to deliver on the cause. The components of this list can be formulated in many different ways, and may vary from issue to issue and sector to sector. With regard to such work, a division of labour has emerged between community-based policy activists and insider policy activists.

My interest is not to pigeon-hole either type of policy activist or their work, but to facilitate a discussion of how various aspects of activist work relate to various parts of the policy process. It must be kept in mind that there can be exceptions—it may be difficult to say whether or not an activist is located in the community or in a government agency. There are certain constraints on the activities of employees of government agencies which have implications for what aspects of policy activism they can pursue. They should not publicly undermine the government of the day. They should not criticise existing government policies in the field in which they work, except as part of government instigated reviews of those policies. They should not provide opposition parties with the means of political advantage, except through formal government channels using official processes of communication. These constraints apply to government employees whether working directly with policy or not. They generally apply only within the person's direct field of work. People who ignore these constraints risk being formally disciplined (including being demoted or sacked) or informally kept away from policy processes. Ways around these constraints have to do with the rights of government employees to participate as citizens in the processes of government. For example, unions or professional associations may provide protected forums in which to speak out and engage in public activities. Political parties may provide closed and protected forums for airing discontent. However, these ways around the constraints imposed on work for government agencies are generally not useful for people in management positions or for those working directly on policy directions. There are other kinds of constraints on activism within non-government organisations who receive government funding or individuals and organisations who wish to enter into and maintain a formal dialogue with government (see Papadakis 1984, pp. 204–8; Dugdale 1992, pp. 99–106).

It is the nature of such constraints which determine the division of labour between insider policy activists and community-based activists. For example, community-based activists must take the running on provoking community debate (for example by staging public demonstrations) and fuelling political point scoring by opposition parties. These activities are things the insider activist usually avoids. There are two things that insider policy activists can do that are virtually impossible for people who have not had hands-on policy experience: the discernment of opportunities or 'issues' in contemporary policy debates, and the practical mapping of a path through the policy process. These are technologies or 'power tools' of policy activism which are based on the personal know-how, the knowledge

111

and culture of the deep throat policy analyst. The ability to deploy contemporary debates is useful for enabling the activist network to strategically tune itself for maximum relevance and effectiveness. The knowledge of how to chart a course through the policy process can help convert activist energies into social change. These two sets of know-how make the insider policy activist highly sought after by both community-based and political activists and confer a certain mystique on the insider. The next two sections consider these activist technologies in more detail.

Recognising the opportunities for policy activism

Specific health policy issues which can form the ground for insider activism arise from the material, historical features of the health system. The first activist technology concerns how these issues are brought to light in such a way that they can be addressed through the policy process. For example, possibilities for insider policy activism arose in relation to some of the major features in the terrain of health policy since the introduction of Medicare. The example serves as a case study of Foucault's (1983, p. xiv) conception of 'analysis as a multiplier of the forms and domains for the intervention of political action'.

The newly elected Labor government introduced the Medicare policy in 1983. It centred around Commonwealth government provision of global funding for the health system in order to drive clear objectives for the health system, and in particular to provide a comprehensive and universal health system. Since then numerous difficulties have intervened in the translation of that simple policy approach to the complex reality of the contemporary health system.

The introduction of a major new policy initiative, such as the creation of a new national health system, extinguishes one series of debates and creates the possibility of a whole new set. The debates that used to be had in health policy before the introduction of Medicare are quite different from contemporary debates. Consider two examples. First, debates on whether a new hospital should be built in a particular area used to turn mainly on political considerations ('porkbarrelling') because there was no real capacity to enunciate the equitable geographical distribution of health facilities as a clear objective. Second, the debate concerning the functional importance of private health insurance and how to increase coverage rates was transformed by everybody in Australia getting public health insurance coverage. This fundamentally changed the nature of private health insurance as a product, turning it from a basic necessity needed to avoid financial ruin, into a luxury product. The new debates which have emerged since the early 1980s are structured by three main themes: the boundaries of the Medicare system; equity issues; and the adequacy of the health system. Each theme has been associated with a whole series of activist causes.

The boundary debates refer to what service areas are to be included within the health system. Does the health system include aged care? Should comprehensive health care include looking after people's teeth (Commonwealth Department of Human Services and Health 1994, p. 161), providing podiatrist services for foot care, or providing financial support for carers? Should psychiatric services be kept separate or mainstreamed into the acute medical care system (New South Wales Health Department 1993)? These boundary issues have been hard fought over the last decade. In many cases, intelligence from insider policy activists has been crucial to the efficient co-ordination of efforts within community-based activist networks in identifying and supporting particular causes.

The introduction of Medicare also created the possibility for a new set of debates on equity in relation to reform of the health system. From the early 1970s until 1984, the central debate in the party political arena had been concerned with the differential access to health services experienced by people of varying socio-economic status (for example, see Opit 1984). Following the introduction of Medicare, the concern for equality of access permutated into a concern with the differential access to health facilities by people from different geographical areas. This concern for geographical equity has become a driver of change in the State hospital systems (Macklin 1991b). Gough Whitlam foreshadowed this in the early 1970s when, according to health policy folklore, he made a pronouncement from the roof of the MLC tower (then the highest building in Sydney) along the following lines: looking below us, we see a community served by one of the greatest collections of hospitals in the

113

industrialised world; looking to western Sydney, we see two million people living with one of the poorest.

From a policy perspective, the introduction of the Medicare national health system in 1983–84 (following the halting progress from 1975 and demise of Medibank: see Scotton and MacDonald 1993; Wooldridge 1991) provided the political impetus for a practical focus on equity of access to health services. Needs-based planning had already become the dominant approach to hospital and health service development by the early 1980s (see Sax 1984).

During the 1980s, with the introduction of the new managerialism, this evolved into a funding formula-based approach in most State health systems. By the mid-1990s, all States and Territories had divided health services into geographical areas and most now fund those areas on the basis of a formula that takes into account the population in the area and its health service needs. I return below to the subject of funding mechanisms with a discussion of the New South Wales (NSW) Resource Distribution Formula.

From a health system perspective, the transformation of equity objectives from a concern with socio-economic status to a concern with geographical location can in part be explained by the injection of increased cash-flow into the public health system in the early years of Medicare. With the increase in the number of people entitled to free care in the public hospital system, concern shifted to the need for increased capital to renovate, upgrade and expand the network of public hospitals. This opened up the tension between refurbishing existing hospitals versus building new ones in relatively under-resourced areas, a cause taken up by many health policy activists, particularly in Sydney. At the same time, the new managerialist approach to the global funding of health services, in the context of universal health service coverage for the whole population, made possible the enunciation of equitable geographical access as a central national objective for the health system's development.

Medicare also introduced a new set of debates about the adequacy of the health system. These have taken at least three specific forms over the last decade. Is Medicare doing enough for enough people? Is the health system keeping up with new technology? Is Australia saddled with a system from 1983 that is unable to respond to events within health services, the health professions and indeed in the biosphere

(Macklin 1991a)? Each of these debates has provided the ground for health policy activist claims to be formulated and pursued.

For example, the HIV/AIDS pandemic brought to light in the early 1980s, was the first major test of the responsiveness of the new Medicare health system to a dramatic new health problem. It brought together a wide range of activists across the gay community, the medical profession, academia, the Commonwealth health department, and the parliament. The Labor health minister who had introduced the Medicare system assumed leadership of the policy response to the pandemic and encouraged activist participation in this response. The response was spectacularly successful (for some discussion of policy activism in this context, see Dowsett, this volume).

One of the major adequacy debates created by the nationalisation of the health system concerns the size of the pie: namely, the total amount of resources to be provided to the public health system. This new policy issue draws on and integrates various lower-level debates about adequacy in health services as well as the issue of the equitable distribution of facilities. Whether the pie is big enough at the national level is an issue that could not be named until a national health system had emerged. Once this debate opened up, it necessarily intersected with wider debates about economic rationalism. Health policy activists could either contest economic rationalist orthodoxy, with its bias towards marketisation and small government, and argue the benefits to community welfare that flow from public sector health financing. Or, they could work within 'fiscal constraints' and direct their activism toward cost-neutral reform options concerning the redistribution of resources. Many activists pursued both these strategies simultaneously.

The political art of interpreting and framing policy

Knowing how to frame policy statements so that they actually make a positive difference is the second power tool wielded by the insider policy activist. It is one of the most difficult and prized arts of government. Its application by the insider activist is both a highly political practice and a great 'intensifier of thought' (Foucault 1983, p. xiv).

The development and deployment of administrative technologies for government is a rapidly changing field. Introduction of a new technology can bring in its wake a profound reorganisation of institutional structures, relationships, roles and responsibilities. Programme budgeting and the purchaser/provider split are two well known examples (Keating 1988; Boston 1995). The changed approach to government, and the associated alterations to the institutional terrain they ushered in, had as much impact on the way policy activism could be articulated as the introduction of a major new policy or programme.

The processes of idea formation, implementation and uptake which constitute policy discourse turn into an assemblage of knowledge, action, relationships and politics. Turning a policy discourse into operational statements is performed by a range of policy actors each of whom occupies a number of subject positions (they talk of the different hats they wear) across a complex range of institutional locations (see Foucault 1972, pp. 50–5). Policy statements are events that function to make particular sense of a general policy field. They are made throughout the policy process from policy conception to implementation. Following Foucault, I suggest that policy statements can be analysed by considering: the objects which the policy governs; the subject positions from which the policies are enunciated; and the conceptual fields the policy statements occur within. These three domains constitute the strategic terrain for the activities of people who work with policy, including insider policy activists.

This perspective can be exemplified with reference to a particular 'policy', the Resource Distribution Formula (RDF) of the NSW Health Department. During the 1980s the operational units of the NSW health system—hospitals, community health centres and the like—were organised into geographically defined comprehensive health services. These have varied in number and changed their names over the years. As of 1997 there are nine Area Health Services covering greater Sydney, the Hunter Valley and the Illawarra, and six covering the rest of NSW. Resources made available by the NSW government for various statewide health service programmes (including population health services, primary and community-based services, acute inpatient services and mental health services) are allocated each year according to the RDF. The formula takes account of the number of people in the area; their health needs as calculated according to their age distribution and modified by factors for

Aboriginality, homelessness and non-English-speaking-background; and their utilisation of private health services (NSW Health Department 1996). The area health services then distribute the resources they receive to health service providers (such as hospitals and community health centres) to provide services for the population.

How is the RDF to be understood as a series of policy statements in terms of its object, subject, conceptual and strategic domains? First, the object of policy should not be conceived as independent of the policy statement. The object of the policy is constructed through the delineation of a reality that does not have meaningful existence for policy until this point. Second, the subject position from which a policy is enunciated involves the policy activist in strategic consideration of: who is speaking; who is enunciating the policy; and what are the characteristics of the space they occupy as a subject.

The Resource Distribution Formula thus represents the bringing into being of a distinct domain of policy action. According to the NSW Government's Economic Statement for Health (1995) the dollar amounts will be calculated as a share of available funds, and these amounts are for a population of people not a collection of health facilities. The NSW Health Department (1996)—a different corporate entity from the government, responsible to, but separate from, the Minister of Health—elaborated these principles into a statement of the detailed maths by which the formula is to operate, and provided guidance on the operational implications it has for area health services (Pearse 1996). Such statements as these, along with a myriad of unpublished letters, memos, and the like produced by policy officers, area CEOs, finance officers and so on, contribute to the delineation of the object governed by the RDF. Together, they constitute a great field of opportunity for insider policy activists.

Third, policy statements are enunciated within a conceptual web of governmental statements and debates that make up the health policy discourse. In the case of the RDF, this web includes: the NSW and federal governments' fiscal policies; a cascading series of performance contracts between Minister and Department; Department and area health service; area health service and hospital; and hospital and clinical unit in NSW (for an analysis of this new contractualism see Yeatman 1995); policies to deal with waiting lists which in the past have required a retreat from resource redistribution due to the short-term inefficiencies it produces; policies concerning people from non-English-speaking-backgrounds (Ferrer 1993); and so on. Activist causes present in any of these fields can be pursued in relation to the RDF.

Finally, it is important to recognise the deep entwinedness of power and knowledge. Part of the struggle within policy work is to promote particular forms of expertise over others. The knowledge base of a new policy field reflects the sedimentation of the power struggles that went into the construction of that field. The RDF represents the outcome of the struggle of policy activists championing the cause of social justice through equitable resource distribution. However, it also presents an opportunity for activists with other agendas to operate across the new governmental terrain opened up by the RDF with its associated structures and processes. For example, those aligned with the new public health movement may argue in the annual budget policy cycle of an area health service for a greater share of resources to go to health promotion.

The effectiveness of the insider policy activist's involvement depends on an understanding (perhaps in a statistical way) of the make-up of the population, its health and health service use profile, the characteristics of and pressures on health services, and of the institutional design of the health system. Knowledge across these fields underpins the relevance, technical acuity and political acceptability of proposals for formula design. What insider health policy activists pride themselves on is their 'feel' for the effects of various formula configurations on the population (or a segment of it) and health service agencies, together with their capacity to recognise and articulate mechanisms which would produce valued changes to the health system. The insider activist's role is to connect the political objectives of the activist's cause—in health, this is more often than not to do with the pursuit of equity in one sense or another—with the administrative technologies available to govern the health system.

Insider activists and their institutional location within government

The preceding sections have explored the motivations, ethics, tasks and technologies of policy activism inside government agencies. Each to some extent has explored how the relationship between insider activism and its bureaucratic location constitutes and structures the subjective experience of the insider activist. Here I take up this thread and reflect on the way the experience of activism within government agencies challenges and shapes the identity of the policy activist.

The starting point for this analysis is the proposition that institutions themselves have an ethics. How can this be so? Public institutions have to frame an account of themselves in terms of specific public purposes that fit the portfolio with which they are engaged: 'We are obliged to document our plans so that they are accessible and we are accountable' (Commonwealth Department of Community Services and Health 1989, p. 4). It is these publicly oriented statements of mission, and their articulation within corporate documents, that provide an important domain for the work of the insider activist. The following example is typical:

> Our Mission. The Central Sydney Health Service is committed to protecting, promoting and maintaining the health of residents in our Area. We also proudly offer the best in sophisticated care to a statewide and national population. (Central Sydney Health Service 1991, p.iv)

By taking such statements at face value, and ensuring that they do not stand as empty rhetoric, the insider policy activist can work towards the ethos of the institution being expressed in the policy discourse. Many health system organisations explicitly acknowledge the importance of equity, of excellence, of effectiveness and of efficiency as components of the ethical mission by which they are oriented.

For activists who are inside government, it is important to be seen to be trying to promote the organisation and its mission, in order to gain a better reception for their ideas by other people in the organisation. It may also enhance their capacity to deploy the organisation's processes for policy and strategic planning.

Such deep insider work may seem to drown policy activism within the demands of organisational loyalty—a classic case of 'co-option'. But this perspective denies the possibility of ethical co-operation, and refuses to appreciate that what is being promoted by the activist can give a legitimate advantage to the institution.

In suggesting that activists can work positively within government agencies, I do not deny that at times the ethos of the institution may be virtually incompatible with the pursuit of any activist cause, except perhaps those which are associated with agendas for smaller government. Periodically, public sector organisations become subject to intense efforts to reduce expenditure or to restructure them. During these periods, the organisation may well be so functionally disabled that it cannot pursue effectively its stated goals, much less respond to any activist agenda of relevance to the community it serves. Insider activists may cope with these periods by putting proactive activist projects 'on the back burner', and by advising community-based activists to not draw attention to any cause which could be detrimentally affected by the fiscal or restructuring agendas in play. A further option is to leave the organisation, a particularly attractive option for the activist–professional who can return to community-based practice. All of these options may do little for the activist's sense of honour or commitment, but survival skills must come into play. Such intense periods of organisational change present the insider activist with both risks and possibilities. They may do well or they may do badly. From personal observation, in times of organisational turmoil, and regardless of the political party in power, junior insider activists tend to do better and senior insider activists tend to do worse. In any case the security and structural location of the activist within the organisation can be as central to policy activism as the pursuit of any particular policy activist agenda or cause.

The need to survive to be useful, the importance of working with rather than against the organisation, the tensions between activist and professional roles, and the technical demands of the exercise of power all have implications for the sense of identity of the insider policy activist. The term 'policy activist' itself is new. Only time will tell if it gains currency and contributes in a positive way to the sense of identity of the people to whom it refers. We can compare the policy activist with Sartre's notion of the committed intellectual: a person with a trained mind, engaged with political and social structures for the benefit of society (see Sartre 1979). This notion implies a sense of self behind the commitment, a self which can be positioned for engagement in some social struggle or other. This description is too self-assured for the insider activist. On this point, Foucault's point about the priority of experience to engagement is instructive.

'Experience with . . . rather than engagement in . . .'. Privileging experience over engagement makes it increasingly difficult to remain 'absolutely in accord with oneself', for 'identities are defined by trajectories, not by position taking'. (Rabinow 1997, p. xix, quoting Foucault 1994, p. 784)

Thus in this chapter I have wanted to emphasise that policy activism inside government agencies is an immanent experience to which the activist gives him or herself, a vocation to which she or he is called. On the one hand, the causes of his or her activism are rooted in prior political and, or, community-based experiences. On the other hand, the activity of the activist emerges immanently from their location inside the agency. Because insider activism straddles this divide, the subjective position of the insider policy activist rarely affords the comfort of feeling 'absolutely in accord with oneself'. It is an immanent, pragmatic ethics that determines the motivation of the activist to be on the lookout for opportunities within the activist discourse; that determines the value of policy know-how as an activist technology; and that allows us to recognise—as did my friend from student politics days—that for the activist, working within government agencies can be an intensifier of thought and a multiplier of the forms and domains for political action.

Acknowledgments

Anna Yeatman greatly assisted with the substantive streamlining and editing of this chapter.

6

Community activism in the health policy process: the case of the Consumers' Health Forum of Australia, 1987–96

STEPHANIE SHORT

The CHF was established to strengthen the 'voice' of the consumer and community sector in health policy decision-making. We believe that a strong consumer voice is one which grounds its arguments in research. For this to be possible, consumers must have access to the resources and education necessary to undertake research work which is of a high quality, as well as community controlled and community based. (CHF to the Commonwealth Department of Health, 24 May, 1989)

In this chapter I aim to explore community activism in the health policy process through analysis of the nature of activism engaged in by the Consumers' Health Forum (CHF) of Australia, from its inception in 1987 through to 1996. The chapter is organised thus: in the first instance I provide a definition of the key term 'health policy'. I then give an overview of the 'imbalanced political market in health care', and define 'policy activism' within this context. I then move on to examine the nature of community activism in the health policy process which was facilitated by the Consumers' Health Forum in its first decade of operation. The case study is based on analysis of relevant correspondence, policy documents and secondary literature, combined with key informant interviews. The Consumers' Health Forum has been chosen as the focus for this analysis of community activism in health, as there is no other country in the world where an organisation such as the Consumers' Health Forum in Australia, representing community interests, has such direct access to national policy makers (Milio 1988).

In this chapter a broad view of the term 'health policy' is taken. 'Generally, the term "health policy" embraces courses of action that affect that set of institutions, organisations, services and funding arrangements that we have called the health care system' (Palmer and Short 1994, p. 23). Thus, it includes actions or intended actions by public, private and community actors (individuals and or- ganisations) that have an impact on health. The term 'health policy' includes also the election and other policies of political parties, that might or might not be translated into government action at a later stage. Thus, 'policy' refers either to a set of actions and decisions, or to a statement of intention. In this chapter I share Wilenski's (1988) view that the dichotomy between 'policy' and 'administration' is no longer useful, as value judgments and choices can be made in any or all of the five key stages in the health policy process: problem identification and agenda setting; policy formation; adoption; imple- mentation; evaluation (Palmer and Short 1994, pp. 33–4). For this reason, also, I am not limiting the notion of 'policy activism' to any one of these stages in the health policy process.

The imbalanced political market in health care[1]

Of the variety of approaches adopted by health policy analysts in the study of health care reform, and barriers to reform, the theoret- ical framework that has been most useful in my own policy analysis work is that of the political sociologist Robert Alford (Alford 1975; Alford and Friedland 1985). Although Alford's work is based on the United States' health care system, the applicability of the underlying theoretical framework has been tested and refined in a number of Australian studies (Duckett 1984; Lin and Duckett 1997; Palmer 1978; Palmer and Short 1994; Sax 1984; Short 1984, 1989).

Alford's thesis is that health policy reform, and barriers to reform, should be seen as the outcome of conflicts between three major health groups, or structural interests.[2] Structural interests are those alliances of interest groups that gain or lose from the health care system the way that it is currently organised. These alliances have been described by Alford as the 'professional monopolists', the 'corporate rationalisers' and the 'community interest'. Established medical organisations and associated interest groups, including private health insurers, and manufacturers of pharmaceuticals and other medical technologies, whose activities and incomes are linked closely to those of the medical profession, benefit from the health care system the way it is currently financed and organised. As the 'dominant' structural interest in health care, they wish to retain the status quo, and are usually very resistant to proposed changes in the health care system. Professionals also tend to support the status quo.

The group of corporate rationalisers comprises hospital administrators, government officials and some health professionals, including some with medical qualifications, whose interests are served by the promotion of greater effectiveness and efficiency in the provision of health services. Corporate rationalisers would normally be members of the health service bureaucracy, though others such as politicians and academics may form part of this group. Corporate rationalisers benefit from reform in the health care system, as their domains of responsibility increase with the implementation of policy reforms such as Medicare, and with managerial reforms such as area health services management or casemix funding for hospitals (Duckett 1984; Lin and Duckett 1997). In this context 'managerialism', refers particularly to the 'new public sector management' in which agencies manage for results and are held accountable for outcomes, as introduced into the Australian Public Service in the 1980s (see Dugdale 1991; Yeatman 1994b).

The community structural interest consists of a variety of organisations and agencies, often representing single client groups, such as those with mental health problems, who have in common their desire to improve the health care available to the community. In Australia there is a wide variety of community health groups, which lobby politicians and health officials, and attempt to attract public and government support. Members of the community participate in the health policy process through non-government organisations such as the Australian Council of Social Service, the Health Issues Centre, the Consumers' Health Forum of Australia and other organisations that seek to promote more equitable access to appropriate health services. Lobbying is usually directed towards Ministers of health, at federal or State levels; ministerial staff; members of parliament; and public servants in departments of health. Compared with other structural interests in health care, these groups are relatively diffuse, not well organised, poorly financed, and generally lacking in bargaining power in the political arena. The community health interest is the least powerful structural interest in the current organisation of health care in Australia.

The relations between these three major groups are characterised by Alford's description of the professional monopolists as being the dominant group, but with the corporate rationalisers seeking to challenge their position of dominance. The community interest is described by Alford as being repressed, but with members of the group trying to become more influential. These structural interests may work together, or in opposition, in particular instances of policy-making and implementation. For example, Stephen Duckett's (1984, p. 960) analysis of the origins of the Community Health Programme pointed to a 'coincidence of interests' between corporate rationalisers and the alliance of community health interests. Moreover, corporate rationalisers and community groups in Australia have allied themselves in defence of national health insurance (Medibank, and then Medicare) for over twenty years (Jackson 1990).

While this characterisation of the imbalanced political market in health care has a good deal of relevance to the analysis and interpretation of health policy in Australia, nevertheless there are several weaknesses in the approach, especially when applied to the Australian scene (Palmer and Short 1994, p. 45). First, the roles of governments and of the political parties as such do not figure significantly in Alford's work. The corporate rationalisers group includes elected and public officials, but they are seen as pursuing their own interests, rather than those of the governments of the day. This analytical omission needs to be remedied, as our analysis of health insurance policies reveals they have been influenced considerably by which political party is in power federally. Indeed, the long-standing ideological polarisation between the Labor and Coalition parties, combined with the highly centralised federal system of government, are conducive to significant health policy changes at the federal level in Australia (Gray 1996).

Second, a further and powerful group in Australia are the trades unions. 'When Labor governments are in power the interests of the trade union movement, as a whole, have been decisive in influencing the direction of health policy' (Palmer and Short 1994, p. 45). The influence of the trade union movement, and especially the peak national body, the Australian Council of Trade Unions, has been crucial in developing and maintaining support for Medicare, as we shall see.

Third, doctors in Australia, and elsewhere, have become a more heterogeneous group than Alford's theory suggests. Although academic medical specialists continue to exercise a major influence of the kind Alford postulates, other medical groups with different values and goals, such as the Doctors' Reform Society on the left, and the Private Doctors' Association on the right, have become increasingly vocal. Unlike most members of the medical establishment, who only become politically active when the prospect of reform is imminent, both these groups actively seek major changes to the status quo.

Fourth, Alford presumes that the possession of superior knowledge and skills by doctors explains their position of dominance in the political market for health policies. While these attributes of the medical profession are no doubt important, clearly there are many other groups, including some non-government organisations and self-help groups, who possess a very high level of specialised knowledge and skills, but lack power. We turn now to examine the notion of 'policy activism' within the context of this 'strife of interests'.[3]

Policy activism and the health policy process

In defining the notion of 'policy activist' in this context two main conceptual notions are available to me. On the one hand, I could equate the notion of 'policy activists' with 'agenda setters', who are, by definition, '. . . those who posit alternative views to the conventional wisdom' (Howe 1996, p. 6). Agenda setters can come from the left of the political spectrum, as represented by the Australian Community Health Association, or from the right of the health policy spectrum, as represented by groups such as the Right to Life Movement.

On the other hand, I could define 'policy activists' as those individuals and organisations who support a more open and participatory policy process, rather than a closed and top-down approach. In this latter definition, policy activism is viewed as a child of the new left, due to its commitment to humanism, post-material values and participatory democracy (Offe 1984; Yeatman, chapter 1, this volume). This contrasts with the 'paternalistic' (see chapter 1) model, in which the medical profession provides the core scientific knowledge and values in the health policy process. Thus, in the health policy arena, policy activists are those actors (individuals or groups) who are willing to challenge the views and dominance of the medical establishment in a democratic way. Given the undemocratic or imbalanced market of ideas and other resources in the health policy arena, it is this latter definition which is used in this case study.

We turn now to consider more closely community activism in the health policy process in Australia. The formal origins of support for active community participation in health policy-making, planning and service delivery in Australia can be traced to the Whitlam Labor government, 1972–75, and especially to 1973, and to the establishment of the national Community Health Programme. The Whitlam policy approach facilitated the 'new public administration' movement which transported the 'new left' rhetoric of participatory democracy into public administration in the 1970s (see Yeatman, chapter 1). In this approach the distinctive contributions of public officials, service providers and clients are accorded visibility and respect in the policy-making process. The Community Health Programme supported community groups wishing to co-ordinate and, or, provide community health services through community-managed community health centres, women's health centres and Aboriginal medical services (Palmer and Short, 1994). In addition, a number of national provider and community-based groups, such as the Family Medicine Programme of the Royal Australian College of General Practitioners and the Australian Community Health Association received funding for secretariat-type functions. This kind of federal support for community or non-government organisations was also evident in other Commonwealth departments during the Whitlam years, including Social Security, Status of Women, Aboriginal Affairs and Overseas Aid (Conley 1992).

During the Whitlam years (1972–75), the ethos of public policy began to be coloured by two intersecting goals: the first was one of extending the availability and accessibility of government provided services so that they contributed to what Whitlam called 'the doctrine of positive equality' (Whitlam 1985, p. 3). The second arose out of the influence of the 'new public administration', which originated in the United States, on Australian State administration. This led to the development of new administrative law which made the internal working of state administration more accountable to the citizenry through mechanisms such as freedom of information and administrative appeals. Over the period of roughly 1975–83 there developed an integrated conception of these goals so that making government services more accessible and equitable was seen to depend also on good administrative process, which required not only a more representative bureaucracy, but being prepared to genuinely consult with citizens and citizen groups. Needs-based planning, for example, was an administrative technology worked up in the area of child care which represented the integration of these goals within the culture of public administration at the time.

The Hawke government sustained this approach to public administration but it began to take second place to what had become the dominant policy concern of the Hawke government: economic restructuring in the interests of making the Australian economy more internationally competitive. Hawke's own inclination toward a consensual approach to the policy process, once married with this governing economic policy agenda and a Labor government's affiliation with the union movement, led to corporatism becoming the *modus operandi* of the Hawke Labor government in the 1980s.

The Statement of Accord by the Australian Labor Party (ALP) and the Australian Council of Trade Unions (ACTU) regarding economic policy was originally struck in February 1983 between the ALP (then in opposition at the federal level) and the ACTU as a bipartite agreement. This 'Accord' was the cornerstone of Hawke's policy agenda, and it set the tone for the policy process in the successive federal Labor governments (Stilwell 1986).

In April 1983, the newly-elected Hawke government invited representatives of business, unions, State premiers and others to assemble for the National Economic Summit in Parliament House.

At the Summit the three parties, government, business and unions, recognised that the development and implementation of a successful prices and incomes policy required supportive policies in other areas of mutual interest, including industrial relations, social security and health.

In the early years of the Hawke government social policy, including health policy, was essentially an extension of the Accord which emphasised economic growth, jobs, voluntary wage restraint, and maintenance of the 'social wage' (Howe 1996).

The nature of Medicare, a universal and equitably funded national health insurance scheme, was outlined in the Accord, on the understanding that the policy would significantly reduce the cost of health cover for the great majority of wage earners, and that it would contribute to the anti-inflationary policies of the Labor government by reducing the Consumer Price Index (CPI) by two percentage points (Appendix A, Stilwell 1986).

In the National Economic Summit Communique, the unions reaffirmed their commitment that they would '. . . accept an offset in wage increases on account of the health insurance scheme' (Appendix A, Stilwell 1986, p. 181). Thus, the Accord involved a trade-off between wage claims and policies such as Medicare, which restored the social wage.

The Accord provided a framework to manage incomes policy in a way which gave the highest priority to economic growth and therefore to employment. Under this approach 'workers could be supported via social wage improvements such as Medicare or tax cuts, allowing the government to maintain a wages policy that made Australia internationally competitive and allowed for growth in jobs without a resurgence in inflation' (Howe 1996, pp. 6–7).[4]

In terms of the policy process, the Summit was significant in that it was a launching pad for '. . . ongoing consultative machinery' (Stilwell 1986, p. 13). This policy machinery, which came to be referred to as 'corporatism', saw the establishment of numerous consultative bodies and mechanisms which *incorporated* representatives from unions, business and other community groups into the policy process. Corporatism rests on the notion of partnership between the state and what are seen to be the key players or stakeholders. The Summit Communique specified that Government had a '. . . responsibility to consult, administer and plan, and make decisions for which they are accountable to the electorate' (Appendix B, Stilwell 1986, p. 182).

Indeed, the Summit called upon the government to publicise the outcome of the Summit widely, and to '. . . encourage the process of consultation at all levels of the community' (Appendix B, Stilwell 1986, p. 183). Thus, bodies such as the Economic Planning and Advisory Council were viewed as '. . . an important source of alternative policy advice for the government and a basis for continuing the consultative process' (Stilwell 1986, p. 14). As Medicare constituted the most significant, and expensive, of the policy initiatives in the social wage area, there may have been some expectation that the Minister for Health would support mechanisms that facilitated community consultation on Medicare and other health issues.

The review of community participation in the Commonwealth Department of Health

In May 1985, several of the community groups who received secretariat support under the Community Health Programme joined with several other non-government organisations to present 'A Petition of Reform Addressed to the Minister' (Attachment A, Commonwealth Department of Health (CDH) 1985). The nine signatories to this petition were the Australian Community Health Association, Australian Consumers' Association, Australian Council of Social Service, Australian Federation of Consumer Organisations, Australian Pensioner Federation, the Council of Social Service of New South Wales, the Doctors' Reform Society, the Health Issues Centre, and Rupert Public Interest Movement. The petition called for greater participation by community and consumer groups in Commonwealth Department of Health processes, in order to bring Australia into line with the World Health Organisation primary health care policy, which called on all member states to formulate national policies to establish ongoing consultative mechanisms with all sections of the community. The petition's twenty-two recommendations were designed to strengthen community participation in what had long been '. . . a secretive, closed and conservative administration' (CDH 1985, Attachment A, p. 2).

The Minister for Health, the Honourable Neal Blewett, previously professor of politics at the Flinders University of South Australia, welcomed the petition and provided the community groups with fees to engage a consultant, plus the services of two departmental officers, in order to review community participation in the Commonwealth Department of Health, with a view to making it more open and responsive to the community (Wadsworth 1989).

Very few public servants in CDH welcomed the petition, but given the clear need to locate new friends for Medicare (a publicly funded compulsory health insurance scheme) and the related aim of developing new strategic alliances with groups across the broad health industry, the subsequent recommendation by a joint committee of petitioners and public servants for the establishment of a health forum was welcomed by policy makers. (Conley 1992, p. 8)

The final report of this review, *The Swinging Door*, established the need for a 'strong cohesive community lobby' to provide the department with information and advice and to act as a balance to the representations of well organised professional, industry and government groups which tended to dominate the health arena (CDH 1985, p. 1).

Establishment of the Consumers' Health Forum of Australia

The proposed terms of reference for the Health Forum included: representation of the community views to the minister and the department; improvement in communication between the community and the department; organisation of a conference of community groups every two years; and monitoring of progress made by the department towards community participation (CDH 1985, p. 1).

The constitution of the Consumers' Health Forum of Australia (1992) specifies that it aims:

1   to provide a means of maximising the participation of consumer and community groups in national policy, planning and service decisions which affect the health of consumers;

131

2 to promote a public and preventive health approach which recognises the health impact of other government policy areas;
3 to promote a just and equitable distribution of resources to redress inequalities in the health status of different groups of the Australian population, noting the pluralistic nature of our society;
4 to encourage the development of health services which are: effective in enhancing the capacity of people to participate as fully as possible in community life and are responsive to consumer needs and preferences; community-based and managed; respectful of human rights; culturally relevant; universally accessible; cost effective;
5 to promote the rights of all consumers to be involved in health policy, planning and service decisions.

Since the Consumers' Health Forum of Australia was established in 1987, it has become the major national organisation which represents the views of community and consumer groups on issues relating to health. In the opinion of Margaret Conley, former executive director of the Public Health Association of Australia, 'The Forum has gone a considerable way towards realising the rather utopian aim of acting as a balance to well organised professional and industry groups' (1992, p. 9).

Conflicting models of community participation

Historically, the model of community participation which informed the establishment of the Forum derived from a good deal of local community development work, and community-based advice, which focused on increasing community participation in health care decision-making at the 'grassroots' level, especially through the Community Health Programme (CDH 1985, p. 45). However, right from the beginning there was tension between this model of community participation, and government-driven needs for consultation. Whilst the notions of 'community development' and 'community-based management' were fundamental to the grassroots nature of community participation under the Whitlam government of 1972–75, the notion of 'consumer consultation' became increasingly popular in Australia under the Hawke and Keating Labor governments from 1983 onwards.

The Constitution of the Consumers' Health Forum reflects these contradictory models of community participation. Although paragraph one is consistent with the principles of social democratic participation, the reference to '(individual) consumer needs and preferences' in paragraph four, is more consistent with the government's need to consult with individual recipients of care. This notion of consumer consultation relies on the notion of the government enabling the rational actor to maximise his or her own benefits, more in line with the ethical principles of neo-classical economics, than with those of community-based participation which are legitimated by the ethical principles of social democratic theory (see Yeatman 1996a). The distinction between these two types of community participation is evident, also, in the use of the economic term 'consumer' rather than the social term 'community group' or the more classical referent, 'citizen'. This tension between community-based participation and government-driven consumer consultation was evident also in the Review of Community Participation in the Commonwealth Department of Health (1985, p. 5).

This emphasis on the value of consultation prior to enacting legislation or implementing policy, has appeared, at least in the economic sector, to contribute to the development of acceptable and successful policies, and to more sophisticated input from the major players, for example through the establishment of the Economic Planning Advisory Council.

The Economic Planning Advisory Council, referred to above, comprised representatives from trades unions, government, business and employer organisations. Under the Hawke and Keating governments of the 1980s and 1990s, the combining of labour, business and government, or more precisely the *incorporation* of trade unions and business into policy-making work, was consistent with the corporatist trend in other Organisation of Economic Co-operation and Development (OECD) countries, notably Sweden, Norway and Austria (Boreham 1990).

Indeed, the history of the incorporation of community groups into health policy development work, as described in this chapter, suggests that the demand for a national consultative structure on health issues was, in part at least, the product of a corporatist culture, as nurtured by Neal Blewett, the Minister for Health. Corporatism was a crucial part of the environment in which the organisational and strategic strength of the community sector in the health industry was consolidated and strengthened. However, whilst the corporatist 'triangulation' of government, employer–industry and labour organisations provided the context within which the Consumers' Health Forum was established, by this time the relevant social movements, including the consumer movement, the women's health movement[5] and the disability rights movement, had not only their own advocates inside the bureaucratic and ministerial advisory agencies, but were also powerful ideational-moral claimants from without.

Consumerism and general management

In the United Kingdom during the 1980s, the publicly owned and administered National Health Service, became permeated with the notion of 'consumerism' due to the introduction of general management principles, and the concomitant challenge to professional medical power (Klein 1990, 1995; Rogers & Pilgrim 1991; Flynn 1992; Paton 1992; Nettleton and Harding 1994). In the National Health Service, general managers needed to build alternative coalitions in order to challenge professional medical power (Thompson 1987).

Consumerism in health in the United Kingdom focused on applying the Thatcher government's Citizen's Charter to the National Health Service (NHS), particularly through the Patient's Charter which emphasised the civil and political rights of each individual citizen (United Kingdom Department of Health 1991). According to Nettleton and Harding (1994, p. 41) this approach to consumerism is likely to '. . . have little real impact on large organisations or established institutions because the UK framework excludes social rights which require that consumers are able to participate through organised representative mechanisms'. The NHS reforms focused on consumer 'individualism' rather than 'collectivism' (Nettleton and Harding 1994).

Although there was tension from the beginning in the rationale of the Consumers' Health Forum of Australia, organised representation for health care consumer groups was its *raison d'être*. In Australia, supportive general managers in the Commonwealth Department of Health, plus an activist Minister, were crucial to support for community activism in the health policy process during the Hawke–Keating years over the period 1985–96. The Forum provides organised representation of the consumer interest at the national level. Thus, while community health activism blossomed within a corporatist policy environment in Australia, its *modus operandi* was consistent with the participatory rhetoric evident in the Community Health Programme, and evident also in the first Commonwealth–State Disability Agreements (Yeatman 1996b), in Chris Ronalds' (1989) Report on the rights of residents in nursing homes, and in the First Triennial Review of the Home and Community Care Programme (the 'Saunders Report', HACC Review Working Group, 1989).

The Consumer Research Development Programme

In 1985 *The Swinging Door* report recommended that the Commonwealth Department of Health allocate research funds to community organisations to research the information needs of their constituency and to carry out 'participatory and social action research'. Then, in the following year, the report of the Better Health Commission recommended '. . . that a national community development fund should be established to assist in, and educate local communities about participation and advocacy projects' (Better Health Commission 1986, vol. 1, p. 75). In 1987 when the Consumers' Health Forum of Australia was established, it had as part of its foundation budget, a small fund ($60 000) earmarked for grants to consumer and community groups for research and development projects.

This grants programme had an important and unique role in research funding in Australia, as the funds enabled consumer and community groups to initiate and conduct their own projects—not to have research done about them by an 'expert', but for the groups to undertake the activities themselves, defined in their terms and by their assessment of the perceived needs and information gaps. 'This tiny fund . . . represented almost the entire monies available for consumer and community controlled research projects' (CHF to Department of Health, 24 May, 1989). Thus, the Consumers' Health Forum enabled consumer representatives to network, and to be resourced with the research and information that enabled them to be properly briefed and knowledgeable in their roles as consumer advocates.

Between 1987 and 1989, the Committee administering the CHF grants programme was chaired by a sociologist, Yoland Wadsworth, a well-known social policy activist and advocate of participatory or action research (Wadsworth 1984, 1989). In 1990, when Wadsworth resigned from the Committee, I accepted an invitation to join the Grants Committee, renamed the Consumer Research Development Funding Committee, and I remained a member until its demise just two years later.

The Consumers' Health Forum research funding programme aimed to fund only those applications which especially demonstrated and furthered a consumer perspective. Grant applicants were asked to specify how consumers would be involved in the management of the proposed project, and groups representing professional, government or commercial interests were not eligible to apply. It was, however, acceptable for consumer groups to seek assistance from another organisation in carrying out its project; the group remained eligible if it was managed and initiated by consumers and genuinely oriented to consumers. The centrality of research to the work of the Forum is illustrated in the following excerpt in correspondence from the Forum to the Department of Health (24 May, 1989):

> The CHF was established to strengthen the 'voice' of the consumer and community sector in health policy-decision making. We believe that a strong consumer voice is one which grounds its arguments in research. For this to be possible, consumers must have access to the resources and education necessary to undertake research work which is of a high quality, as well as community controlled and community based.

Between 1987 and 1992 seventy-five consumer research projects were funded under the Consumers' Health Forum research development programme, to the total value of $364 000. Groups in receipt of funds included the Congress Alukura Council, Maternity Alliance, the Schizo-phrenia Fellowship of Victoria and the Older Women's Network. This research, and research conducted by the Forum, underpinned the Forum's policy advocacy work in Aboriginal health, maternity care, mental health, aged care, and so on, as illustrated below.

One of the more prominent projects was conducted by Congress Alukura, an Aboriginal women's organisation based in Alice Springs in Central Australia. I quote from correspondence received by the Consumers' Health Forum (4 April, 1991):

> The Congress Alukura would like to share some information with the Committee that the years of political lobbying, negotiation, Aboriginal self-determination and tremendous community involvement and participation have now been rewarded. ATSIC [the Aboriginal and Torres Strait Islander Commission] have given approval for the Congress Alukura to purchase land and to construct a new building.

Congress Alukura, which represented the views of one of the most disadvantaged groups in Australian society, received funding in 1987, the first year of the funding programme, to enable Aboriginal women from remote and rural areas to attend a workshop where they discussed the notion of 'borning' and knowledge of the Grandmother's Law. Knowledge gained from this workshop, and from other sources, aided them in gaining government support for a community-controlled Aboriginal Women's Health Centre in Alice Springs. It is interesting to note, too, that the parent organisation, the Central Australian Aborig-inal Congress (commonly referred to as Congress)[6] was originally established as a political advocacy organisation, with funding from the Department of Aboriginal Affairs in 1973. The continuity between this Whitlam-led initiative, and the commitment to community development, research and policy activism evident in the Consumers' Health Forum research development programme, is evident.

Why did funding for the consumer research development funding programme end?

Just one month after taking over responsibility for the newly created Department of Community Services and Health (DCSH), in March

1990, Minister Howe approved the restructuring of the Community Health Programme and three related programmes which were administered by the two previous departments, to form the Community Organisations' Support Programme (COSP). The objective of this new programme was '. . . to provide funding for infrastructure support to community organisations with a primary focus of relevance to the portfolio' (Commonwealth Department of Health, Housing and Community Services 1991, p. 47). The House of Representatives Standing Committee on Community Affairs (1991) aimed to achieve rationalisation in the funding and administration of peak health and community organisations within the new department. The terms of reference for the conduct of the COSP review included reference to the kind of accountability that could and should be expected by the funding department, and the outcome measures that could be required from the funding authority as a condition of funding. The report stated that the main task facing the DCSH and the Committee was '. . . rationalise arrangements which had evolved separately in different Departments' (House of Representatives Standing Committee on Community Affairs (HRSCCA), 1991, p. 2).

Funding for the Consumers' Health Forum research funding programme ceased in 1992, after implementation of the major recommendations from *You Have Your Moments* (HRSCCA 1991), the review of the Community Organisations' Support Programme (COSP), under which the CHF was funded.[7] This led to a reduction in the amount of core funding received by the Consumers' Health Forum and by many other peak health and community organisations, from the 1992–93 financial year (HRSCCA 1991). In the 1996–97 federal budget, after the advent to power of a new Liberal–National Party government under Prime Minister John Howard, COSP was restructured, and renamed the Community Sector Support Scheme (CSSS). The Commonwealth then commissioned the consulting firm, Coopers and Lybrand, to review the funding for national secretariats of community organisations. The aim of the consultancy was to investigate and make recommendations about the purpose, nature and level of funding for secretariats of community organisations under the Community Sector Support Scheme and to recommend which organisations were to receive funding from 1 July 1997. From

July 1997, portfolio funding to national secretariats was more closely linked to measurable outcomes relevant to the provision of health and family services in the community. The rhetoric of the corporate rationalisers in health care, and of the new public sector management, in which agencies manage for results and are held accountable for outcomes, is evident in this scheme, rather than the language of community rights and participation.

The Consumers' Health Forum grants programme was never popular with the professional monopolists in the National Health and Medical Research Council (NHMRC), partly because the funds were not allocated by the NHMRC in line with its own processes of peer review, and partly because Minister Blewett imposed an allocation of $40 000 of NHMRC funding to the programme just prior to his resignation from the health portfolio, in the wake of the 1990 federal election. Concern about the grants programme was also expressed by the chair of the health Ethics Committee of the NHMRC (CHF to R. Kalucy, 21 Sept., 1989), as the NHMRC guidelines on ethical research and the requirement that researchers seek ethics approval from an institutional ethics committee consti- tuted along NHMRC lines were not being adhered to by the Forum. The Forum drew up its own 'Fair Play Guidelines' for consumer researchers in 1990 (Matrice 1990).

The Consumers' Health Forum research funding programme also attracted considerable critical scrutiny from managers in the federal health authority, some of whom considered that all health research funding should be administered under the one professional umbrella, the NHMRC. This managerial imperative to rationalise the funding and administration of health research received a further boost under the new Liberal–National Party government in 1996, which saw several research programmes rationalised. In the 1997–99 triennium the Public Health Research and Development Committee was incor- porated into the much larger and longer established Medical Research Committee. The Research and Development Grants Advi- sory Committee (RADGAC) was terminated, also, on the understanding that health services research would be undertaken through the normal NHMRC grants process.

There was concern, too, from health officials about accountability to the minister, with monies going directly to community groups, and the possible publicity that this could attract. Public sector emphasis on upwards accountability became more evident in correspondence between the department and the Forum from 1991 onwards. For example, in 1991 the covering letter to community groups in receipt of funds under the programme included the caution: 'This offer is made on the understanding that you are not in receipt of funds for this purpose from any other source'. This caution was intended to prevent organisations from 'double dipping', or attracting funds for a project from more than one source. Whilst the Consumers' Health Forum Research Development Programme was nurtured by Minister Blewett until he left the portfolio in 1990, his successor, the Honourable Brian Howe, did not choose to defend the programme against the criticisms coming from the professional and managerial interests in the health arena. It could be said, however, that the viability of the Consumers' Health Forum itself was strengthened during Brian Howe's tenure as Minister, as the increased conformity with public sector management principles such as public accountability,[8] during his tenure, made its core funding base more secure.

A high water mark for community activism in the health policy process

The Consumers' Health Forum research funding programme (1987–92) represents a high water mark in terms of community participation in the health policy process, during the Hawke and Keating years. Whilst the Consumers' Health Forum was born of community activism and nurtured by a Minister, Neal Blewett, who believed in strengthening the community constituency for reform in health care, medical bodies resented the threat to their monopoly of control over health research, and many managers in the health bureaucracy were not supportive of the openness and unpredictability that the programme brought.

The funding programme (1987–92), and its demise, brought to the surface fundamental tensions in community participation initiatives, such as the Consumers' Health Forum; especially the tension between gaining legitimacy with allies in the health bureaucracy, whilst avoiding co-option into the formal system to such an extent that the challenge is rendered ineffective (Conley 1992, pp. 3–4). With implementation of the major recommendations of the review of the Community Organisations Support Programme (COSP), stricter public sector accountability arrangements were applied to the community organisations funded under the programme. The Consumers' Health Forum could not justify having its own research funding programme, when no other COSP-funded community group had such a programme.

From 1991–92 all Community Organisations Support Programme grants were subject to the intensified requirements of managerialist forms of auditing. As a result, 1992 was the last year in which the Consumers' Health Forum provided funds to community and consumer groups to enable them to conduct their own research. The issue was principally one of public sector managerial concern about accountability associated with the untied money distributed to community and consumer groups. Core funding to the CHF from the Commonwealth health authority peaked in 1991–92, but funding for the forum overall continued to rise each year after this, due to additional project-based funding which was initiated by the department. In 1995–96 the Consumers' Health Forum of Australia (1996) received more than $1 million from the Commonwealth government, and over two-thirds of these funds ($680 000) came through special project funding commissioned by the Commonwealth Department of Health and Family Services. Much of this project funding was devoted to the conduct of consultations on departmental programmes in areas such as pharmaceutical education, general practice, women's health and rural health, which is consistent with a consultative rather than a community development approach to community participation in health policy development. Thus, in the period 1992–6 increasing emphasis was given to the consultative function of the Forum.

On the significance of the public policy context

This chapter has traced the origins and development of the Consumers' Health Forum of Australia, established in 1987, from its early origins in federally-supported local community development work, to its current status as a 'one-stop consultation shop' for the Commonwealth Department of Health and Family Services. The CHF is the major national organisation which represents the views of community and consumer groups on issues relating to health in an imbalanced political market that systematically favours the dominant professional monopolists or the challenging corporate rationalisers.

The chapter has indicated that the forum has undergone two distinct phases of development. In the first six years (1987–92), emphasis was given to the development of a strong cohesive community-based lobby which could provide the Commonwealth health authority with information and advice to act as a balance to the representations of well organised professional, industry and government groups. Since 1993, and implementation of the recommendations from the review of the Community Organisations and Support Programme, however, increasing emphasis has been given to the consultative function of the forum, which is consistent with a managerialist rather than a community development approach to community participation in the health policy process.

In the 'heyday' of the reform-oriented Labor government (1983–87), progressive public servants were able to develop significant programme innovations, in the name of making public services more accessible and responsive to the needs of individuals in the community (Yeatman 1996a, p. 285). As financial restraint played a more important role in the public policy environment after this period, there was increasing emphasis on managerial control and accountability. This managerial climate was evident in the COSP review which was initiated by Brian Howe, in 1990, and which led to the rationalisation of the Community Organisations and Support Programme, and to termination of the Consumer's Health Forum Research Development Programme. This decision has been traced principally to managerial concerns which focused on accountability for public funds. The analysis in this chapter noted, too, that this concern on the part of federal health officials coincided with the professional monopolists' concern to control health and medical research funding and administration under the single umbrella of the National Health and Medical Research Council. Thus, the tide ran out on the consumer-managed Consumer's Health Forum Research Development Programme when there was a coincidence of interests between the professional monopolists associated with the NH&MRC and corporate rationalisers in the federal health authority.

Perhaps most importantly, Neal Blewett, the Minister for Health between 1983 and 1990, wanted to win friends for Medicare, and he needed to strengthen support for the Hawke government's key economic policy, the Accord. The community development approach, which underpinned the high water mark in community activism in the health policy arena during the Hawke and Keating governments was more appropriate for a government with an activist reform agenda (the Accord).[9] When Brian Howe replaced Neal Blewett in the Health portfolio in 1990, the Consumers' Health Forum and other community-based health organisations were reorganised in line with the new managerialist emphasis on fiscal restraint and public sector accountability that was dominant at the time in the Australian Public Service. After 1993, Consumers' Health Forum activities shifted from community development to consultation. This scenario suggests that the high water mark of community activism in the health policy process (1987–92) during the period of the Hawke and Keating governments, 1983–96, occurred due to an alliance of interests between a reformist Minister (Blewett) with progressive public servants and community activists.

This case study of community activism in the health policy process has also brought to light the fact that the broad public policy agenda of the government of the day plays a crucial role in facilitating and, or, resourcing community activism in the health policy process. During the Whitlam years there was an unprecedented level of political and financial support for community development and community activism in the policy process, across the public policy spectrum, including health. The Hawke government came to power in 1983 with a reform agenda, and a commitment to control wages and prices through the Accord with industry and the unions, and to protect the social wage through initiatives such as Medicare. Between 1983 and 1996, industry, professional and community groups were incorporated into the policy process, and national consultative mechanisms and processes such as the Economic Planning and Advisory Council and the Consumers' Health Forum were established in order to maintain support for wages restraint, and for the social wage, and components such as Medicare. This period saw public resources devoted to consultation rather than community-based participation, and with the new manageralism evident in the Australian Public Service, there was decreasing support for community activism in the health policy process. This chapter has focused on the rise and demise of the Consumers' Health Forum Research Development Programme, 1987–92, as it represented a high water mark for community activism in the health policy process during this corporatist period of Labor governments.

Given the imbalanced political market in health care, one could expect the nature of community participation in the health policy process[10] to reflect the shifting alliances and balance of power between the professional monopolists, corporate rationalists and the community. In Australia, this structural interests' perspective requires recognition, too, of the influence of governments and of political parties, of trade unions, and of heterogeneity of medical lobby groups within Australia, as indicated at the beginning of this chapter. In examining the applicability of this analytical framework to the case study analysed in this chapter, it would appear that the public policy environment of the Accord, and the political needs of the health minister, Neal Blewett, were crucial in facilitating and resourcing the Consumers' Health Forum of Australia. Policy activism, in the form of the 'Petition of Reform' from community and consumer groups, was received sympathetically by supportive public officials in the Department of Health, and with Ministerial support, the Consumers' Health Forum, and the grants programme were born.

Perhaps Alford's (1975) structural interests' perspective is most useful in helping us to understand and explain barriers to reform in the health policy process. Medibank was progressively dismantled under Coalition governments, between 1975 and 1983, and funding for the Consumers' Health Forum research and development programme ceased due to resistance from both professional monopolists and corporate rationalisers. Thus, the conceptual framework offered by the notion of the 'imbalanced political market in health care' goes a long way towards explaining the forces which work to *constrain* community activism in the health policy process on an ongoing basis.

When we turn to moments of progressive reform in the health policy process, as in this chapter, several ingredients appear crucial. First, a commitment by the government of the day to the reform process, in this case by the Whitlam and then the Hawke governments, second, support from the Minister of the day, and in this case study the role of Minister Blewett was crucial, third, support from progressive public officials, ministerial advisers and so on who champion the community activist role, and who do a great deal behind the scenes to facilitate it, and fourth, the existence of democratising social movements such as the women's health movement and the Aboriginal rights movement, who are not afraid to challenge the hegemony of the professional monopolists in the health policy process.

Thus, the case study of the rise and fall of community activism in the health policy process offered in this chapter, suggests that the historical conjuncture of a reformist government, a progressive minister, sympathetic public servants and democratising social movements *facilitates* community activism in the health policy process. And, by the same token, it is the relative absence or weakness of these forces which constrains and diminishes the role of community activism.

Acknowledgments

I would like to thank Ben Bartlett, Margaret Conley and Denise Fry, who provided me with dates and information, and staff in the Secretariat at the Consumers' Health Forum, who assisted with the data collection. I thank, also, Anna Yeatman for her most useful feedback and ideas.

7

Discourse analysis and policy activism: readings and rewritings of Australian university research policy

GAR JONES, ALISON LEE
AND CATE POYNTON

Introduction

In this chapter policy-making and policy activism are understood as being matters of discursive and textual practices. In making this point with respect to policy analysis, it is first necessary to situate the chapter within some broader sociocultural considerations. In general, we recognise that Western forms of life are more and more complexly *written*. In part, this means that more and more domains of ordinary life have become subjected to, and shaped by, the explosion of 'information' through the massive capitalisation of the print apparatus and by the new information technologies. Forms of life increasingly become 'scene(s) of discourse' (McCormack 1991). More particularly, as Norman Fairclough (1996a) notes, late modern or advanced capitalist societies are marked by rapid change in the form of the incorporation of vast new areas of social life into markets and by the 'colonisation of ordinary life by economic and bureaucratic systems'. This rapid social change, according to Fairclough, is 'increasingly centred upon cultural change, and cultural change often takes a pre-eminently discursive form' (Fairclough 1996a, p. x).

More specifically, the point is made in chapter 1 of this book that there has been a massive proliferation of public policy over the past forty years. The subjection of more and more domains of social life to policy takes the form of the 'writing' or 'textualisation' of those forms of life. This proliferation of public policy discourse acts to construct whole new populations, by means of ways of naming, organising and governing. The policy process is, as much as anything, a process of the generation of massive amounts of text, in the form of policy documents, submissions, press releases, implementation guidelines, databases, evaluation reports, and more. To play a part in the policy process, whether in the development, the implementation or evaluation of policy, whether in interpretation or in contestation, is to engage in language practices. That is, the policy process needs to be understood as centrally and iteratively involving processes of speaking, of writing and of reading. This has a material effect in terms of how the everyday practices of policy formation and policy implementation are carried out. It similarly raises important questions concerning what counts as policy activism. That is, policy activism may in large part consist of chasing and contributing to various kinds of paper trails. These include government publications in glossy covers, the construction of national databases and multiple readings and re-presentations of data. To be a policy activist is to be centrally involved in the generation (writing) and interpretation (reading and rewriting) of text.

The particular policy site with which we, as authors, are centrally concerned is current university research policy. This is a site which, since the late 1980s, was increasingly subjected to the policy regime of the Labor state in its agenda of bringing higher education under the umbrella of its broad economic rationalist reform process. It is a site which is currently undergoing, as is the whole of higher education, massive destabilisation within the new policy environment of the Coalition Liberal–National government. The sector is facing major reductions in funding, at the same time as increasing regulation of its activities. These changes have profound implications, particularly in terms of new conditions of 'knowledge production' and questions of access and equity. The role of universities in relation to new knowledge is increasingly constrained by government policy decisions informed by largely economic considerations. Since the higher education sector was restructured in the late 1980s, and new universities[1] were formed within the 'Unified National System'

(UNS), research dollars have been spread increasingly thinly as more universities and more individuals within those universities have begun to undertake research and to compete for funding. This, combined with funding cutbacks for other aspects of university work, and the consequent massive increase in the workload of academics, has effectively ensured that research for many is becoming more and more difficult to undertake at all. Of all aspects of higher education, the activity that has been subjected to the most detailed interventions by government is research. This is possibly because research is seen as most closely tied to 'the national interest' via the direct linking of research and development (R and D) to economic growth and development.

Within this policy context, we occupy positions which have a number of important commonalities and which bring us together as analysts and activists. As members of 'new' universities (the University of Western Sydney (UWS) and the University of Technology, Sydney (UTS)), we experience the restructuring of the higher education sector and the changes to research policy in terms of a set of effects in the constitution and reconstitution of institutional positionings and identities. These effects are differentially experienced across the higher education sector, with new universities, which attract only small portions of the government research dollar, rendered particularly vulnerable to policy changes. Our particular institutional positions, as co-ordinator of a university research office (Jones), as director of a research centre (Poynton), as members of university research management bodies (Jones, Lee, Poynton), and as researchers, provide us with cross-disciplinary and cross-sectoral knowledge of this policy context. As makers and implementers of policy within our local institutions, we are concerned to develop a critical analysis of national research policy developments. The productivity of this particular collaboration lies in the collective endeavour of two academics and an administrator working together upon such an analysis. We bring together particular expertise, as a professional with intimate knowledge of the complexity of this policy site and as academics with expertise in various forms of discourse analysis. This allows us to construe policy work in terms of text-work and hence to understand our own work in analysing activism in terms of discourse analysis.

The particular concern of this chapter is to explore productive ways of thinking about discourse analysis as a form of policy activism. If 'discourse analysis' can be construed most generally in terms of close attention to text and to the practices of reading and of writing, then a great deal of policy work as text-work can be understood in discourse–analytic terms. While there is a considerable literature on specialised forms of technical analysis of text and discourse that goes by the name of 'discourse analysis', what we are concerned to do in this particular chapter is to see discourse analysis more broadly in terms of the daily work of reading and writing that happens 'on-the-job', in the interests of direct intervention in the policy process. In complicating this apparently self-evident point, however, we bring a perspective that is informed by the academic field of discourse analysis, particularly, an understanding of the *productivity* of discourse—that is, its capacity to 'bring into being' what is being talked about. That is, discourses, in Foucault's (1977, p. 49) terms, are 'practices that systematically form the objects of which they speak . . . discourses are not about objects, they constitute them and in the practice of doing so conceal their own invention'. As analysts we are concerned, not so much with negative critique of the undesirable effects of the exercise of power through policy, though contestation of particular policy effects is sometimes necessary, but rather, with the conditions of possibility of policy meanings and policy effects, and with the positions made available for individuals and institutions within those meanings.

Attention to texts and 'readings' of texts crucially goes beyond a 'realist' conception (Van Maanen 1988; Lather 1991) of the policy process in terms of 'what happened', who said and did what and with what outcomes. A realist text is one which claims to be a 'neutral medium for conveying pre-existing facts about the world' (Woolgar 1991, p. 28). Attention to the textualisation of policy supplements and often unsettles such 'realist tales'. This process of unsettling and rewriting is a matter of paying close attention to questions of language, particularly with regard to the question of representation. The word representation suggests that what language does is 're-present' what already exists outside language: that language is merely a convenient form of packaging of 'reality'. All kinds of critical approaches to text and discourse agree, however, that what language does is to constitute or construct the world we live in, and ourselves as part of that world. It does this by making available, as resources for 're-presenting' the world, templates which incline us to read that world in particular ways. Discourses may thus be understood in terms of such resources.

Language is not just about representation, however. Texts such as policy texts are incitements to action, necessitating not only 'encoders' and 'decoders' but also 'actors'—those who will 'interpret' the requirements of policy into specific sets of actions understood as capable of realising the goals of the policy or of problematising and deflecting those goals, that is, rewriting them.

Despite the increasing proliferation of policy texts, there does not seem to be a great deal of attention paid to language as the 'stuff' of which those texts are made. There are important developments in policy analysis that attend to these questions of the productivity of text and discourse (Yeatman 1990; Ball 1994; Poulson 1996). It is part of the task of this chapter to contribute to an analysis of the policy process in making an argument for the use of discourse analysis for the purposes of policy activism. It should also be noted at this point that the focus on language is not intended to ignore the importance of other resources for textual meanings. Indeed, the particular salience of numbers and the readings to which numerical modes of representation are put form an important part of the analysis in later sections of this chapter.

In what follows, we first present a 'realist' tale, a relatively 'straight' and singular coherent narrative about the development of research policy in the decade since the higher education reforms were first begun. The particular focus of this narrative is the move to 'performance-based' funding for research and the direction this policy initiative took in Australia towards the quantitative measurement of research output and the development of the measurement instrument known as the Research Quantum. The following section will then subject this tale to a series of readings and rewritings, focusing on the ways in which these new texts themselves count as interventions into the development of research policy in our respective institutional environments and within the national arena. We then explore how attention to policy as text and as discourse can generate different critical and enabling readings of policy texts as they are received, interpreted and implemented within the specific institutional site of the creative arts. This field, newly constituted as a university discipline as a result of the incorporation of colleges of advanced education into the unified higher education sector, is of particular significance in the universities of which we are members. As a case study for the ways in which policy discourse works to constitute new objects and new populations, it is instructive.

University research policy and the Quantum: a realist tale

In 1993, the National Report of Australia's Higher Education Sector (Department of Employment, Education and Training (DEET) 1993) highlighted how 'the performance and funding of research in Australia has differed significantly from the majority of Organisation for Economic Co-operation and Development (OECD) countries because of the relatively dominant position of government' in funding research and development (R and D), as opposed to the 'relatively low level of performance and funding of R and D by the business sector' (DEET 1993, p. 247). This alliance or dominance of government and the academy meant that the higher education sector was a major provider of research and development in Australia. The latest data shows that this situation has not changed substantially (Australian Bureau of Statistics (ABS) 1996).

Not surprisingly, the focus on research and research performance dominates much of the public debate surrounding the Australian higher education sector, yet, in the Australian context, the flagship nature of institutional research activity has been a relatively recent phenomenon. As the National Report slyly noted, within the Australian university sector of the early twentieth century, 'little money was available . . . to support research, especially at the University of Melbourne' (DEET 1993, p. 4). Indeed, many commentators in this period saw Australian universities as costly toys (DEET 1993, p. 4).

The recent phenomenon of a strong public policy focus on research grew out of the major restructure of the higher education sector that occurred in the late 1980s, the plans for which were outlined in the 1988 Commonwealth Government White Paper on higher education

(Dawkins 1988). One of the most significant changes to occur in this period was the dismantling of the binary divide, that educational schism characterised by universities on one side, colleges of advanced education and institutes of technology on the other; one side awarding degrees, the other diplomas. The abolition of the binary divide saw the creation of many new universities, sometimes out of amalgamations of colleges of advanced education, either with one another (for example UWS) or with institutes of technology (for example UTS), or by the merger of such institutions with established universities. The results were dramatic. At the beginning of the 1980s there were nineteen universities and forty-six colleges of advanced education. By 1991 the Unified National System (UNS) was in place, involving only thirty-nine institutions (DEET 1993, p. 30). These reforms and the subsequent growth in funding significantly increased the opportunities for more individuals to obtain a university education, as well as enabling many more academic staff to undertake research (Brennan 1993, p. 92). As the Industry Commission noted in its 1995 R and D Report, university staff describing themselves as engaged in 'teaching-only' fell from 35.5 per cent in 1988 to 13.6 per cent in 1991 (Banks, Owens and Hall 1995, p. 341). This was a significant cultural change.

These structural reforms were promoted on the basis of efficiency, effectiveness and rationalisation of resources. As David Phillips, former head of the Higher Education Division of DEETYA (previously DEET, reconstituted as the Department of Employment, Education, Training and Youth Affairs) argues, the reforms employed:

> . . . a policy model based on the view that the most effective use of limited public resources would be achieved through a co-ordinated, systemic approach. The Unified National System was a mechanism to restrict the distribution of public resources to a

Table 7.1   Changes in Australian higher education 1982–92

A system changes	1982	1992
Institutions	87	39
Students	341 390	559 365
Academic staff	23 705	31 345
Research funding	$69 million	$280 million

Source: Department of Employment, Education and Training (DEET) 1993, p. xxix.

specific group of large institutions, with conscious attempts to limit the duplication of expensive infrastructure.

It was taken to be self-evident that there was a role for government, not just in funding but in ensuring that funds were distributed in an efficient manner. (Phillips 1997, p. 12)

A less benign interpretation might argue that these changes occurred in the context of international movements linking education, including higher education, to employment via what Lingard refers to as a 'micro-economically refocused human capital theory' which is about 'education's contribution to the production of multi-skilled workers to assist in the international competitiveness of national economies' (Lingard 1996, p. 78).

Within this same context, the 1988 White Paper on higher education committed the Labor government to the development of performance indicators within the higher education funding process, outlining, in the language of economic rationalism and the performance contract, the desire for a 'funding system that responds to institutional performance and the achievement of mutually agreed goals' (Dawkins 1988, p. 85). The White Paper outlined the need for performance indicators to cover a wide variety of higher education functions, involving such things as student demand and course completion rates, quality of teaching and curriculum design, research performance and indicators of performance against equity goals, as well as measures of organisational efficiency.

From the perspective of the late 1990s, however, the anticipated performance measures relating to teaching quality, student experience, equity and efficiency have not materialised. Only research performance has been established, together with simple calculations regarding student completion rates. As the National Board of Employment Education and Training summarised it: 'the original goal of the White Paper of allocating all operating grant resources on the basis of output or performance measures has not yet been achieved' (cited in Anderson *et al.* 1996, p. 84).

Yet, in terms of research funding, performance measurement became deeply entrenched. As the Higher Education Council noted:

. . . core funding of Australian universities for research purposes is now almost entirely performance based. This is a major turnaround from the situation a decade or so ago. Then, core funding of research was implicit and effectively confined to the group of nineteen institutions comprising the pre-1987 universities. (Anderson *et al.* 1996, p. 47)

No other aspect of higher education performance has been reviewed, analysed, celebrated and worried about as much as research, in terms of its funding, focus and productivity. This obsession with research performance has been somewhat of an international phenomenon, although it is interesting to note that Anderson *et al.* found the actual use of performance-based funding quite limited: 'of all the OECD countries in our survey we found only five examples (apart from Australia) where funding for a national system is linked directly to performance to any significant extent' (Anderson *et al.* 1996, p. 59). This list of countries included Denmark, the United Kingdom, Germany, the Netherlands and Sweden, as well as a model operating in Tennessee, USA. Examination of such overseas models highlighted a range of performance funding systems that were significantly different from the Australian model, often being implemented in order to 'achieve specific targets: more student enrolment, or more students of a certain calibre, or . . . improvement on a number of specific and agreed targets' (Anderson *et al.* 1996, p. 76). The Research Assessment Exercise operating in the United Kingdom was, in its 1996 operations, focused on research quality via an examination of the productivity outputs of research active staff across the sector in sixty-nine subject units of assessments (Anderson *et al.* 1996, p. 9).

The history of how performance funding for research was embedded in the Australian higher education sector is complex. In 1990, via the Relative Funding Model, the government attempted a one-off equalisation of institutions' operating grants, involving, in the teaching component, the average costs of delivery of a variety of undergraduate and postgraduate courses in groups of disciplines (Anderson *et al.* 1996, p 147). In tandem with this one-off equalisation came the development of the research component of the operating grants, known as the Research Quantum. In this model, the teaching component accounted for 94 per cent of the total operating grant across the sector and the Research Quantum 6 per cent. Between 1990 and 1994, the Research Quantum was distributed in proportion to each university's success in obtaining National Competitive Grants (via Australia's prestigious national research agencies). The intention was to build into the model research output measures (publications, disseminations) in the near future. The Research Quantum was not, however, redesigned and redistributed until 1995, when input measures were broadened to include industry funding and other public sector support for research, while also taking into account research output measures relating to the number of research and scholarly publications produced by staff and students and the number of higher degree research completions (Anderson *et al.* 1996, pp. 47–8).

These changes were announced in December 1993 and the first data collection was undertaken in 1994, organised by the Australian Vice-Chancellors Committee (AV-CC), involving 1992 and 1993 data. In the December 1993 announcement, the Minister for Employment, Education and Training also announced that the Research Quantum would no longer be a percentage of the total operating grant for the sector but a defined sum of money. In terms of the 1996 and 1997 Research Quantums, this has meant that the actual amount of money for distribution has fallen to around 5 per cent of the total operating grants (DEETYA Research Branch 1997, p. 1) and, until the redesign for the 1995 Quantum, institutions were being assessed on their 1988–89 performance. This was an inadequate state of affairs, particularly for those newer universities that had been making inroads into the research funding capital of the sector via competitive grants and industry funding. As the Industry Commission Report on Research and Development noted: 'the Research Quantum reflected past rather than current performance [and] does not recognise the need for special treatment of emerging disciplines or those of national importance with low student demand' (Banks, Owens and Hall 1995, p. 386). The model adopted by the Commonwealth possessed no mechanisms for examining and rewarding developing institutions.

The output measures relating to publications have had a tortuous history (see Appendix for details of the different models of the Quantum). For the 1994 collection (Quantum I), the publication measure involved eight categories: books, chapters, journal articles, reference works, reports, reviews, conference proceedings and patents. By 1995 (Quantum II), the list of allowable disseminations had expanded to twenty-two categories but, by March 1997, further revision had reduced the publications' categories to four traditional measures (Quantum III). This latter change was argued for on the basis of efficiency—in terms of both the resulting distribution of funds as well as a reduction in the administrative effort required by universities to produce the more complex publications data outlined above. Throughout this exercise of legitimising and delimiting diversity in research activity, there were different positions taken. Established universities were not keen to see newer universities and newer disciplines rewarded for high productivity. Newer universities were keen to have their development recognised, but fearful that the still heavy reliance on external grants would see the bulk of the Research Quantum, on average 65 per cent, continue to be returned to half a dozen institutions. The Research Quantum, in its many manifestations, has highlighted how closely policy on research performance has been related to government concerns with efficiency, effectiveness and the rationalisation of resources (Department of Employment Education and Training 1993, p. xxvii).

Given the reliance of the higher education sector on traditional modes of research production, such as the refereed journal article, it was surprising that creative works were ever considered acceptable publication outputs. It was also surprising that the sole-authored research book, the prestige output most common in the humanities and social sciences, stood at the pinnacle of each version of the publications model. In many disciplines, particularly the sciences (as the model of research that many researchers saw as being forced onto the entire higher education sector), the sole-authored book is a largely non-existent output. Thus, one of the consequences of performance funding of research output has been to promote an unprecedented degree of visibility for the book, particularly advantaging faculties of humanities and social sciences, now identified and rewarded for producing most of the nation's books (approximately 72 per cent of output in this category for 1994). Whatever happens to the Quantum in future policy developments, there is no easy path back from such transparency, subsequent changes rendering disadvantage to individual disciplines and institutions all too visible. It is the common multiple-authored paper of the sciences whose 'value' has been somewhat dissipated, although it is important to remember that team-based scientific effort results in a relatively large number of refereed journal articles whose combined value per year is easily likely to exceed the value of a book that is produced over a three to five year period.

It has taken almost ten years to play out the enunciated policy position of the Labor government with regard to performance funding. From the Green Paper of 1987 to the revised 1998 Quantum, universities have been progressively transformed by the dominant agenda of restructuring the public sector in line with the general efficiency goal of doing more with less as well as with the additional goal of promoting competition where possible. The application of such sustained policy in higher education has left the individual researcher within the academy confused about what exactly the academy stands for. Judgment on academic productivity is increasingly directed by often reactive academic managers faced with looming deficits and a shortfall in research funding. In many 'post-1987' universities, this may lead once more to some kind of renewed binary system, with funding and enrolment shortfalls encouraging certain universities to consider reconceptualising themselves as predominantly teaching-only institutions.

'Strategic information': rewritings

The formation of the ensemble of policies that has culminated in the current measurement instrument of the Research Quantum has been a process of the subjection of the domain of research to greater and greater forms of specification. Those concerned with the implementation of policy at university level are required to deal on a daily basis with an ever increasing proliferation of text; in particular, with the government driven requirement to produce ever more extensive and ever more detailed data for national data collections. Research productivity, in Australia at least, has become an exercise in quantification, as the term 'Quantum' eloquently testifies. In contrast to other comparable countries, for example, Britain, research is measured simply as amounts of items, hierarchically measured within particular grids of categorisation. This has led to the assessment of research productivity in terms of standards for validation of performance that are supplied by the accountancy discipline of auditing.

The publications component of the Quantum repositions both

individuals and fields of scholarship within the academy and plays a significant part in constituting how those individuals and fields are understood and measured. The Quantum is in effect a calculus of who people are and can be, for instance, as 'productive' or 'unproductive' academic researchers within the prevailing discourses of what counts as research. This has a material effectivity within many universities, where departments and faculties seek from central research offices a snapshot of who is producing, and who is not. Within many universities, the Research Quantum has become in effect a management artifact, a fiscal disciplinary tool used for promotion and tenure purposes internally. Externally, it is used for marketing purposes, to attract both further research funding and new research-only staff. This is despite the fact that, as the Anderson report noted, 'annual fluctuations in performance are only to be expected, and provide no sensible basis for funding of intrinsically long-term institutions' (Anderson *et al.* 1996, p. 76). An economic rationalist discourse, producing artifacts such as the Research Quantum, has repositioned the complex process of knowledge production within a model of adequate returns on human capital.

In what follows, we return to considerations of how particular kinds of attention to the effects of the proliferation of text and to changing discourses can come to constitute critical intervention into particular policy trajectories. We do this via, first, a critical rereading of the discourse of quantification in terms of the commodification of research and of what Fairclough (1996b) terms the 'technologisation' of public policy discourse. Here, we begin the task of opening up the possibility for strategic 'rewritings' of the dominant narratives of research policy, within our own specific institutional sites. We then proceed via a case study detailing the effects of the changing rules for what counts as 'research' on one domain of scholarly endeavour. This site, the creative arts, is of particular importance for the productive output of many of the 'new' universities.

Quantification and commodification

The Quantum implementation guidelines text titled 1997 Higher Education Financial and Publications Research Data Collection (DEETYA 1996b) presents Quantum data collection as a minutely complex book-keeping exercise, exemplary in its work of specifying precisely what activity is to occur as a direct result of the production and dissemination of the text through the university system. The text itself is twenty-eight pages long and is accompanied by detailed descriptors of publication categories, the specification of verification requirements for the different categories, and specifications for the 'fields of research' and 'socio-economic objectives' classifications.

It is easy to point to the development of such exercises as 'technologies' which represent the possible excesses of an economic rationalist approach to management, especially when an eye is cast over the shoulder at the decade and a half of research policy developments in Britain. It is similarly an easy matter to construe the newly constituted 'researcher' as the latest instance of the invention of the 'calculable person', with reference in particular to Hacking's work on statistics in the constitution of new populations in Britain in the nineteenth century (1982). Nevertheless it is important to attend to the conditions of emergence of this text and the readings that might be made of it; to consider, that is, what discursive effects are made possible in this instance through this apparatus.

Measurement, as Johnston points out, 'allows us to grasp and control (part of) a complex situation . . . Clearly, measurement can increase information, improve planning and equally clearly it permits greater control' (1997, p. 2). Measurement 'reduces complexity by focusing attention on a single dimension, by a (violent) breaking of wholes into pieces, by giving number to value'. Measurement by number works by reducing unlike objects to a single linear scale which gives a numerical value to the object; the object can then be compared to other objects and subjected to a systematic economy of exchange. In this sense the quantification of research output is an exemplary instance of commodification: how a discourse of 'use value' (research as the generation of useful knowledge) gives way, in large part, to exchange value (points and funding).

There is no doubt that research and scholarship have been significantly commodified. The publications component of the Research Quantum is now effectively aligned to a financial audit process. It is highly likely that a multinational accountancy firm will be employed by DEETYA to validate the research artifacts of Australian academics for the 1998 Quantum. Acceptable proof becomes a challenge in itself, as outlined in the Quantum guidelines. Knowing something has been refereed, knowing as an author that responses have been rendered to referees and portions of the text have been rewritten, will, in the end, be meaningless, unless the physical evidence is provided that the journal article was indeed refereed. Reputation and peer knowledge about the disciplinary 'lie of the land' will be nullified, for the auditor may ultimately demand a copy of the letter that stated that a paper had gone out to referees, although a certain privileging will occur for those journals listed on American based citation indexes.

One of the discursive effects of this attention to the quantifiable specification of research productivity is that it runs the constant risk of setting up and promoting a binary relation between 'quantity' and 'quality'. That is not to suggest that the government texts explicitly invoke this binary, nor that such an effect is an effect of policy intention. Indeed, the explicit intention of the Research White Paper (Dawkins 1989) is the pursuit of 'excellence'. Rather, the effect is a result of omission. The definition of 'research activity' in the data collection guidelines text is thus: 'The essential characteristic of research activity is that it leads to publicly verifiable outcomes which are open to peer appraisal' (DEETYA 1996b, p. 11). This definition is not incongruent with the emphasis in the White Paper on excellence and the 'best researchers' (Dawkins 1989). Nevertheless, in the absence of a technology for the establishment of quality, other than with reference to 'peer review', the insistence on the salience of the quantitative constitutes, by default, 'research productivity' as an amount. Moreover, amounts of research output which translate into amounts of money in funding returned to universities have to be measured against amounts of money required to generate the accounts of the amounts of research output. Thus, Anderson *et al.* (1996, p. 56) noted in anticipation of the modifications to the Quantum categories from Quantum II to Quantum III: 'less verifiable categories could well be discontinued in the interest of cost-efficiency'. Further, despite the immense effort to specify in minute detail the essential differences among the categories, anybody charged with administering the Quantum exercise is faced with enormous discrepancies, both in scale and in 'standing', among items ostensibly in the same category. Despite these complexities, research productivity, as quantified by the Quantum, has become 'strategic business information', particularly for corporate activists who wish to give their institutions the best possible 'product focus', usually articulated in 'boys' own' narratives: 'we got the most money'; 'we published the most books'; 'we had the biggest growth in funding'.

In this environment, those responsible for managing research in individual institutions are regularly involved in complex and seemingly endless data collection exercises in response to federal government requirements to build up its national research data collections, data which are still not easily and centrally accessible. There is, for example, no easy world wide Web access. Yet the generation of this 'strategic information' for purposes of policy formation sees more and more of the research activity of individual universities made visible and represented in particular ways. For example, senior policy makers such as Max Brennan, immediate past Chair of the Australian Research Council, have developed what is termed the 'Brennan Index', where algorithms are produced, positioning universities differentially in terms of such matters as their relative capacity to support research degree students. One such algorithm sees the 'sandstone', or established, universities represented in terms of the relatively much higher amount of research income per research higher degree student, in comparison with 'new' universities. The conclusion drawn from this algorithm is that 'sandstone' universities are better able to support research degree students (DEETYA 1995).

It is possible, however, to re-deploy or 'rewrite' such data, once in the public domain, in the interests of generating different narratives. For instance, once research performance is commodified in this manner, it is possible to tactically appropriate the discourses of economic rationalism in the generation of alternative 'value-for-money' narratives, such as the following. In the period 1994–95, the University of Sydney received, on average, $63 million per annum in external research funding and produced, on average, 4753 publications output per annum. In a calculation based on a direct relationship between income and output, each publication cost $13 237. Similar calculations see the University of Melbourne's output costing $16 466 per item and the University of Adelaide's costing $19 528. Publication costs across the Australian Unified National System averaged $11 900.

In contrast, the University of Western Sydney during the same period received, on average, $4.3 million per annum in external research funding and produced on average, publication outputs per annum of 883. Based on the same calculation, each publication cost $4849. Similar data are available for the University of Canberra, whose publications each cost $6514, and Deakin University, whose publications each cost $3814. The conclusion might be drawn from these data that researchers in these newer universities are more productive than their counterparts in more established universities and that their research environment is a more dynamic one that may be more conducive to successful research degree training.

These retellings, then, are different representations of research productivity, generated in the interests of changing the relations of distribution of government research funding within the higher education sector. Such retellings, when publicised in appropriate forums such as the national press and academic publications such as this book chapter, constitute a particular form of activism in the sense of the generation of open public debate. They function, then, both as incitements to action and to the renegotiation of policy initiatives such as the Quantum.

Creative arts and the academy

Authoritative accounts of what counts as research are produced by official texts of public policy such as those from the OECD or the Labor government's research White Paper (Dawkins 1989). Such accounts construct research and researchers in ways which have material effects in the constitution of new objects and new populations to be governed. In the case of research, the creation of the Unified National System saw, first, new institutional entities come into being under the umbrella of the prestige term 'university' (UTS and UWS were two of these newly constituted entities). Second, since universities have come, largely since the Second World War, to be substantially defined by their role in producing research, the consequences of this policy development was the reconstitution of the populations working within these institutions as 'academics' and, hence, as 'researchers'. Such developments are not without complexity and contradiction, however, and policy effects may be as unintended as they are profound, as the following case study illustrates.

The OECD defines research and experimental development (R and D) as 'creative work undertaken on a systematic basis in order to increase the stock of knowledge, including knowledge of man [sic], culture and society'. In addition, 'R and D activity is characterised by originality. It has investigation as a primary objective, the outcome of which is new knowledge, with or without a specific practical application . . . R and D activity ends when work is no longer primarily investigative' (ABS 1993, pp. 3–6). The ABS includes creative arts in the definition of R and D activity. In the Australian context, the 1992 Statement of Purpose, argued that universities were expected to provide 'an intellectual climate within the institutions that encourages the questioning of currently accepted knowledge and modes of inquiry, its foundations and its suppositions' as well as 'achieving scholarly depth and perspective in matters relating to society, technology and culture' (National Board of Employment, Education and Training (NBEET) 1992).

Within Australian universities, the creative arts academic who engages in 'research and scholarship' as officially understood, sees themself as questioning modes of inquiry and challenging perceptions. For example, in performance studies, the creation of a performance can represent a complex and analytical inquiry into the form and nature of culture, with the presentation of the performance being an aesthetic synthesis of the research results. Increasingly, the visual is being read as academic 'text'. The academic outputs that emerge from research in the creative arts can be reproduced, reviewed by fellow academics, cited in articles and journals and can inform other research. The traditional notion of the text has been redefined over the last two decades and now incorporates the analysis of many cultural forms and artifacts. Increasingly, the interdisciplinary nature of research has given impetus to the confluence of disparate disciplines. Academics within visual arts and design collaborate effectively with engineering, computer sciences and architecture to explore new ways of imagining and representing knowledge, culture and society. Original creative work in the visual and performing arts can examine a culture's knowledge base in a systematic way, and scholarship and conceptual innovation are often the potential outcomes of research in the creative arts. Within the creative arts, peer review is prized. Yet tensions remain between traditional and non-traditional measures of research productivity. A sizeable part of the academy cannot 'read' the output of this newly constituted academic discipline. These tensions have been played out through the emergence and reconfiguration of the publications component of the Research Quantum.

In the period from 1992 to 1996, the Faculty of Performance, Fine Art and Design at UWS Nepean witnessed substantial growth in students, staffing and research activity. Its academic staffing complement in this period (including casual staff) went from 52.61 to 80.28. For a developing faculty, and a faculty staffed overwhelmingly with academics whose teaching and research grow out of their professional practice as visual artists, performance artists, designers, dancers etc., the effects of the Research Quantum in the assessment of their research productivity are dramatic. Figures in the following tables are based on information that has been collected and analysed by the research office at UWS Nepean.

In Quantum I, which judged the faculty's performance on indicators that included no creative arts measures (such as exhibitions), performance was, not surprisingly, limited. Yet even within such limitations, the faculty displayed some traditional research outputs and seemed to be developing rapidly. The faculty's weighted publications output for Quantum I can be seen in Table 7.2. The changes that occurred in Quantum II had significant impact on how the faculty could both report its research activity and be judged. Under the revised scenario, the faculty had accounted for almost 7 per cent of the total Unified National System output of visual arts (Category J3 and J4; see Appendix). In its own terms it had become 'research active'. This occurred despite the fact that (a) its performance academics, in theatre and dance, could not report any of their creative works, since performance did not 'count' as research, even in Quantum II, and (b) the weightings given to those creative works which were recognised were low. As Deane *et al.* noted, 'a major international exhibition that is curated and reviewed, and based on two

Table 7.2 Research quantum

Quantum I	1992	5.00
	1993	19.09
Quantum II	1994	34.73
	1995	40.28
Quantum III	1995	5.00

years of research, is only worth 40 per cent of the weighting allotted to a refereed journal article and less than that given to a written conference proceeding' (1996, p. 8). Yet the desire of research policy managers at the national level for orthodoxy and simplicity appeared to be conspiring against recognition of the achievements of creative arts academics.

The stringent revamping that occurred in Quantum III has all but decimated the recognised productivity of the faculty's active researchers—see Table 7.2. Had Quantum II been used to measure the faculty's 1995 productivity, a different story would have emerged: a figure of 40.28 compared with 5.00 previously.

The high productivity of creative arts academics was highlighted by Deane *et al.* in their study on women and research productivity in the post-1987 universities (1996, p. 126). The dismantling of the Quantum II grid, which recognised this productivity, and its replacement by Quantum III have had major effects on how such academics are positioned within their institutions. Lest this case study be viewed as idiosyncratic, it should be noted that, at UTS, in the same period of the shift from Quantum II to Quantum III, in the comparable faculty of design, architecture and building, claimable output was reduced by almost 90 per cent in one year. The clear message articulated in Quantum III is that only certain traditional research outputs will 'count'. This situation has clear implications for the diversity that characterises the research profile of, particularly, the new universities. As Anderson *et al.* (1996, p. 81) note: 'when performance-based funding is used across the system it can, like a Procrustean bed, force institutions into the one mould, lopping off divergent features and reshaping others'.

The ongoing impact of such procedures on the constitution of the 'population' of university researchers has been, and continues to

165

be, enormous. The effects of changing research policy are diverse, and depend on the disciplinary area of the individual researcher. For creative arts practitioners, their rapid transformation into valued researchers earning dollars and prestige for their institutions has been followed equally rapidly by the 'dismantling' of this new kind of academic person. Barely had a space been created for a new kind of subject position, in relation to university, disciplinary and professional institutional practice, than that space was deemed no longer to exist. For humanities researchers, on the other hand, at least for the time being, their most prestigious traditional output, the sole-authored book, is still given high (quantifiable) value, thereby implicitly endorsing that traditional and problematic figure of the 'heroic' individual scholar. This case study demonstrates graphically the productivity of discourse, new discourses bringing into being new kinds of persons (in this case, a new kind of 'calculable person') and 'knowing' them in new kinds of ways. The work of the discourse analyst lies in vigilant readings of the technologies through which this 'knowing' is brought about, and in strategic retelling of the effect of such technologies.

Conclusion

The discursive effects of the Quantum on institutions, disciplines and individuals have been complex. A more comprehensive account of this policy site would situate these effects within a history of the discursive constitution of research and of the figure of the researcher. There is a need for a genealogical perspective to generate accounts of how new kinds of persons and new practices have been brought into being through the exercise of policy. There is also a need for a more ethnographic perspective on the 'underlife' of policy (Ball 1994), in terms of the effects upon individuals and groups as they experience the implementation of research policy developments within their own institutions. For instance, many academics have developed negative reactions to being constituted within the regimes of their university's research management processes as 'productive' or 'unproductive' researchers; reactions range from cynicism to exacerbated vulnerability, as colleagues and managers take up a range of possible positions, from reactive pragmatism to refusal and, for some, a great enthusiasm to 'play', their desire for success effectively performed through number. Researchers within many disciplines experience the benefits of increased transparency for existing research funding, research practices and outcomes, and the partial displacement of the pre-eminent positioning of the sciences and of scientists within the university.

Yet this displacement, together with many more of the localised effects of the policy of performance-based funding for research, has received little public comment. Public discussion about research policy in Australia in general has most typically been limited to high-level federal government bureaucrats and senior academics who have moved into management roles within universities and from there into policy-making bodies such as the Australian Research Council and the AV-CC. It is arguably the case that such senior figures, by and large, have little investment in extensive open debate about the merits or otherwise of the particular policy directions of research management. They stand to gain more by general compliance with these government-driven agendas, including the Heath Robinson-esque Quantum machine.

It is also rare to find people responsible for the implementation and administration of research policy inside universities being concerned to tell 'counter-narratives' or to intervene in the directions taken by government policy agendas. Typically, such people are 'administrative', or 'non-academic' staff, themselves constituted as particular kinds of persons through the discourses of public service as distinct from academic work. There is a particular 'class' relationship between these two categories of persons within the academy, where the administrative staff member is the 'arm' of the senior manager, typically the Pro Vice-chancellor for research, and responsible for carrying out, rather than formulating, policy. It should be noted, however, that, in the current environment of the restructure of higher education, the binary divide between academic and general staff is being eroded, and the privilege of the former is disappearing. A major point of change is precisely around the management of the Quantum, where administrative staff of research offices are charged with various degrees of bureaucratic harassment of academics in the completion of the Quantum exercise and, more significantly, of exercising judgment over the standing of academics' research outputs.

At the same time, the changing relations between academics and administrators offer new possibilities for policy collaboration and forms of policy activism.

What, then, are the possibilities and spaces for activism in research policy, and how can discourse analysis enable these? More particularly, what are the possibilities for using discourse analysis in relation to the research futures of the new universities? There are several orders of response to these questions. First, as policy workers within our own universities, we are all involved in internal policy formation and implementation within the terms of the specific ecology of our respective institutions. Vigilant readings and critical retellings of the micro-effects of research policy within specific sites such as creative arts faculties generates the space for more generative responses by university management bodies.

A second order of response concerns the humble, everyday work of *reading*, of attending carefully to questions of representation of the research policy question in the public domain, particularly the national press. An example of the benefits of such close reading can be seen with reference to a recent piece by Donald Horne (1997, p. 28). In a rare polemic on the topic of the Quantum, Horne speculates on what might have happened over the last decade had universities been 'left without the benefits of superficial enquiries and thoughtless number crunching . . . and . . . spared the naive and slapdash attempts at measuring performance'. His conclusion is that universities may have been left better equipped to pursue a role for themselves outside the framework of the dominant economic rationalist discourse. Leaving aside the colourful language of oppositional critique within which Horne's piece is couched, what is most striking in his account is the 'idea' of a university that is sufficiently autonomous to be able to imagine and pursue a role for itself outside of the current financial control of governments. His piece is useful in articulating a space of imagined difference from the current trajectory of government; yet that difference needs to be conceptualised in terms of direct engagement within the terms of that discursive trajectory, rather than simply a refusal of it. What comes after Quantum III is a matter of conjecture (and possible future contestation), but it is unlikely that it will develop in a space that can be imagined outside of the 'colonisation of ordinary life by economic and bureaucratic systems' noted by Fairclough (1996a), in all of the complexity and contradictoriness that this implies. Activism in terms of attention to text and discourse has to be conceptualised in terms of the generation of reimaginings and retellings that are plausible and actionable.

Finally, we view (and intend) this chapter to be itself an intervention in this terrain, mobilising policy knowledge, as part of a larger strategy of 'retellings' of the research policy narrative. Such work includes academic publication in the policy field, as well as other forms and domains of writing, including research policy conferences and the national academic press. (It should be noted parenthetically that this chapter contributes, albeit in modest fashion, to the Quantum calculus of our respective universities at the rate of 0.33 points per author!). Whatever the direction research policy takes in the next decade, the existence of texts that critically engage with the discursive conditions and effects of these policy developments is a resource for shaping those directions.

Appendix

Composite index publications data: weightings used for 1995 Research Quantum allocation (Quantum I)

Publications category weighting

Books   3.0
Book chapter   1.0
Journal article   1.0
Reference works   0.5
Review article   1.0
Conference publication   0.5
Contract report   0.5
Patent   1.0

Composite index publications data: weightings used for 1997 Research Quantum allocation (Quantum II)

Publications category/sub-category weighting

A Books
A1 Authored—research   5.0

169

A2 Authored—other   2.0
A3 Edited   1.5
A4 Revision/new edition   0.5
B Book chapter   1.0
C Journal articles
C1 Article in scholarly journal   1.0
C2 Other contribution to refereed journal   0.5
C3 Non-refereed articles   0.2
C4 Letter or note   0.2
D Major reviews   1.0
E Conference publications
E1 Full written paper—refereed proceedings   1.0
E2 Full written paper—non-refereed proceedings   0.3
E3 Extract of paper   0.1
E4 Edited volume of conference proceedings   1.0
F Audio-visual recordings   1.0
G Computer software   1.0
H Technical drawing/architectural and industrial design/working model   1.0
I Patents   2.0
J Creative works
J1 Major written or recorded work   1.0
J2 Minor written or recorded work   0.2
J3 Individual exhibition of original art   1.0
J4 Representation of original art   0.2

Composite index publications data: weightings used for 1998 Research Quantum allocation (Quantum III)

Publications category/sub-category weighting

A1 Authored—research book   5.0
B1 Authored research chapter   1.0
C1 Article in scholarly journal   1.0
E1 Full written paper—refereed proceedings   1.0
Source: Research Branch, High Education Division, DEETYA 1997

170

8

Pink conspiracies: Australia's gay communities and national HIV/AIDS policies, 1983–96

GARY DOWSETT

That was good. Thanks.

Yes, it was, wasn't it . . . *Can you just move your leg a little?* Ta.

It's Bill, isn't it . . . sorry . . . I'm no good at names.

Will, actually, and I know you're Peter, 'coz you're famous.

What do you mean, famous? . . . *Oooh, do that again!*

I know about your position on the Ministerial Advisory Committee and on the protease inhibitor trials, and I read your pieces in *Outrage* and in *HIV Treatment News*. But I never thought I'd meet you, let alone . . . *Ummmm.*

Well, I didn't expect on yet another trip to these bloody panic sessions in Canberra to meet the likes of you. Where have you been all my life . . . sorry—dumb line.

S'okay. I suspect waiting for just this moment. *Ooow, that hurt . . . but just enough.*

So, what are we to do today—bonk some bureaucrats, sodomise a few socialists, lust after a few likely liberals, or exercise our enormous lobby power and turn the Australian government completely queer before lunch.

If only. But seriously, we can't let the drongo from the Minister's office continue to spin the line that leaving the words 'gay men' in the national AIDS policy document would be an act of discrimination. For God's sake, doesn't she know her epidemiology?

They're under pressure from the Right to 'de-gay' the epidemic before the by-election in Queensland, irrespective of the fact that over 80 per cent of HIV infections occur among faggots in this country.

When are they gonna do *health* instead of politics, I ask you? *Only after you move that there and put those here and wrap the rest of you around this. Now shut up, and we'll worry about the bureaucrats after a little buggery.*

The gay lobby

It is as you expected. Pillow talk drives HIV/AIDS politics. The gay lobby does exist, networked together in such moments of perverse pleasure, undermining the democratic process, and debauching public policy with its dangerous desires.[1] These slippery little sessions of concupiscence between gay men generate a synergistic immensity in lobbying power clearly outclassing the Returned Services League, the Shooters' Party, the Mining Industry, the Australian Council of Trade Unions and all the Old Boys Clubs in the country. Well, on that last example . . .

The phrase 'gay lobby', all that it stands for and silently gestures toward, is a permanent aspect of politics in Australia nowadays. It is invoked in annual debates about the Sydney Gay and Lesbian Mardi Gras, in specific moments such as the 1995–97 New South Wales (NSW) Royal Commission's inquiry into police corruption and paedophilia, and most often and importantly in relation to HIV/AIDS. The gay lobby is portrayed as dangerous, insidious, as a 'passing' (as in passing for 'normal') internal (unsafe) threat to the commonly understood (safe) practices of politics. They're everywhere (they're not, actually); you can't tell them from anyone else (tell that to a drag queen); and their agenda is *by definition* perverse and perverting (stopping humans from dying).

The gay lobby is also argued to be incredibly successful, even overwhelming the influence of Australia's medical–scientific establishment by distorting Commonwealth and State health policy on HIV/AIDS. Often it is said that the gay lobby has captured various health ministers' ears (and occasionally other body parts), despite the usually anti-gay media coverage of HIV/AIDS that informs the generally homophobic Australian electorate, and the fact that in electoral politics only one 'pink' electorate actually exists—the NSW Legislative Assembly seat of Bligh in inner-eastern Sydney.

The gay lobby is also seen to have successfully diverted ever-diminishing government funding from more pressing (read deserving) diseases. This particular claim attempts to position other needy causes (often breast cancer) as somehow marginalised and sidelined by HIV/AIDS, implicitly indicating that the 'everlasting secret family' (Moorhouse 1980) is somehow more influential than the combined might of the Australian women's movement and our cancer research institutions. It is rarely reported that the evaluation of the second national HIV/AIDS policy (in place from 1993–95 to 1995–96) found that only 10 per cent of available education and prevention funds was actually spent on gay and other homosexually active men, despite such men accounting for over 80 per cent of HIV infections nationally (Feachem 1995).

Treichler (1988) coined the epigrammatic phrase that AIDS was an 'epidemic of signification'. Certainly, the notion that gay men 'spread their legs with an unquenchable appetite for destruction' (Bersani 1988, pp. 211–12) haunts HIV/AIDS, irrespective of the worldwide epidemiology of HIV infection relating to heterosexual as well as homosexual transmission. It has even been argued that this discursive positioning of gay men at the centre of the pandemic actually led to the curious, initial classification of HIV as a sexually transmissible disease rather than the more accurate classification of blood-borne virus (Horton with Aggleton 1989), revealing a partisan aspect to medical science that some might care not to notice. It is almost as if gay men *were* the virus and that they, rather than it, caused the pandemic.

There is significant documentation of this pervasive thread in the weaving of HIV/AIDS into a significant moment in late twentieth century history. Watney (1987) produced a stinging account of the British and United States media dealings with AIDS (in Australia, see French and Duffin 1986). There is no other disease in recent times (except for the longstanding and ever-present trope of prosti-tutes and sexually transmissible diseases) where the most affected population has been regarded as at fault in the way gay men have been in this pandemic. This can only be explained by adverse social and political responses to homosexuality itself being allowed to infect the conceptualisation of this health crisis so effectively that, like racism, most commentators cannot see the dynamics of homophobia in operation in even the simplest processes.

This positioning of homophobia as a central theme in Australia's HIV/AIDS history is no simple claim about anti-gay sentiment; rather, it borrows from Sedgwick's (1990) argument that homophobia is the driving force in homosociality—those social relations between heterosexual men binding patriarchy together and structured by the refusal of anal desire. Too large a conceptual leap? Try it this way. Gay men violate masculinity by exposing all men's penetrability and the instability of heteronormative desire. Homophobia becomes essential to the smooth operation of power among men as a way to avoid the dangers of intimacy and, subsequently, betrayal; it is not accidental that men refer to being double-crossed as being 'shafted'.

The refusal of same-sex eroticism is central to the relations between men in Western societies such as Australia, and that refusal effectively excludes gay men from fully exercising male power unless they remain hidden or 'closeted', thereby proving the insidious secrecy and conspiracy of which they are always suspected. The exclusion of gay men from positions of power in many HIV/AIDS institutions, apart from the gay community-based ones, has been noted by Plummer (1996), and is one way in which the effects of any gay lobbying is strategically minimised. So how is it that the gay communities are seen as being so insidiously effective?

Gay men and HIV/AIDS

The Australian national HIV/AIDS policies *are* exemplary. Few countries have achieved such sophistication and effectiveness, and even fewer can demonstrate the sustained slowing of the epidemic that can rightly be claimed here. The story of our national policies has been told elsewhere and will not be repeated here. Ballard (1989, 1998) in particular has watched the development of HIV/AIDS policy from its early days of the first Hawke Labor Commonwealth government to the release of the third National HIV/AIDS Strategy in

1996 (Commonwealth of Australia 1996). Its predecessors (Commonwealth of Australia 1989, 1993) codified policy initiatives and practices developed in the main from the 1984 Commonwealth election onwards, stimulated by the then Queensland State government's cynical attempt to use as an election issue the death of three babies as a result of HIV-infected blood transfusions whose donor was a gay man. The then Commonwealth Minister for Health, Dr Neal Blewett, and his advisers read the political and public health tea leaves and provided rapid, proactive and sophisticated leadership at that time. Ballard, viewing the action from the Political Science Department at the Australian National University in Canberra, documents this history well. But it is a view from Canberra.

From the gay 'ghettos' of Darlinghurst in Sydney and St Kilda, Fitzroy and Collingwood in Melbourne the HIV policy scene before 1984 did not appear so active in Canberra. Indeed, there has been a significant tendency in Canberra, partly in an understandable attempt to emphasise the successes of the national policies themselves, to write out of the history of HIV/AIDS the contribution of others in the game, most notably the gay communities, but also some State health departments and other community sectors, particularly sex workers and those affected by haemophilia.

This is a key issue: how to position community activism in the effectiveness of HIV/AIDS policy and practice in Australia? In this chapter I shall concentrate on the gay communities alone, first, for they are communities that partly grew initially out of an engagement with political activism itself and, second, for the sheer size of the epidemic among their ranks, which compelled them to become the major community sector in HIV/AIDS activism and service delivery.[2]

There are at least four factors that need to be recognised about Australia's gay communities which are important in the HIV/AIDS story. First, it is necessary to audit the resources available in the gay community which came to bear on HIV/AIDS. In 1982, the time of the earliest diagnoses of HIV infection in Australia, gay politics were far from dead, even if 'gay liberation' was transforming itself into what is now known as the 'gay community'. National homosexual conferences were yearly events from 1975 until 1985 (unlike in the United States and Britain) and what became HIV/AIDS was on the agenda at the 1983 Melbourne conference, where the already formed,

State-based AIDS Action Committees and other gay/AIDS groupings came together, recognising thereby the national public health threat in the epidemic. A meeting with Blewett at that time was to be an important move and, although the Commonwealth was slow to respond, and the community sector was less than fully aware of what it wanted from the government, this moment represented the earliest engagement of two of the major protagonists that were to enter the fray.

Second, key gay community leaders emerged at this time, drawn from two groups: gay activists who had been working, many since the beginning of gay liberation, for homosexual law reform, other gay rights and, in particular, in the human services sector; and other gay men drawn not from gay liberation but from the rapidly developing gay communities, and whose connections were with political parties and more professional networks. This factor is often unnoticed: there were many gay activists and professionals working in education, health and community services, trade unions, professional associations, in policy development in the public sector, and in the academy, who were skilled at reform agendas and in community and policy activism.

Third, from the early 1970s, in seeking to reform the various States' anti-gay laws, a form of skilful political bargaining, community mobilisation, and a radical critique of the state and its 'role' in sexual matters had created among gay men (and lesbians) a 'workforce' that provided the gay community with a leadership that was to be important in HIV/AIDS work. Some, indeed many, are now dead; this was leadership from within the epidemic, not just around it. But it is important to note this level of activist skill already in play at both national and State level, working with both conservative and progressive political parties and networked nationally around a reform agenda in relation to sexuality. There was also a familiar form of civil rights activism within the gay communities able to be readily mobilised, and its strength and character are best found in the origins of the world-famous Sydney Gay and Lesbian Mardi Gras, initially a street celebration and demonstration in 1978 raided by NSW police. By 1984, the 'gay liberation movement' and the 'gay community' had become a single, if multifaceted, entity—a constellation of various forces, skills, experience, expertise, leadership, and international networks that combined to provide a wide-ranging response to the increasingly complex epidemic.

A fourth factor is the international nature then (and now) of gay politics. The first reports of what was to become AIDS were carried in Australia's then nascent gay community press, at the beginning and since, the most important source of information and debate about HIV/AIDS issues for Australia's gay communities. Similarly, the main public health response to the HIV pandemic—safe sex—was devised by gay activists in the United States, based on their (accurate as it turned out) judgment about a possible causative agent and its modes of transmission (for example, Callen 1983). Gay men invented safe sex in their bodies and their experience of sodomy, and the world should be grateful for that. We should also not underestimate the importance of international airline stewards in disseminating the latest news about HIV/AIDS and safe sex quicker than almost anyone else.

This internationalist component of gay activism is often under-rated, partly because most accounts of the influence of United States gay HIV/AIDS activism ignore its international effects, and the North Americans are usually ignorant of indigenous activism in other countries. To Australians working internationally in HIV/AIDS it is a constant surprise that our obviously successful efforts are still unacknowledged and unknown abroad. By the same token, the influence of other gay communities abroad in providing a remarkable resource for gay activists here is an often neglected aspect of our HIV/AIDS story.

There is undoubtedly a true tale to be told (and I cannot tell it, for I am not privy to its ins and outs) about the influence of both apparatchik and bureaucrat advisers to Blewett, who were/are gay. There were times when Blewett himself was on the receiving end of none-too-veiled speculation about his sex life by those who saw some 'pinko-poofy' plot at play and wanted things to be handled differently. The contrast with Aboriginal and Torres Strait Islander, ethnic or women's health issues could not be greater: in these instances, politicians would be criticised for *not* having advisers from the particular stakeholder grouping or community. Although there is no doubt that these gay advisers had some influence, that this should often be cast as malign is itself an interesting twist. It may be that the wisdom of their influence on Blewett arose expressly *because* of their connections with gay communities here and abroad and a consequent, almost prescient, recognition of the dimensions of the epidemic. This assisted in the gearing-up of Australia's health system and policy framework faster and more precisely than was possible elsewhere.

Yet, in reviewing from hindsight the evolution of national HIV/AIDS policy one can see other logics at play. One is the general context of reform in public administration in the direction of policies of consultation and participation during the 1980s, partly due to the influence of 'femocrats' and multicultural politics (see Yeatman 1990). More specifically, there was the growing impact of the Ottawa Charter, developed by the World Health Organisation, and its encouragement of community consultation and participation in framing the 'new public health', at a time where the paternalistic welfare state was becoming unsustainable in developed countries (and impossible in developing countries). There were other initiatives in the health system in Australia which changed the resources and policy processes available to HIV/AIDS, such as the restitution of a national health system, Medicare, under Blewett's leadership. This achievement was already providing a battleground for the Labor government and the medical establishment. The Commonwealth and the State governments then led by Labor knew that any new public health crisis might re-elevate the doctors to the pedestal from which they had slipped in the 1970s and early 1980s.

The early HIV/AIDS policy frameworks were certainly attempting to mobilise countervailing forces to the medico-scientific establishment. The most noticeable symbol was the 1985 appointment of media personality, Ita Buttrose, to head the National Advisory Committee on AIDS (NACAIDS), later disbanded, which provided a platform for other health professionals, the community sector and people living with HIV and AIDS to be consulted and to participate in the full gamut of policy and programme development (see Altman 1992 and Plummer 1992 for a more detailed examination).

The gay communities were under no illusions about the medical establishment: years of electroconvulsive aversion therapy, institutionalisation and hormone treatments had led to a scathing critique of medical science and practice as a powerful discourse, and gay liberation had followed closely the analysis of feminism about the importance of women's 'control of their own bodies'. The early responses from the (medical) Working Party on AIDS, established in 1983 under the auspices of the National Health and Medical Research Council (again, see Ballard 1989; Altman 1992) and led by Professor David Penington, left no illusion among gay men that were medical practitioners to be in sole control, gay men would again suffer at their hands.

The Working Party, re-formed in November 1984, and eventually becoming the National AIDS Task Force at the same time as NACAIDS was established in 1985, did little to calm the gay communities' fears about the medical profession over the next two or three years. The eventual formation of the Australian Federation of AIDS Organisations (the national 'peak' HIV/AIDS community sector organisation) provided the clout at the national level which was needed in the political shifts that occurred from 1988 onwards as the national HIV/AIDS policy was refined and refreshed. Eventually, the Australian National Council of AIDS (now the Australian National Council on AIDS and Related Diseases) joined these entities together in 1988. But, by 1989, when the first national HIV/AIDS strategy (in a single policy document) was implemented, the stakeholders were well entrenched and a process of policy formation involving them had long been set in train, and continues to operate today.

In sum, Blewett and the Commonwealth had little alternative to the inclusion of the community sector in the constellation of forces mobilised to deal with HIV/AIDS. By the time of the first major Commonwealth initiatives in late 1984, the gay communities had already established the first HIV prevention activities (their major preoccupation over the next decade) and the first community-based, volunteer, home-care and support programmes for people living with HIV and AIDS. The Commonwealth was centrally involved in turning these community-based initiatives into the 'AIDS Councils', the first semi-professional AIDS service organisations (as they are now called), and which have been the major service providers in Australia. Blewett's greatest achievement lay in finding the policy framework that would do this so effectively. Even so, he could not ignore the gay communities: they were already effective and in action, and by virtue of the trajectory of HIV in Australia inextricably linked with it.

From that time, each successive national AIDS policy has contained various and complex arrangements for community consultation and participation in all forms of policy formation, on Commonwealth and State committees, and elsewhere, thereby recognising the forces already in play. These forces need no further explication here except to say that this 'partnership', as this elaborate consultative and participatory process eventually became known, has always involved the community sector and, most often and in largest numbers, gay men from the AIDS Councils on most policy advisory committees and in programme development and evaluation processes. That the Councils are also the major providers of prevention education, other health promotion, and care and support services to people living with HIV and AIDS is, however, as much a product of their own early organisation, as it is of Commonwealth recognition, incorporation and funding.

It is important to remember in this current era of ever-shrinking governmental service delivery, that the greater part of service delivery since the epidemic started (outside of hospital and clinical care) has always been the responsibility of gay communities. These communities are legitimate stakeholders in any issue and process related to the epidemic. It is the breadth of the fields that gay community activists must cover in order to participate which defies any notion of HIV/AIDS as a narrow public health arena. Apart from prevention education, gay men (and people living with HIV and AIDS) must deal, for example, with: medical and social research and its conduct and funding; clinical drug trials, drug regulation and approval processes; epidemiology and surveillance policy guideline monitoring and development; national health promotion policy development and programme design; provision of hospital beds, 'HIV/AIDS' wards, hospice services and home-based care programmes; reform of laws on prostitution, drug use, euthanasia; the development of HIV/AIDS education programmes for schools, ethnic communities and for people with disabilities; Australia's international development aid programmes focused on HIV/AIDS programmes; to name but a few. What began as community activism focusing on an immediate health crisis has become a major input into many public policy domains in Commonwealth and State policy processes.

Political and community action

I now turn to the types of activism that have been brought to bear by gay communities on HIV/AIDS policy development and implementation processes since the epidemic began. The first of these kinds of activism looks remarkably like that seen in gay liberation activism and traditions of civil disobedience. During the first decade of the epidemic, the gay communities have at times invoked or resorted to *direct action* to make otherwise ignored ideas and needs felt. These actions have taken the form of street marches on parliaments, State and Commonwealth, protest activity against various politicians, policies and commercial organisations (particularly the wealthy drug companies), and the kinds of print, performance and rhetoric that accompanies such direct action.

The net effect of this kind of action is hard to gauge directly, in terms of cause and effect. Newspaper reports of attendance numbers at rallies are always disputed. Politicians alternately address or refuse to attend such events depending on who is in power and who wants to be. There is always considerable behind-the-scenes activity choreographing the public spectacle, including the many more 'cultural' events that have become ritualised now as part of the culture of HIV/AIDS, for example the annual candlelight rallies, the always moving unfolding of the quilt memorialising many who have died, the annual World AIDS Day programme, and HIV/AIDS fundraising events during Mardi Gras and so on. Although these are not those acts of civil disobedience that underpin many other 'direct action' gay community responses to HIV/AIDS politics, there is no doubt that these 'cultural' actions do galvanise the gay communities at times and do attract additional media and broader public attention to an epidemic in danger of being forgotten as time wears on.

This kind of activism with its liberationist origins has profoundly affected the representation of HIV/AIDS in many forms. Just a few examples suffice. The major underpinnings of early HIV prevention activity drew more on the experience of gay community mobilisation practices than traditional health promotion practice: the community was urged to shift collectively toward safe sex to save itself. Being HIV positive (i.e., infected with HIV) was initially regarded largely as a personal issue to be kept quiet or hidden for fear of discrimination and stigmatisation. By the late 1980s, the notion of 'coming-out' as HIV-positive was seen as a central aspect of getting to grips with one's infection and confronting the silence that has often accompanied HIV/AIDS as a result of stigma and marginalisation. This was a direct transfer from 'coming-out' as 'gay', a chief tactic of gay liberation for much the same purposes. Following from this 'coming-out' were notions of 'HIV identity' and 'HIV community' (see Ariss *et al.* 1992).

These aspects of what is now referred to as 'identity politics' set the scene for establishing a quite different understanding of the experience of disease, not unlike the claims made by people with disabilities in the late 1970s, but vastly enhanced by HIV/AIDS so as eventually to affect other conditions and diseases, for example multiple sclerosis. People living with HIV and AIDS fought vigorously for 'living with' not 'dying from', a claim to inclusion, to speaking for themselves, and to repositioning the patient as partner in disease management. These configurations invoke a politics of civil rights, particularly the right not to be discriminated against on the basis of a medical condition. Legislation enshrining this for people with HIV and AIDS has now been passed in a number of States and at Commonwealth level.

A rhetoric surrounding HIV infection developed internationally from this kind of gay activism. The distinction between HIV and AIDS was eventually made explicit and demanded in all situations, so that the infectious agent and its epidemic, HIV, were distinguished from AIDS, the syndromic diagnosis of consequent illnesses (Watney 1987). Sympathetic onlookers and supporters, and those seen as enemies or threats, found themselves castigated for using phrases such as AIDS 'sufferers' or 'victims'. The very phrase itself, always so carefully presented—'people living with HIV and AIDS'—represents a demand to control the representation of living with HIV infection in terms derived from the experience of HIV infection rather than from its medical management or political purposes.

Distinctions between modes of infection—sexual, medically

acquired, neo-natal—were regarded with great suspicion, particularly as the idea of the 'innocent victim' of AIDS gained currency in the public domain. Gay communities heard the implied spite in that term, and recognised the homophobic attempt to reconfigure gay sex as guilty by definition. This was resisted so vigorously that, at times, the specificity of other modes of infection was lost to view. This is particularly the case with the infection of haemophiliacs, and it also underpinned gay community opposition to monetary compensation to those with medically acquired HIV infection.

Perhaps a shining moment of this kind of activism can be found in the activities of the AIDS Coalition to Unleash Power, or ACT-UP as it was better known. Organised largely in response to Australia's then notoriously slow and bureaucratic, if thorough, drug approval processes in 1990, ACT-UP was based on street action, notions of consciousness raising, and the 'zap', whose origins again are readily recognisable *inter alia* in early gay liberation activism. This was a further example where an American gay-activist strategy became for a time a global force in HIV/AIDS. ACT-UP's presence was felt globally in such activities as the 'trashing' of multinational drug companies' stalls at international AIDS conferences, actions against various stock markets over the issue of drug company profiteering (repeated again in New York in April 1997), and against governmental inaction, particularly the notorious neglect of the Reagan administration in the United States throughout the 1980s.

It was on the issue of drug approvals that ACT-UP's activities in Australia had the greatest impact. ACT-UP demonstrations in Sydney in the early 1990s were often emotional and dramatic (see Duffin 1997), but were one vital contribution to the eventual and much-needed overhaul of the drug approval procedures in 1992. A controversy about Duffin's account of these events in the pages of the *Sydney Star Observer* (1997a), a weekly gay and lesbian newspaper, reveals the difficulty in evaluating the effect of this kind of activism: a letter to the editor from a government bureaucrat involved at the time in response to Duffin's article discounted the impact of ACT-UP on the drug-approvals issue and claimed more credit for the behind-the-scenes bureaucratic and political process. This example reveals some of the tension in the relationship between those within bureaucracies who regard themselves as activists and those working from a community sector base.

This *politics of authenticity* among people living with HIV and AIDS in Australia is wonderfully documented by the late Robert Ariss (1998), an anthropologist and one of the founders of People Living with HIV/AIDS (NSW). The claims to HIV identity and community, and the actions of groups such as ACT-UP, brought with them a claim to proper representation, that is, that only people with HIV and AIDS could truly represent their own situation and must therefore have a voice in all that concerns them. In the gay communities, historically marginalised and stigmatised, this was an immediately resonant claim, and was widely and rapidly embraced. In effect, it led to the formation of local and national associations of people living with HIV and AIDS, and a now standard inclusion of HIV-positive representation on all HIV/AIDS committees, boards, panels and processes. Of particular note here is the participation of people living with HIV and AIDS on the various types of committees and boards overseeing the three national HIV/AIDS research centres, all kinds of drug trials, and the national HIV/AIDS policy evaluation processes.

This kind of representation leads toward incorporation within governmental processes, an embracing of the state in a way gay communities and early gay liberation activism had never done before, in marked contrast to the Australian women's movement, and it was discussed and debated at great length. As I argue in more detail elsewhere (Dowsett 1998), until HIV/AIDS there were no 'poofycrats' alongside the 'femocrats'. It would be a mistake to see the inclusion of people living with HIV and AIDS, and for that matter gay men, in such processes as a tokenistic gesture by the then Commonwealth Labor government and the various State governments of both political persuasions, or as some wily insinuation by the 'gay lobby'. As already noted, the 1980s and 1990s were a period of great increases in similar community consultation processes by government in many portfolios.

Moreover, the inclusion of gay communities (and at times other community sectors) and also people living with HIV and AIDS has been at times tense and difficult for those gay men who are HIV-positive and in that sense members of both communities. Simply put, this tension resides in the, itself simplistic, division between prevention education (preventing further infection of uninfected men), for which the AIDS Councils are mainly funded, and care and support for those already with HIV infection and/or AIDS (health promotion and community-based programmes of home care and social–emotional support). For gay communities then there have always been two main games, and the competition for funds for both has been a potentially divisive issue, so far well managed.

Yet, perhaps nowhere else is it possible to see the tremendous impact of the engagement of the national HIV/AIDS policy with gay community activism than in their HIV prevention activities. Some of this work in the 1980s and 1990s has been described in Dowsett (1992, 1996a) and Parnell (1992, 1997).[3] It is this work, its innovation and daring, its libidinous imagery exuding homoerotic desire, that captured gay men's sexual culture and attached it to HIV/AIDS prevention in a way no public health issue has previously achieved. For it is in such 'ownership' of HIV/AIDS that the successes of the gay communities lie, in reducing the rates of new infection among, and surviving the tremendous losses to, their ranks. This activism finds its manifestations in cultural and expressive forms that run the full gamut from street-wise drag show to full-length ballet, from eye-catching beer coasters to magnificent internationally acclaimed art (see Gott 1994), from autobiographies of the experience of living with HIV and AIDS (Michaels 1990; Conigrave 1995) to the crafty inclusion of condoms in pornography and other erotica.

Professionalisation of HIV/AIDS policy activism

Few governments pursue strategies of funding community groups to the extent that the gay communities were funded from 1984 until the present. Without some evidence of significant success on the part of those gay communities, it would be politically unsustainable. In this regard, when the AIDS Council of NSW became one of the larger non-governmental service organisations in Australia (eclipsed, for example, by Family Planning, the Cancer Council, and various religious charities and welfare bodies), this was not due simply to successful activism; it was largely due to effective and efficient service

185

delivery. In other words, the continuing funding of gay community-based programmes and the pursuit of the policies of partnership that saw the continued representation of people living with HIV and AIDS and gay men in various consultative and decision-making processes was based on the proven capacity of the gay communities to deliver the goods—this in a political climate where anti-gay forces regularly hectored governments about the influence of the 'gay lobby'.

The professionalisation of these AIDS service organisations and the significant professional skills of the (largely) gay men who managed and staffed these organisations (often drawing on the resources of their gay liberation and, or, professional activities noted earlier) produced a highly experienced and skilled labour force. And yes, 'they' were everywhere. There were medical practitioners of the likes of the late Dr Ralph Deacon, himself an HIV-positive gay man working out of the Albion Street HIV/AIDS clinic in Sydney, or Don Baxter, early gay liberationist and university librarian, the longest-serving HIV/AIDS programme manager in the community sector before his recent decision to move on from the AIDS Council of NSW to other things. Even this author, whose days in gay liberation seem so far away now, is one of but a few academics working continuously since 1986 in social research on gay communities and HIV/AIDS.

These examples represent the bringing of professional skills *and* an intimate knowledge of and participation in gay community life to bear on HIV/AIDS. There are hundreds of other examples, right across the country, in clinical trials, behavioural research, health promotion, home-care service delivery, and even more directly in the development of policy. The specially established Commonwealth and State HIV/AIDS policy units and bureaux have often recruited staff from the community sector, particularly the gay community sector, as the ever-extending endeavours of these workers provide a unique blend of skill, experience and commitment. From the earliest of this kind of appointment in Victoria (discussed in Ballard 1998), this crossing-over of gay men from the community sector to public health bureaux has been an interesting advance. Although there have long been complaints about 'professional AIDS faggots' and 'AIDS career-ists' from those with 'purer' activist credentials, there is greater evidence that, partly as a result of the national HIV/AIDS policy itself and partly because of the duration of the epidemic, there is now a highly skilled, long-serving, professional, gay, HIV/AIDS workforce that crosses sectors effectively, able to bring to the policy development process a unique contribution.

In developing responses to HIV/AIDS, these gay professionals were able to raise and drive gay and lesbian issues within their organisations and workplaces. This in turn facilitated high quality professional advice being fed back to the gay communities as these professionals became more actively engaged in their communities, often as a result of the urgency and immediacy of the epidemic. There was considerable professional skill available to the gay community from other gay men and lesbians involved in the parliamentary processes, various party-political activities and public bureaucracies, who clearly increased the communities' capacities to negotiate the political minefields of HIV/AIDS politics and policy processes at both State and Commonwealth levels. It is hard to ignore this galvanising effect of the epidemic on gay men (and among lesbians), perhaps previously 'closeted' or occupied more with careers than gay politics. The stakes in HIV/AIDS were so high—the life or death of oneself, one's friends and one's lovers—that gay communities undoubtedly strengthened during the late 1980s and early 1990s directly as a result of the epidemic, at the same time as AIDS itself took its terrible toll on those same communities.

'Professional' does not always mean paid to be so; the volunteer workforce in the gay communities of nurses, lawyers, doctors, journalists, social workers, teachers, and even politicians, often doing unpaid professional tasks, but as often working as carers, condom distributors, fundraisers, entertainers and unpaid general labour, at various times and ways over the last fourteen years has involved an enormous level of skill and dedication. The epidemic insinuated itself into the very core of almost every gay man's life, his sexuality, and could not be escaped.

This was exemplified at the international level in Berlin at the IX International AIDS conference in 1993. There, in a final plenary, Meurig Horton, a staff member of the World Health Organisation's Global Programme on AIDS, presented a paper challenging any lingering concept of the displacement evident in 'us/them' in dealing with this pandemic, its workforce and those infected. Horton revealed to the thousands assembled what a few friends privately knew: that he was, at one and the same time, a medical anthropologist by training, a United Nations bureaucrat working in health promotion in the developing world, a gay man, from an ethnic minority (Welsh), and HIV positive (Horton 1993). Horton's 'self-outing' was not a confirmation of the 'they-are-everywhere' paranoia; rather, it was a demand for an end to the absurdities of the dichotomies of us/them, HIV-positive/HIV-negative, gay/straight, patient/medico, client/ professional, and so on. It exposed forever the absurdity of, and homophobia underlying, that often-heard complaint about the effects of the 'gay lobby'.

Activism and the containment of the epidemic

The irony in this anxiety about the gay lobby is that Australia's response to the HIV epidemic has been exemplary by world standards. Not only has the epidemic in Australia been brought under control in those populations where it first took its devastating toll, but the potential transmission of HIV among other populations, especially the so-called 'general' (read heterosexual) population, did not happen.[4] This kind of transmission did happen elsewhere, and specious arguments in retrospect about the fact that the heterosexual epidemic did not happen here refuse to recognise that, maybe, this was not an accident but the effect *inter alia* of the enormous efforts undertaken to make sure that it did not.

Like other Western nations such as France and the United States, we could have had a general population epidemic; we did not, and we should thank our lucky stars . . . no, we should thank our HIV/AIDS policies and our gay communities (and sex workers) for that. This is an issue rarely 'unpacked' in the popular HIV/AIDS debates, and it is worth spending some time on as one way to assess Australia's policy response to the epidemic.

One of the features in viral transmission through penetrative sex is that any entry point for the virus into a given population will provide the beginnings of a sexual network through which subsequent infections occur. Closed communities, either through cultural or geographic boundedness, will experience an intensity of infection;

infections beyond those communities depend on the effective operation of those boundaries. A good example of this is the now
well-known effect of truck drivers and the armed forces moving along
highways in a number of developing countries transmitting HIV as
they go, mostly through vaginal intercourse. In this example, roads
breach both geographic and local social (even national) boundaries
and allow the infection to multiply. In the case of countries where
the epidemic was initially and principally transmitted through anal
intercourse between men, the potential for further infection among
other populations depended on the security of the boundary between
homosexuality and heterosexuality—two notoriously unstable categories just over one hundred years old in conceptualisation and use
(Foucault 1978; Weeks 1985; Halperin 1990).

We do not need the category of 'bisexuality' to tell us that the
virgule in homosex/heterosex is shaky; Kinsey *et al.* (1948) did that
fifty years ago. Although their report on high levels of male-to-male
sex has never been replicated and may not represent Australian
sexual culture well, this should not obscure one of their most telling
points, that is, that sexual activity is contingent. If Kinsey's figures
are a product of the mobilisation and mobility of males during and
immediately after the Second World War, we must reckon with at
least a situational and circumstantial fluidity in desire, if not a deeper
structural instability in the categories by which we so fondly police
ourselves. If lots of soldiers and sailors find it untroublesome to
'come across' in a brown-out, we must acknowledge a highly con-
ditional sexual culture where same-sex relations are not simply the
preserve of private schools, prisons and football clubs.

I have argued elsewhere (Dowsett 1996b) that there is a perversity
in Australian masculine sexual desire, endlessly able to pursue the
sexual possibilities of the male body well beyond the confines of
heteronormativity. If that is the case, the potential for the transmission of HIV is, in theory, enormous: beyond the politico-psychic
category of 'gay' and the cultural boundary of 'gay community',
through the non identity-related sex practice of anal intercourse
between men, to so-called heterosexual men and, ultimately, their
female partners. This possibility parallels the substantial number of
women in the so-called heterosexual epidemics largely in the developing world, infected by their philandering husbands and

boyfriends—although female sex workers are usually regarded as the 'villains' at source in these cases.

There was a potential for an Australian general population epidemic in the mid-to-late 1980s, particularly in relation to the likely contribution of other vectors of infection operating right from the start, viz., illicit drug injection, medical transmission (until 1985 among blood and blood product recipients), and from mother to child *in utero*. So how is it we have not seen this patterning in the Australian epidemic? Why did the general population epidemic not happen?

One explanation is that we are a sexually boring and unadventurous nation, that is, many of us do not go beyond the bounds of the hetero/homo divide. That boundary is certainly policed heavily. During the early days of the epidemic, sex between men was illegal in most Australian States, and despite increasing historical evidence of a long-standing homoeroticism in that great Australian tradition of mateship (Hughes 1987), there is an equally well-known, perhaps directly related, tradition of 'poofter bashing'. This is not an easy country to be gay in, and there is a lot of direct pressure *not* to explore same-sex eroticism.

These statutory and cultural forms of policing the sexual boundaries do achieve some firmness in the virgule, and this indeed *may* account for a significant reduction in risk situations where sexual transmission of HIV between men might occur. I say 'may' because we will never know: few Australian men will tell us how frequently they resist the ever-present possibility of 'fooling around' with another bloke; beyond their own mates, gay communities are highly visible and not hard to find if you are interested in the odd bend in your sexuality.

So, policing of the sexual boundaries may account for some Australia-specific diminution in the transmission of HIV beyond the gay communities. Indeed, only seventy-eight Australian women to date attribute their HIV infection to heterosexual sex with a man who has also had sex with men (National Centre in HIV Epidemiology and Clinical Research (hereafter NCHECR) 1997). There may be something in the 'we are sexually boring' argument after all. But also, at the onset of the epidemic, Australia had only a small population of illicit drug injectors, and the early, national implementation of needle and syringe exchanges and harm reduction pro-grammes led the world in this kind of prevention strategy with remarkable success. Consequently, only fifty-eight women and sixteen men to date attribute their HIV infection to sex with a drug-injecting partner (NCHECR 1997).[5] This example reveals how arguments about potential 'leakage' of HIV from one population to another—gay men to bisexual men to the latter's female partners, drug injectors to their sexual (not just injecting) partners—are often thin in their understanding of the complexity and structuring of interpersonal relationships on a society-wide scale.

These factors explain some of our success in achieving such reduced transmission of HIV beyond the original affected popula-tions. There is sufficient evidence also to suggest that the prevention efforts undertaken among and by Australia's gay communities may have had greater spin-offs than we usually understand or can readily investigate. The success of their efforts is revealed in ever-decreasing rates of new HIV infection among gay men. The HIV epidemic is waning here, though the epidemic of AIDS is still with us. Behaviou-ral data, from a number of studies undertaken from 1985 to 1996, reveal: huge and sustained increase in condom use (in a population that never needed them before); greatly reduced frequencies of unpro-tected anal intercourse; and sustained levels of other safe sex behaviours (Kippax, Connell *et al.* 1993; Kippax, Crawford *et al.* 1993; Kippax *et al.* 1994; Richters *et al.* 1996). In other words, most gay men are having safe sex most of the time with most partners, and that 'most' has been sufficient to produce the slowing of the epidemic documented in the epidemiological surveillance.[6]

This success has led, first, to Australia having a smaller pool of virus than if no reduction in unsafe sex had been achieved among gay men. Second, over time, the pool of virus has been largely confined to gay communities and its sexual transmission beyond became less likely. This is also a result of the enormous uptake of safe sex by gay men as more than a sex act: safe sex has become a feature of cultural formation in gay communities. Third, safe sex was and is most likely to be the mode of sex between gay men and other homosexually active men, including those who are bisexually active, predominantly heterosexually active, and even among the heterosexually identified (these are not the same thing) who dabble in same-sex activity within the blurred sexual boundaries.

These accumulate to produce greatly reduced levels of risk taking in male-to-male sex in Australia, much of which is incalculable, since studies, with their usual sampling biases toward the literate middle classes, the willing and the unashamed, produce a certain pattern of findings. But even assuming that there are those who do not come forward (and therefore might provide a larger pool of wayward men having unsafe sex), the sheer stability of the epidemiology over the past twelve years in terms of newly diagnosed HIV infections and in AIDS diagnoses would have revealed by now any seriously different pattern of transmission in these blurred boundaries within Australian sexual culture. The very nature of the disease means such patterns cannot stay hidden for that long. One cannot ignore this stability; it speaks volumes about our successes to date. In this way, much of the success of Australia's response to HIV/AIDS must be logged onto the ideas, discourses and practices of gay community activism. In contrast to activism in such issues as housing or unemployment, gay community activism on HIV/AIDS is lodged in the very bodies of gay men and the very collective acts of sexual pleasure they so responsibly pursue.

Conclusion

When the 'gay lobby' is invoked as a signal that 'our AIDS policy is off the rails', this seriously fails to recognise the level of skill, experience and commitment in evidence in gay men's participation in HIV/AIDS work. When the story of HIV/AIDS in Australia is told in such a way as to locate the action in Canberra or for that matter in only ministerial and public service offices, a great disservice is done to our gay communities and their contribution to fighting this epidemic, politically and sexually. But, more importantly, the lessons learned from the quite remarkable success Australia has achieved in managing this terrible epidemic are lost to us if the story is not told in full. The evolution of the national HIV/AIDS policy in Australia from its faltering start in 1983 to its endurance in the face of the federal electoral victory by the conservative Coalition parties in 1996 is a fine example of policy activism in play, and to overlook a key player is to misread the game.

Well, at least she gave in and added 'gay men' to the document.

I know, but I think that had more to do with the upcoming Health Ministers' meeting where they're going to have to haggle about funding service delivery.

I s'pose so . . . but who else is experienced and geared up enough to deliver services to gay men in these days of small government? They can't *not* work with us! They've kinda trapped themselves on that one, haven't they.

Yeh. Oh, here's the taxi. Where are we going? Your hotel or mine?

Acknowledgments

My thanks to John Ballard, Don Baxter, Ross Duffin, Michael Hurley and Anna Yeatman for their constructive criticism and helpful advice in the writing of this chapter.

9

Policy activism, community housing and urban renewal: Bowden–Brompton 1972–96

GAEL FRASER

Introduction

In this chapter I examine the nature and impact of policy activism in Bowden–Brompton over the period from 1982–96 in relation to the common objectives of community housing and urban renewal. The focus is on a group of activists who worked along a continuum from community-based activism to policy activism. Work that began with the fight to save the area from demolition moved towards improving the availability of affordable housing in the area, and to the establishment of the first housing co-operative in the area. A number of people involved in this process were linked to the development of community housing as a State government programme. The emergence of community housing in South Australia, its definition in legislation and its support from both the community and government sectors, is explored in this chapter as the visible and valued 'contribution to policy of public officials, direct deliverers and clients' (see chapter 1, Yeatman, this volume). The interviews and reading which I undertook for this work revealed the importance of valuing community in the contribution it makes to quality of life and in its contribution to policy and systems change.

I consider here the contribution of the people (residents, students, public servants) who were central to the revitalisation of the area and to this policy process. In this work I draw on interviews and other data which I have collected for a more extensive examination of the place of community housing in urban renewal.[1] This study takes into account the various changes in political environment brought about by changing government ideologies and the impact of these changes on the role of the public service. During the past ten years the State government's urban renewal and housing policies have been supportive of inner area redevelopment and community housing. Policy activism which led to the renewal of Bowden–Brompton occurred in two distinct stages.

The first stage (1970–82) was an organised reaction against the State government's transport and highway policies which were perceived as collusion between local and State governments with industry against the interests and wellbeing of the local residents. The second stage (1982–96) entailed the establishment and development of tenant-managed housing as a precursor to a community housing programme which spread across the State. The first stage was reactive. It was not so much aimed at the development of policy in relation to housing, rather, it sought to stop the destruction of the local community ecology and to build among local residents the capacity to veto what was perceived as unjust action on the part of government. By the second stage, the focus had become proactive and focused on the introduction of co-operative housing. This was a concerted effort from local community members with key support from Housing Trust staff: together these established a policy agenda for community housing. It is this shift from the reactive activism to save the area and housing for local residents to a deliberate activism to establish and build housing co-operatives that is the centre piece of this chapter. This shift from reaction to proaction was also a move to a conscious and strategic ambition to influence the policy agenda and its implementation.

The Bowden–Brompton area sits within the Charles Sturt Council (formerly Hindmarsh Council) in South Australia and is a notable example of urban renewal in an inner Adelaide suburb. The stimuli for this renewal process, the key participants and the continuing dynamic have all contributed variously over the past twenty-five years to reshape both public and private housing in the area. An increase in the proportion of social housing in this area has occurred against a backdrop of ongoing conflict between residents and heavy, noxious industry. While this conflict continues today, albeit to a lesser degree, there is now pressure being placed on the local council to continue and extend the greening of the area. This study traces the origins of tenant-managed community housing in the strong community activism which was characteristic of the area in the early 1970s. What began as community-based activism to regain residential rights turned into concerted determination to develop one of the first tenant-managed housing co-operatives in South Australia (SA). The subsequent development of four more housing co-operatives, several housing associations and an increased number of South Australian Housing Trust units contributed to the significant proportion of social housing in the overall redevelopment of the area. The level of social housing in Bowden-Brompton has had a direct impact on slowing, although not preventing, the gentrification of the area. Gentrification which is often developer led is in evidence in the developments which border Torrens Road on one edge of Bowden–Brompton.

The first activists in this case study were influenced by the student union activism and the community development movement which flourished in the 1970s and 1980s. There were (and are) many people involved across the Bowden–Brompton redevelopment and the growth of community housing in South Australia. We can speak indeed of a community housing movement. Many of the people involved whether directly as residents or as external 'supporters' were champions of this movement and became directly involved not only in the changes to the Bowden–Brompton area but also in the development of community housing in South Australia through the Community Housing Assistance Service of South Australia, the framing of the *South Australian Co-operative and Community Housing Association Act* (1991) and the establishment of the SA Community Housing Authority as an organisation which grew out of and separated from the South Australian Housing Trust in 1991.

This process involved a range of activists who were engaged for different reasons: students; residents; local government and State public servants and politicians. They were variously involved in preventing the destruction of Bowden–Brompton and in contributing to the redevelopment of public and private housing in the area. For all of these participants the common factor was sharing, to different degrees, the sense of a better future for (variously) their children, themselves and the community. I construct three profiles of individual activists who made significant contributions to this process. While some would identify themselves as fighters for change, they would be unlikely to think of themselves as 'policy activists'. They are more likely to emphasise the positive impact of collective action on the futures, outcomes, of residents in the area.

What is evident among the larger group who were involved in the area and who constitute the policy actors is the conscious and unconscious operation of a network stretched over community, bureaucratic and political sites. In relation to the growth of a community housing policy agenda, there is evidence of a shift over time from a reactive, intuitive, but committed intervention aimed at improving conditions and in particular housing opportunities for the local community to rational interventions (planned, deliberate policy and a budgeted programme) which have influenced the growth of community housing throughout the State.

My particular interest in this story is the insight it affords into sustainable urban renewal as an organic process. The outcomes may be intended but they are not limited to those which arise out of linear processes of traditional town planning nor indeed of any rational planning process. There is also recognition from the activists in their retelling of their story that individuals have grown through an evolving process. The nature of individuals' participation has occurred in relation to their needs and capacity: some stayed involved for the whole process; some came and went several times over the period of change; and some were clearly part of a defined stage or part of the process.

In telling this story I have identified three key themes which seem interesting in constructing an analysis of this instance of an activist engagement with the policy process. The first theme concerns the creation of a sense of community across what Yeatman (chapter 1, this volume) identifies as bureaucratic, professional, practitioner and consumer activist networks. The second theme centres on the accumulation of experience, skills and achievements and the learning they involved for the range of activists concerned. Through this accumulative process of learning and achievement individual activists were

197

drawn more fully into the policy process. For example, the residents who became local councillors, the student professional who became a champion for community housing development and the resident housing co-operative member who, through her activist role and experience eventually became a member of the first public authority for community housing. The third and final theme that is reflected in this story is a continuum which runs over time from the reactive and intuitive community activism, which was oriented to stopping the policies aimed at destruction of the area, to a deliberate and conscious policy activism which had a direct impact on setting the community housing policy agenda.

Community activism: laying a foundation for renewal 1971–82

Historically, the Hindmarsh Council area including Bowden–Brompton, was one of mixed residential and industrial use. Its origins from 1853 lay in the formation of small cottage industries which grew up supported by both residential and industrial expansion. Following the First World War more noxious industry began to move into the area and the wealthier residents began to move out. It was still a good place to live and by 1931 over 14 000 people lived in the area. After the Second World War many houses were demolished for industrial development. At the same time the area attracted many Greek, Italian and Yugoslav migrants because of the low cost of housing. For the past twenty-five years the issues of balance between the mix of residential and industrial uses and the quality of life for residents has been the subject of much debate, writing, action, planning and change.

Bowden–Brompton has long offered cheap, low rent housing close to the city. It was equally attractive to industry because of its proximity to the city and main transport routes. Active concern for Bowden–Brompton as a legitimate place for people to remain living as part of a community and as part of the mixed economy of the area began with recognition of the likely impact on the area that would follow upon the controversial Metropolitan Adelaide Transport System (MATS) plan. In 1968 this plan identified Bowden–Brompton as the potential site for the largest highway interchange in the new system. The acceptance of the MATS plan by the State government resulted in the compulsory purchase by the Highways Department of over three hundred houses. There are many stories of these houses being destroyed and falling into disrepair over the years as the MATS plan was first fought and then shelved. Gradually much of the housing was annexed by industry. Local residents saw this as a deliberate ploy by both State and local governments to remove residents from the area.

The State government proposed the MATS plan in 1968. In the decade that followed, the perception of residents was that private industry together with the highways department and the local Council were working to turn the area into an industrial park. While the Council wanted to retain the West Hindmarsh and Croydon areas as residential it saw considerable financial advantage in the development of an inner suburban industrial park. What ensued over the next fifteen years was a sustained struggle on the part of local residents and community development workers. It was characterised by continuous community intervention. The MATS plan was successfully resisted and, subsequently, the demolition of the area by industry, the Council and the highways department was resisted. Many groups and individuals were involved: one person who spoke to me recalls that during this period 'people from every street would come to meetings'.

The community's concern was that Bowden–Brompton was becoming increasingly hazardous as a residential area because of noise and air pollution and that dangerous industrial practices were incompatible with residential living. It was unsafe for children and older people as a result of the heavy industrial traffic on narrow streets formerly used by neighbourhood residents. What emerged in interviews and other material was a strong sense that the community fabric was being deliberately destroyed and sacrificed to industry and that this process had the sanction of both State and local governments. While there was a growing need for low cost housing, residents' groups were well aware of the common practice employed by the highways department of cementing up toilets to prevent the houses from being habitable. In the early 1970s significant resistance began against this continuous degradation of the area. From the stories told to me it appears that the original activism stemmed from several sources—residents, external student activists, unionists and community workers. While these groups had some common aims there was often considerable friction between their approaches to change and their different ways of working. The Bowden–Brompton Community Centre was formed in 1971 to provide the focal point for community development in the area. It was funded through the Commonwealth government's Australian Assistance Plan. The Centre was a base for a range of community services including legal aid, women's and children's groups, food co-ops, information and advice and it supported the development of the community farm and Bowden–Brompton Community School. One description referred to 'a rough rolling caravan' of students, residents and other activists who got involved in the struggle for the area. They worked together with local groups including the Hindmarsh Residents Association and the Bowden–Brompton Community Centre, the newly formed Shelter SA, the squatters group and the Low Income Action Group ('a shelf company of sorts') and the Brompton Park Residents Group.

Some residents began restoring run down houses and others were supported in resisting what was perceived as a campaign of intimidation aimed at (especially elderly) residents in an effort to get them to sell up and move away. In the video documentary *Give Them a House and They Take a Street* (Anderson 1984) it is clear that from the beginning of this urban resistance movement there were some central and key participants. Many of these were involved through residents' groups and housing co-operatives from this period and are still community members. From this time there were three key issues: pollution, housing and the preservation of a residential community. Underlying these was a commitment to people's rights and to the principle that it was worth fighting for the community's future. The tactics employed by the activists took a variety of forms. Different people and indeed different segments of the 'resistance' movement undertook varying activities sustained over a ten-year period. These included squatting in houses targeted for demolition, re-roofing and renovating government owned houses targeted for bulldozing, writing submissions, plotting strategic action, lobbying politicians, gaining funding for the Community Centre, picketing industry and watching over vulnerable houses, and building alliances with unions. This resistance developed a charisma and a resilience which captured the imagination of many outside the area.

What had been to this point a dispersed community development process essentially evolved into a more deliberate mainstream strategy on the part of residents when they formed the first Hindmarsh Residents Association (HRA) in 1981. The HRA began to campaign against pollution and housing demolition. It put pickets on houses to stop development by industry. It articulated the feeling of mistreatment of residents by both levels of government. It lobbied the local Hindmarsh Council because there was a strong feeling that the Council was not looking after residents but was 'siding' with industry in order to gain a stronger tax base. It was clear in my interview with a key participant in the Association, who eventually ran for and was elected to Council, that even then there was concern to retain low levels of industry to counteract potential gentrification and potentially high increases in land and house prices. The Association urged the Housing Trust to purchase older, run down houses and to renovate them in co-operation with developers. The target group of tenants included existing residents of the area on low-to-middle incomes.

The Hindmarsh Council was a central element in the dynamic of changing the area. The relationships with the Council and its elected members and administrative staff were important particularly because of the planning powers of the Council and what was perceived by activists as the unsympathetic approach of the then town planner. Residents who were concerned about saving the area decided to have a legitimate voice on Council. They campaigned and the result was that various of the activists were elected to the Council in an attempt to at least be heard and to participate in the Council's decisions. Over time several members of the Association were elected to Council. I interviewed two of these people and they were both clear that the Council did not particularly alter its approach to Bowden–Brompton until after the State government changed its own plans for the area. These representatives were therefore under no illusion about their influence on the Council but for each it was a significant experience. Both told the story of arriving an hour before the regular Council meeting to deliver some documents which had been misdirected, only to find the rest of the Council members in a meeting. This meeting was apparently a regular caucus meeting of the old guard on the Council before the Resident's Association member arrived.

An eleven-month picket on houses which were eventually demolished at least got the State government to realise that the residents were serious. There was a feeling that progress was slowly being made. In 1981 the new State Liberal government decided to build a remand centre on a large block of land in the area. The land was picketed by a team of residents so that there were four picketers at all times on a two-hourly roster. In 1982 following the election of a Labor government and with support of the unions who blackbanned the site, the remand centre plan for the area was withdrawn.

At the point when it took an active role in the redevelopment of the area, the State government decided that the constant battle between industry and residents should be tackled. The then Chief Executive Officer of the Department of Environment and Planning, at a public meeting with residents, announced the government's commitment to injecting housing into the area as well as wanting to improve the poor relationship between industry and residents. In 1983, the State government announced a major redevelopment in the area with the goals of arresting population decline, resolving the conflict between industry and residents, improving the environment and involving the local community. There were several key consultation and planning reports prepared for and by the State government. These were predicated on the predicted population base, household formation, the need for low to medium cost housing as well as a concern to balance this development with industry retention and limited development. The reports also acknowledged the potential for gentrification which would have a detrimental effect on maintaining affordable housing in Bowden–Brompton. The draft plan released by the Department of Environment and Planning in 1984 was not accepted by a number of local citizens. Several different groups (the Community Planning Group, the Hindmarsh Residents Association and the Urban Permaculture Consultants) responded by developing their own Community Strategy Plan. Eventually, a final and agreed upon version of the plan was released. As a result there followed significant residential development on vacant land, the involvement of both the private sector and the Housing Trust and the upgrading of some physical and social services in the area.

Hindmarsh Housing Co-operative 1982–94

In turning to the establishment and growth of the Hindmarsh Housing Co-operative I want to shift the focus from the political activism of the early years to the development of community housing. In particular I will recount the ten-year process (1984–94) undertaken by the co-operative to complete the major 'new build' project commonly referred to as 'the ASC (Australian Servicing Contractors) site development'.

What became the Hindmarsh Housing Co-operative was originally established in 1982 as the Hindmarsh Housing Association[2] with the help of the Residents Association to provide low cost housing for the (traditional) residents of the area. The Housing Association was set up for a variety of reasons: to provide secure and affordable housing to local residents; to present a positive alternative to industry expansion; to counter the negativity associated with the activist resistance in Bowden–Brompton; and to preserve residential properties in this area. This Association was one of the first housing associations established in South Australia along with the Women's Shelter Housing Association and the Northern Suburbs Aged Housing Association. Of these the Hindmarsh Housing Association was the only tenant-managed association. One of the first actions of the Association was to save six Trembath Street houses from demolition and to have them renovated for resident members who had been active in the fight to save the area. This step was hugely symbolic of progress to reclaim the area for residents. This achievement was made in co-operation with the State government and with the South Australian Housing Trust in particular. By all accounts the development of the Hindmarsh Housing Association was the result of persistent submission writing, as well as the strategic and relentless pursuit of the relevant Labor branch. Its existence is owed to the constant encouragement of members and other residents to attend meetings, and the detailed attention to finance in order to convince the government of the broad support for the project and its viability. Four of the key people who established the Association became involved in the subsequent campaign for the Australian Servicing Contractors (ASC) development site and were members of the initial site committee.

The Hindmarsh Housing Association was a milestone in the emergence of co-operative housing in South Australia for two reasons. It promoted the concept of tenant-managed housing, and it fostered many of those who were to hang in for the long haul of getting a policy of co-operative housing established. The next struggle was with the broad policies of the SA Housing Trust. At that time public housing tenants had the usual tenant landlord relationship with the Trust. Houses in any location were assigned to those on the waiting list. The Trust then undertook the general landlord functions of rent collection and maintenance. The view of the Hindmarsh Residents Association was that tenants should have the opportunity of being involved in managing their own housing and should have a say in where they lived. It was hoped that this would help to build community and to decrease the cost associated with housing management and maintenance.

The Association gained the support and subsequent intervention of some South Australian Housing Trust staff. It borrowed money on the private market to purchase highways department houses which otherwise would have gone to industry and the Housing Trust subsidised the loan repayments. In 1984 the Housing Trust purchased the ASC site which became the focus of a ten-year building development programme for what, by then, had been renamed the Hindmarsh Housing Co-operative, initially in partnership with the Trust and subsequently with the SA Community Housing Authority, set up in 1991.

The development of the ASC site (formerly owned by industry and still surrounded on two sides by industry) on behalf of the Hindmarsh Housing Co-operative was managed by a Site Committee. The membership of the Committee fluctuated over the ten-year period of development reflecting the capacity of and need for individual involvement. The Committee included at various times Hindmarsh Co-operative members, Residents Association members and a number of people who became (and still are) involved in the growth of community housing in South Australia at a policy and programme level. One resident, Mary, who had been active in forming the Resident's Association and in the activist fight for the area remained involved throughout the development of the site from 1984 to 1994.

The ten-year period of development of the site into co-operative housing was a complex interaction between government, community and industry. The housing co-operative members I interviewed spoke of learning about all aspects of development: planning, design, getting Council approval, commissioning architects and builders, managing the allocated finance and negotiating with the South Australian Housing Trust and subsequently with the South Australian Community Housing Authority for funds. In order to purchase the property an arrangement was reached with the Hindmarsh Council and the Hindmarsh Development Committee on the land. This arrangement included an agreement that the adjoining block of land immediately to the west of the site would be developed by the Council as part of a greening strategy for the area and to provide a much needed barrier between the residential housing and industry. To date no action has been taken and the land remains much as it was.

What was not anticipated was the prolonged and complex process of soil remediation. The question of contamination was faced when some local members painstakingly photographed the cleaning fluids being dumped on the site. In itself this issue provided the State government with some new challenges in managing the removal of toxic substances and involved at least four Ministers over ten years including the Ministers for Environment and Planning and the Ministers for Housing. As an unintended consequence of this project, as with other cases, the government developed policies on land contamination and remediation.

Some of the housing for the ASC site was designed by a local architect who specialises in environmentally sound construction and who was himself a housing co-operative member. He has also designed the housing in his own local co-operative (MERZ Inc.) which uses the same principles of modern design, good light and cooling together with environmentally sound construction. The designs for this site (and indeed others in the area) make use of rammed earth construction. Several housing co-operatives have houses which are co-located on this site. Another design completed last year for an offshoot of the Hindmarsh Housing Co-operative, Paris Flat Housing Co-operative, has used a cluster housing design for its Green Street site. This project incorporated the original old house on the building site into the new plan and used rammed earth walls internally with a corrugated iron exterior. As with a number of the cluster designs this group of houses were built around an internal shared garden area. Co-operative members were involved in the design, costing, planning approval processes and then in the negotiation with the Housing Authority for funding. Paris Flat's Green Street site came in under the allocated budget.

The transition from community-based political activism to policy activism: the activists

From the interviews and records, particularly the community newspaper *The Pughole*, it is clear that many people were involved in fighting against the destruction of the area and in working to establish and build co-operative housing. Records of meetings show attendance of sixty to seventy people was common in the early years. Over time of course, the groups and individuals involved have changed. People were passionate about the cause, committing long hours and making personal sacrifice to the reclamation of Bowden–Brompton. Over the past six months I have interviewed a number of people involved in the renewal of Bowden–Brompton. Some were active in the early changes in the area during the 1970s. This initial group of residents, students and workers in the area first recognised the health impact of pollution from industry and the potential for saving this inner suburb from destruction by industry and government. Some of those I interviewed continue to live (and work) in the area. Some have contributed to the establishment of the first housing co-operative in South Australia. Some are still residents of this housing co-operative (Hindmarsh)—or of the other co-operatives in the area. Some continue to live in Housing Trust accommodation which they first moved into many years ago.

Most of the people I interviewed were drawn into the process of community action by their own belief in a future for the area and their own convictions about the need for healthy local communities.

They were committed to this local area which had a dynamic community spirit and sense of history. Most are still residents in the area, many of whom live in community housing. Others who are residents were active in challenging government to support these changes from a position of activist politics as well as a shared commitment to the notion and principles of community housing. And still others (known but not interviewed) are acknowledged as the 'friends' of the area who worked actively in the bureaucracy and through political channels to bring about positive change to the area.

In addition to the activists associated directly with the housing changes I discovered that there had been a richly differentiated group of community-based and community-oriented activists working towards change in this area. It involved both residents, and professionals working as policy activists in education, community and legal aid services in the area. Many of the professionals employed by the State government or in government funded programmes who initiated community-based services such as the Bowden–Brompton Community School, the Bowden–Brompton Community Centre and the Bowden–Brompton Community Legal Service became involved.

What seems to have occurred here is a shift from activism to policy activism. The policy activists in this study are particularly interesting if we consider the distinctions between bureaucratic, professional, practitioner and consumer activists. In the case of Bowden–Brompton sooner or later all are in evidence; some have ceased to be activists and still others have moved to other areas. Their relationship to and impact on the process of urban renewal that took place in Bowden–Brompton involved a movement from an unconscious to a conscious espousal of the collective action required for sustainable development. This can also be regarded as a shift from activism to policy activism. This case is an example of the sort of interactions which characterise this sort of policy activism and its impact on the nature and form of urban living.

It is important to reflect on how is it that a community-based movement not only turned out to nurture and create effective policy activists but also contributed innovative conceptions of community development to the policy agenda in the areas of residential housing, community renewal and sustainability. In part this was due to the hothouse effect of a localised set of issues which not only drew on established community attachments but developed them into a tenacious and passionate set of commitments. The residents' resistance movement to the MATS plan development developed a passionate commitment to the survival of the area against the opposition of the Hindmarsh Council and the apparent indifference of the State government. For the size of the area there were large numbers of people involved from the outset of the process beginning with the student and resident activists in the 1970s. As I mentioned above, residents' meetings numbered between seventy-five and one hundred people which for a small area like this was significant. Even the ASC site committee for Hindmarsh Housing Co-operative had variously between six and twenty people on the committee throughout its ten year life from early planning to the completion of the buildings in 1994. There was an acknowledged leader particularly for stage one of the renewal process. All of the people I interviewed referred me to one[3] in particular who is seen as the key leader and strategist from the very early days of developing community resistance through to the completion of the building on the ASC site.

As I progressed through this search and interview process I discovered a South Australian 'Who's Who' network of community development champions in legal services, education, community services and public, or, community housing. There are two observations which flow from this discovery. The first is that the network of people who were involved was not in itself a conscious strategic effort. That it had a strategic impact is due to its emergent synergies rather than due to any rational planning and forethought. The second observation is, using the benefit of hindsight, what started as a local and community-based process had an impact on the development of government policy at the State level and contributed to the emergence of community housing at a national level. This is especially noteworthy since there had not been so much a conscious desire to influence social, urban, policy on this scale as much as a genuine commitment to making positive difference at the community level. Over time, however, this kind of policy ambition and awareness became manifest in individuals who took up leadership roles in both the community housing organisations and the State government bureaucracy. The combination of skill, creativity and passion, all required in maintaining a successful local struggle are likely to have been key elements in their success.

A nucleus of people emerged who forged the housing co-operative movement in South Australia which resulted over time in the development of over eighty housing co-operatives, the formation of the Community Housing Assistance Service of South Australia, the *South Australian Community Housing Association Act* and the establishment of the South Australian Community Housing Authority. A brief portrayal of three people who were involved variously with the urban renewal of the area, with the emergence of the Hindmarsh Housing Co-operative and with the development of a discrete Community Housing infrastructure in government gives an indication of the range of actors who both got caught up in and contributed to the shift from a reactive community-based politics to a proactive role in setting the policy agenda. These three were members of the ASC site committee in its work over ten years, Mary being the one continuous member throughout the life of the Committee.

Mary: resident then and now

Mary is a long-time resident of the area who became involved with the early resistance in the 1970s. She was a founding member of the Hindmarsh Housing Association. Mary did not envisage that she would demonstrate against government policy, become elected to the Hindmarsh Council or be seen by a generation of housing co-operative members as one of the founders of tenant-managed public housing in the South Australia. In some ways she embodies the shift from an unconscious to a conscious and deliberate activism. Mary played a key role in 'talking up' the changes, and the need for involvement from all levels of government. She articulated the concerns of community members at meetings, on videos and in the council: namely, we like the feeling of community here; we want to be able to live here in decent housing and in a healthier environment with our children.

As a member of the Hindmarsh Housing Co-operative management group Mary stayed continuously on the ASC Site Committee over the ten-year development period. She subsequently moved to

Paris Flat Housing Co-operative when it was formed and continues to be involved and articulate in her community.

Alan: *former student from outside the area*

Alan acknowledges from the beginning of his involvement with Bowden–Brompton he came in and out of the renewal process as part of a broader political commitment to housing change and as part of a group of student activists (unionists). He did not really get involved until the early 1980s. With others he was to have a significant impact on the emergence of community housing as a force in social housing in South Australia.

Alan was a student when he first became involved with Bowden–Brompton. He was involved in much of the political activity in the early 1980s and was involved in Tent City set up in Victoria Square, designed to demonstrate a broad alliance for affordable housing. His contribution to the Bowden–Brompton area is recognised still by many of the first group of people I interviewed who told me I must speak with him. He helped to found the first peak community housing body in South Australia which eventually became the Community Housing Assistance Service of South Australia (CHASSA). Subsequently, as first a former Commonwealth public servant, and now a community services manager in local government, he has taken his activist years with him into the development of policies and programmes associated with social housing.

Sandy: *former resident and founding member of South Australian Community Housing Authority Board*

Sandy became a member of Hindmarsh Housing Co-operative and subsequently of the Paris Flat Housing Co-operative. She was enormously active in both co-operatives and in elected positions in the peak body, CHASSA, whose executive she chaired. Sandy was a founding Board member of the South Australian Community Housing Authority, and has subsequently worked as a consultant to government and community in housing related work. Most recently she has remained active in the emerging peak body policy framework for community housing organisations (the bringing together of housing co-operatives and housing associations) in South Australia.

All three openly acknowledge that the process was messy, complex and evolutionary. As a policy process it is a good example of emergent strategy (Mintzberg 1987) where deliberate policy change (tenant-managed housing) and existing policy and programmes (Housing Trust) merged to become the new direction: community housing. It required the diverse skills and contributions of many people who played a part at various times in the renewal of the area. No one of these could have foreseen the evolution of policy activism as it characterised the development of particular actors' roles and contribution.

Three of the activists have been engaged directly (Sandy and Mary) or indirectly (Alan) in the coproduction of viable co-operative housing in South Australia. The notion of coproduction was described in a CHASSA project[4] which identified some good practices in co-operative housing management in South Australia. The documentation of this project proposed the notion of coproduction between community and government as the basis for the joint management of key resources in housing co-operatives: people, property, finance. It provided an example of a new framework for analysing joint government and community programmes. It is an important concept because it shifts the focus away from seeing the government–client relationship as an active–passive one, to a conception of government and community as joint actors whose 'jointness' is central to the delivery and effectiveness of, in this instance, a community housing programme.

Conclusion

What is presented in this account is a type of policy activism which lies across the intersection of a community-based politics of urban renewal and the governmental policy process. It brings out the complexity of the roles and relationships which get caught up in this intersection. The process includes particular individuals who find themselves at different points of their career as policy activists in

211

different locations, for example at one point operating out of the community base, at another point operating out of the bureaucracy. The process goes beyond the individual to a policy activist network which comes to span both of these locations. Just as an individual policy activist who comes to operate in both locations at different times does not segment these experiences into isolated compartments but integrates them within a continuing narrative of what is important, how things get done, who is involved, and where things need to go, the network itself ensures that those who are consistently located at one point or another (the community as distinct from State government, for example) draw on the experience, cognitive maps and policy imagination of those who are located at other points within the same network.

I offer this story of urban renewal in Bowden–Brompton as an example of organic change. It was simultaneously both a deliberate and an unconscious process which developed a model of sustainable development with its roots firmly attached to community-based and collective action. It is deliberate because the people involved were committed to making a difference to their own lives and to the community in which they lived and worked. The changes which came about to land use and housing were the results of a passionate commitment to social and environmental change and of the planned and unplanned action to bring these changes about. While the activism evident in both stage one (1970–92) and stage two (1982–96) was not planned or implemented around a conscious framework of sustainable development (Jacobs 1994), it provides us with an excellent example of this new model for community driven change.

Bowden–Brompton has offered South Australia examples of demonstrated options in environmental housing design, attractive low cost medium density housing, and land reclamation. In co-operative housing it has provided an example of the benefits of a coproductive relationship between government and community. Just as importantly it has given South Australia a widely acknowledged story of how ordinary people from their community and places of work can influence government policies and programmes. The story lives in the recollections of individuals, in the videos and archives of community groups and in the records of government reports and plans.

The journey which began with the action in the 1970s has been a longer one than the participants at the time might have thought. It has been a process which over the years has involved different State governments, local governments, residents' groups, senior bureaucrats and ministerial policy advisers. The area has been a focus of environmental policy changes in managing degraded and contaminated land, the location for the first housing co-operative in South Australia as well as, more recently, the site of some major joint private and public initiatives in medium density housing. A number of the most noxious industries have left but some still battle on even in these days of industrial site development and relocation by government. The newly amalgamated Charles Sturt Council has yet to reveal a clear supplementary development plan for the area and there is still considerable scope for greening and for interleaving more parks and recreation spaces into the area. There are still contaminated sites which stand unaltered and untouched due to the unknown cost of decontamination. The greatest danger for many residents especially of the older part of Bowden–Brompton is that the gentrification of the area has occurred and that this area will be lost to low income earners if there is not a continuous and effective commitment from the State government to maintain affordable accessible social housing in the area.

Acknowledgments

I would like to thank Anna Yeatman for her encouragement and contribution to the thinking in this chapter which has been critical to the final piece of work.

10

Activists in the woodwork: policy activism and the housing reform movement in New South Wales

JULIE NYLAND

We had to learn the more delicate arts of negotiation and finesse, of wheeling and dealing and the political necessities of compromise. Some people didn't learn these skills, some people thought they had learnt these skills and hadn't, some people learnt them all too well, and some people yearned for the good old days of the shoot-out at the not-so OK Corral. (interview)[1]

Farewell to the OK Corral

The policy 'shoot-out'

Traditionally, academic discussions of policy actors involved in policy reform have focused on the controllers and initiators of public policy at one end—politicians, reforming bureaucrats, 'policy entrepreneurs'—and the policy 'opposition' at the other end—interest group representatives, community activists, non-government sector lobbyists. From either perspective, the scenario presented usually involves a struggle between the opposing interests of the policy makers inside government, and those organised forces seeking to influence policy from positions outside government.

This construction is reflected in the contrast between 'top-down' explanations of policy-making and 'bottom-up' explanations. In the former, policy decisions are taken by government policy actors inside the policy process, and then implemented. In the 'bottom-up' version, policy-making is driven by claims and demands made on the state by outside interest groups, to which government policy makers are forced to respond. These constructions have been somewhat superseded in recent policy literature by analyses that attempt to synthesise the two approaches (Sabatier 1986) or that bring policy makers together with outside interests in 'policy networks' (Atkinson and Coleman 1992; Cawson 1985; Van Waarden 1992).

Despite the contributions of these later analyses, it is the more simplistic picture of government policy makers in conflict with non-government activists that frames the experience of many who have worked in the bureaucracy of government, or the organisations of the community sector. For those who see the rightful job of government to be the setting of policy without undue interference, community organisations and interest groups are a potential disruption to the smooth planning of government business (conforming to Majone's (1991) description of the 'received view' of policy-making). For those who see the role of community organisations to be one of advocacy for the community, governments are the often immovable objects to which the irresistible force of community activism must be applied (for example, Knoke 1990).

The concept of community activism, and the identity of community activists, are derived in part from their connection to the notion of applying force to governments in order to bring about policy reform. In Australia, particular meanings and identities developed around the concept of activism during the intense period of social reform in the 1970s and early 1980s. As the quote above implies, many community activists of the time saw their contest with governments as a form of 'shoot-out' over the content and direction of policy. They located their activism in their pursuit of policy reform against a dominant policy agenda, using methods such as public campaigns or lobbying activities to apply pressure to politicians or government bureaucrats. They saw their involvement in community sector organisations or groups, as opposed to public sector organisations, as intrinsic to their identity as activists.

This identity, and the concept of activism itself, was also challenged during this same period in Australia, when, as a result of changes in governments and reforms in public sector administration, 'activists' began to also work in government agencies. The most notable group were the feminists who entered the bureaucracy to work as 'femocrats'. Their activities sparked strenuous debate in the feminist movement about whether it was possible to work 'on the inside' of the state, or whether 'co-option' was inevitable (Eisenstein 1996, pp. xv–xvi, 20–21, 74–78; Dowse 1984, p. 146; Watson 1990, pp. 8–10). Could one be simultaneously a worker for the state and an activist working for policy reform? This question certainly split opinion among those activists who remained on the community sector side of the fence. Many feminists were highly critical of the 'femocrats' inside government, and saw these moves as akin to an 'act of treason' with regard to the women's movement (Eisenstein 1996, p. 90).

While the movement of feminists into the bureaucracy has been well documented (Eistenstein 1996; Franzway *et al.* 1989; Sawer 1990; Watson 1990; Yeatman 1990), the movement of other types of activists into government positions has been neglected. In New South Wales (NSW) in the late 1970s and early 1980s a number of people active in social services reforms, such as welfare, housing, planning and child care, left their posts at the barricades of the 'OK Corral', and moved into positions inside government bureaucracies. This was prompted by a change of State government in 1976, and a set of public administration reforms promoted during the mid to late-1970s under the Wran Labor government (Wilenski 1977). The reforms replaced systems of seniority with employment on the basis of merit, and, in so doing, opened government authorities to the recruitment of a new breed of public servant. This was particularly evident in the social service bureaucracies where many of the 'new breed' bureaucrats were either recruited from the community sector or from local government.

A similar set of concerns about co-option existed for these people as existed for the femocrats. In both cases these political debates tended to overshadow the fact that, although tensions and conflicts existed, connections remained between those involved in community activism and those who became bureaucrats. Many community sector feminists supported the femocrat strategy, and retained their working relationships (not to mention private friendships and love affairs) with women in the bureaucracy. In the case of femocrats, this is rarely documented, although Eisenstein provides an example of networks across the sectors (1996, pp. 25–6). In a much earlier study of the emerging women's movement in the United States, Freeman argued that a 'symbiotic relationship' existed between feminists outside government and what she called the 'woodwork feminists' inside government (Freeman 1975, p. 230).

In looking at a case study of housing activists, I have found a similar set of connections. In the case of housing policy reformers, many of those who remained in the community sector retained strong alliances, working relationships and friendships with those inside the bureaucracy. Networks formed across the two sectors, linking activists in the community sector with activists who had moved into the public sector. Those who entered the bureaucracy retained their opposition to certain dominant policy agendas, continuing to work for reform from within government agencies. Those who remained in the community sector put aside direct action tactics in favour of 'the more delicate arts', using strategic alliances with those inside the bureaucracy to gain access to the policy-making process.

The picture is no longer a simple scenario of public policy makers locked in policy combat with community activists. In between these protagonists were the 'policy activists', who pursued policy reform across a range of arenas, in collaboration with one another across the institutional boundaries of public and community sectors. Using informal policy networks, they burrowed deep into the policy-making processes and into the very woodwork of the public sector.

Policy activism and the housing reform movement

I first became aware of 'policy activists' and informal policy networking across the public and community sectors through my own involvement in reforms that took place in NSW public housing policy during the early 1980s. As a participant in events which led to some of these reforms, I had the opportunity to watch the way in which they took place, and this experience left me with a number of questions about the way in which these reforms occurred, and the role played by community sector activists.

The housing reform movement began during the late 1970s in

NSW, when momentum gathered among community sector activists agitating for policy reform in public housing. This movement gathered strength and numbers during the early 1980s, when activists battled unsuccessfully to make an impact on the housing policy of the time. Reform began to occur with a change of Housing Minister in 1983. Over the next few years, the NSW State housing authority (the NSW Housing Commission, which became the Department of Housing in 1986), underwent a major restructure and a reform of housing policy in a number of areas, including eligibility criteria, scope of programmes offered, participation of tenants, operational policies, and support for home purchasers and private renters.

Although the change of Minister was the catalyst for the reform of the housing authority's legal constitution, management structure and operational activities, there were many factors that contributed to these changes taking place. One of the key factors was the employment of a number of new staff in the Housing Commission, in a newly established section dealing with community-based programmes. These people all belonged to a loose network of housing activists and their allies, and they became the 'new guard' within the crumbling control of the 'old guard' of the Commission.

The policy actors involved in the movement for housing policy reform cannot be adequately described within simple identities of 'bureaucrat' or 'activist'. Some of the policy activists had been working as bureaucrats for some time, but were also key players in the community sector lobby groups. One interview respondent confessed to late night poster pasting expeditions, protesting against the policies of the Housing Commission, using the official work vehicles of another department. Those who moved into the Housing Commission worked as subversives, consciously pursuing policy and programme reforms that were not generally supported by the senior management of the Housing Commission. They were no longer community activists working from the outside of government, but neither were they faithful and compliant members of the public service. It should be added, however, that they were change agents both licensed and encouraged to act as policy reformers by the Minister for Housing at the time, Frank Walker.

Those that remained in community sector organisations began to work in different ways. Their connections to people who had moved inside the bureaucracy gave them an 'inside' access to the policy process, and altered the strategies that they used to pursue reform. They spent less time 'chucking rocks', as one interview subject described it, and more time planning 'wheeling and dealing' strategies with their bureaucratic allies.

In terms of their relationships to the policy process, all these players were 'activists', with a shared focus on policy reform. They were also all 'policy makers', in the sense that they were shaping a policy agenda, and the policy responses that the government eventually adopted. The alliance between the two sets of policy activists created a different point of access to the policy process for the community sector activists, by engaging them in policy formulation informally with those inside the policy process. Key to this was the fact that they worked across the boundary of the public and community sectors in a collaborative way that broke the rules of hostile engagement.

I first began to use the term 'policy activist' in thesis supervision sessions prior to discovering that the term 'policy activist' had been used by Heclo in his work on informal policy networks, or 'issue networks' (Heclo 1978, p. 103). Although he coined the term, Heclo's concept of policy activists is quite limited, referring primarily to groups of policy 'experts' located within the federal government administration in Washington. Like the policy actors I am describing, Heclo's policy activists are policy actors 'who care deeply about a set of issues and are determined to shape the fabric of public policy accordingly' (p. 105). They connect and link to others with similar concerns, forming 'issue networks' based on shared interest in shaping particular policy agendas, from which they work for policy reform.

Heclo's emphasis on the expertise of the policy activists, as 'specialised subcultures composed of highly knowledgeable policy-watchers' (p. 99) constructs them more as policy technocrats than activists. Although he portrays his policy activists as policy actors who 'care deeply', they do not necessarily work with the sort of zealousness one usually associates with activism. The term 'activism' implies that the players have some degree of enthusiasm and strong belief for their cause, which Heclo's policy activists appear to lack.

Activism also implies that the activist is working against the current or prevailing forces. Heclo's players are often in the position of advisers to policy makers and, thus, are players within dominant policy agendas. The policy actors in the housing reform case study worked with strong commitments to policy reform, and against a dominant policy agenda.

Policy reform and informal policy networks

The other significant feature in the case of the housing policy reform movement is the informal network between the policy activists, and the part that this networking played in bringing about policy reform. What struck me at the time of my own involvement was that policy decisions appeared to be more effectively influenced by personal networking and strategic activity within government, than by the political lobbying of activist organisations external to government. Private discussions between friends and acquaintances generated the ideas that became new housing policy. Through the development of policy critique at an informal level within this network, policy activists influenced policy-making at the point of setting agendas and defining policy problems. Strong alliances between people located in different positions across community, bureaucracy and parliament proved to be extremely powerful forces for policy reform.

This type of network also provides a link between the 'top-down' elements of the case study and the 'bottom-up' elements. Policy activists within the bureaucracy were linked to policy activists in the community sector via the informal processes of the network. By studying the activity of these policy activists and their informal policy networks, I want to show that it is possible to observe an informal level of engagement with policy processes that is a form of middle ground between 'top-down' and 'bottom-up' explanations of policy reform. This is an alternative and potentially complementary approach to formal policy network explanations such as corporatism which also form such a bridge. Corporatism entails *formal* consultative relationships between government, employer associations, unions and other key stakeholders (for further discussion of the corporatist approach of the Hawke Labor government, see Short, this volume). This case study requires us to emphasise *informal* policy networks which may affect and inform formal networks. While the latter are publicly acknowledged, informal policy networks operate privately and often intersect with friendship and personal ties between activists.

The informal network, and the type of intervention in policy made by policy activists, raises issues about the relationship of community sector policy activists to the policy process. In the case study, I document the movement of a number of these policy activists from positions outside the policy process, as external agitators, through increasing engagement in the policy process, and thence into positions that were effectively in control of the policy agenda. During the process of the reforms those of us who were in the community sector were presented with an opportunity to enter a part of the policy process from which we had previously been locked out. We moved from positions as external agitators and lobbyists to being active participants in the design and formulation of new policy directions, and into policy advice positions legitimated by the state. This took place in the context of increasing housing department legitimation of community sector interests in policy setting through consultative, advisory and, ultimately, corporatist structures.

Housing reform in NSW

The process of policy reform in housing moved through three phases. The early community activism provided a base of community support, and raised public awareness about some of the issues. The formation of the network of collaboration between political, bureaucratic and community sector policy activists was vital for achieving bureaucratic and political support for the reforms, allowing the development of specific programmes and policies, and for the negotiation of hurdles within the bureaucratic and political systems. Finally, the movement of activists into the Housing Commission consolidated the reforms, and replaced the dominant policy agendas of the 'old guard' with the reform agenda of the Minister and his 'new guard'.

The barricades

By the late 1970s, a strong and vocal housing reform movement was active in NSW, with links to housing activist groups in other States. The NSW housing reform movement was composed of a small cluster of lobby groups set up in the mid-1970s, of which the widest ranging was the State-wide group Shelter. The activities of these organisations primarily involved lobbying politicians at both State and federal government level, organising public protest, as well as some degree of local organising and information dissemination. Their concerns were about the loss of low cost inner city housing through gentrification, the scarcity and poor location of public housing, the rights of public and private tenants, and the lack of self-managed housing alternatives (such as housing co-operatives). Specific interest groups, such as women's refuges, were also active in housing reform, and ran campaigns about issues such as priority access to public housing, and longer term supported housing for victims of domestic violence.

The activists involved shared a common framework of analysis which encompassed strongly held values and beliefs about social justice and equity, community control, responsiveness to need, and active engagement in the policy process. These more general values underlay a series of analyses and criticisms of the government's housing policies and housing delivery which, in turn, drove a series of specific policy goals that the policy activists pursued.

With the exception of private tenancy issues, the NSW Housing Commission which later became the Department of Housing, had responsibility for all these areas of concern. The Commission became the main target of the groups agitating for change, and these lobby organisations were highly critical of the Commission's operations, the planning and development approaches of the State government, and the housing authority, and the way in which tenant and landlord relationships were regulated and conducted. These criticisms were based on activist beliefs that housing had a vital impact on people's wellbeing, and that it needed to be subject to the principles of equity, local control and sensitivity to needs being promoted elsewhere in social services.

Those involved in the reform movement shared a number of broad goals. They wanted to raise the political profile of social housing, increase the amount of quality public housing, and make better use of housing stock. This was reflected in lobby organisation demands on the Housing Commission to support 'public housing not welfare housing', build more public housing, make better use of vacant government property, and to cease building inner Sydney high rise complexes and 'broad acre' estates on the margins of Sydney.

They were intent on changing the way in which low income people accessed housing and the type of service they received as tenants, and to this end they demanded that the Housing Commission change its eligibility and priority access criteria, provide better legislation and support for private tenants, and provide better internal systems and participation for public tenants.

They wanted a housing system that would recognise and be more responsive to people's needs. This was reflected in their attempts to redefine homelessness and housing need, broadening it to include the support needs of people made homeless for reasons such as domestic violence, housing dislocation, psychiatric disability or other personal problems. It was also reflected in their call for increased control by housing consumers over their housing through the development of community housing alternatives, including housing co-operatives, rental housing associations and housing projects for those with special needs, such as women leaving refuges. At the height of their assault, they ran a campaign calling for the sacking of the then Minister for Housing, using the length of the public housing waiting lists as their primary criticism of his agency's performance.

The bureaucracy

At the time, the Housing Commission was an older style public service authority, constituted as a commission rather than a department, with a Board of Commissioners who directed the activities of the organisation through the management of a paid chairman. By the late 1970s, the Housing Commission had gained a reputation among those seeking change in housing policies as a conservative and unresponsive organisation. It was variously described by activists reflecting on the period as 'moribund', 'gummed up', 'back in the dark ages', insular and with little policy capacity.

The community activism in housing reform had very little impact on the commission. It remained predominantly resistant to any forces of change until the change of Minister in 1983. As one interview respondent commented, 'it really wasn't interested in doing anything other than building boxes and managing them on a rental basis'.

The structure of the commission, with its appointed Board, meant that the Minister did not have the sort of 'top-down' power that a

Minister might usually have. In order to counter this, and to build a strong policy development base, the Minister moved a number of bureaucratic positions out of the Housing Commission, and into his own office. This located both policy expertise and resources under his immediate control.

The new Minister found that, in order to bring about significant policy change, significant 'cultural' change was also going to be necessary. Among other strategies, he deliberately sought out people within the Housing Commission that he perceived to be progressive, and made contact with them. He moved to locate new people interested in the same reforms as himself in key positions within the Housing Commission. The purpose of this was to import particular points of view, as part of 'a very deliberate policy to drag in as many people as we could into the system who had the right attitudes' (interview), and to bring in skills from the community sector that he believed were lacking within the commission. As a consequence, he actively supported the development of new community programmes, and the employment of staff from outside the commission in these programme areas.

The Trojan horse: community housing programmes

Although the Housing Commission was not the only State government authority considered by many to be still in the 'dark ages', it contrasted markedly with departments like the Department of Youth and Community Services, which had opened up under the influence of public sector reforms at State government level. By the early 1980s, the Department of Youth and Community Services had a significant contingent of staff recruited from the community sector and local government, many of whom were committed to community development principles. A specialist unit with an explicit mandate to promote community development and investigate innovative service delivery had also been established.

The development of the first 'community' housing programme actually took place within the Department of Youth and Community Services. In 1981, an opportunity arose to make use of a federal government funding initiative to subsidise low income private renters and those in mortgage difficulties (the Mortgage and Rent Relief Scheme). NSW housing activists were opposed to this type of subsidising, as it was considered to be a short-term 'band aid' response to problems, and potentially inflationary in its impact on private rental charges.

Informal discussions between a bureaucrat in Youth and Community Services and community housing activists outside the bureaucracy resulted in a proposal that became the Community Tenancy Scheme. The Community Tenancy Scheme was a programme that funded community-based organisations to provide low rent housing, with a high degree of tenant participation in the management of the organisations.

When the new Minister took up the housing portfolio in 1983, he also took up the welfare portfolio, and the stewardship of the Department of Youth and Community Services. As part of his strategy to extend the activities of the Housing Commission, he moved the Community Tenancy Scheme across to the Housing Commission, where it joined an embryonic division of community programmes. As one former staff member put it, 'he was always very supportive of the scheme from the beginning because I think he saw it as an opportunity to rattle the bars in the Housing Commission a bit. He was using it as a way to infiltrate some people with progressive thinking into the organisation' (interview).

The Community Tenancy Scheme did indeed prove to be somewhat of a successful Trojan horse, importing the core staff that would expand the Community Programmes Division, and provide key personnel for a bureaucratic coup d'état. Over the next four years, a further seven programmes were added to this division, and its staffing complement rose to over sixty people, mostly employed from the community sector. More significantly, it was people from these areas who then rose quickly through the management ranks, aided by restructures, resignations of old guard senior managers, and the creation of new positions, to take effective control of the organisation. As his coup de grâce, and in order to move the impediments to effective Ministerial control, the Minister engineered a statutory restructure of the Housing Commission and, in 1986, it was replaced by the Department of Housing. By this time, people from the Community Programmes area occupied over one-third of the senior management positions in the organisation.

During this period, the housing authority reformed a number of its operational policies. Most notably, it expanded its eligibility criteria to include single people, and introduced a system for tenant involvement in decision and policy-making. It also introduced programmes and policies for a number of special needs groups. These included women, Aboriginal people, and people with disabilities. The range of services and programmes offered by the authority expanded dramatically, primarily through these specialist programmes for specific population groups, and a number of other 'community' programmes.

The new department was created with expanded functions, which included responsibility for other housing tenures (private purchase and rental). By 1987, it was providing funding to the key lobby groups that had previously been strong critics of the old Housing Commission. Groups like Shelter were funded to provide policy analysis and advice to the department. Others were funded to provide direct support to other housing organisations, or direct services to people needing assistance.

From the beginning of establishing the new community programmes, the policy activists, with the Minister's support, had also established 'Ministerial Advisory Committees' to guide policy formulation and implementation. These committees were primarily composed of community sector appointees, and representatives from the programme areas concerned. The development of the Ministerial Advisory Committees was a successful strategy for protecting programmes against the Housing Commission old guard, as these Committees had the power to bypass the commission senior management and advise the Minister directly. As the Minister gained more direct control over the commission, these committees remained as an accepted method of involving non-government stakeholders in the policy process. They functioned as formal 'policy networks', and were part of an increasingly corporatist culture of policy consultation and negotiation that was part of the reform movement, and of the style of Labor governments of the time.

From barricades to bureaucracy

The policy activists

There were a number of significant characteristics that the policy activists in the housing reform movement shared, and that formed a basis for the informal network between them. The information about their activities is based on interviews with a number of key players.

They were generally of the same 'generation', and had common experiences from their relationship to the social movements of the late 1960s and early 1970s, being in their early to mid-twenties at a time of immense social change. This is a key factor in the development of broad philosophies, ideals or critiques that individuals held. For many, this was reinforced by their experiences in the radical university environments of the early 1970s. Two-thirds were university students in the early 1970s (half of whom had graduated in social work). For some, their university education in social work developed quite specific critiques of the social welfare and related systems. For others, early Marxist or socialist influences developed critiques along similar lines.

A number had been influenced by direct experience in social services, primarily through student or paid involvement in welfare or accommodation services. Over two-thirds of these people cited this type of direct experience as significant in the development of their ideas, and in their coming into contact with other activists.

Their involvements had been concentrated, geographically, in the inner city suburbs of Sydney, where they had been located in organisations that had close working relationships. As a consequence, many of the key players came into contact with one another through their student placement or work activities. Over time, they became increasingly interlinked, activating network relationships based on common policy interests and ideological frameworks. They mostly all knew each other, were aware of joining a network of sorts, and had a sense of personal connectedness. This was expressed most often as being a combination of shared political beliefs, shared commitment to action, and, in the case of particularly close sets of connections between subgroups within the network, personal friendships and relationships.

As the network grew, often through the activity of key mentors, these activists influenced and reinforced one another's thinking, developing and extending their own ideas through their activities. As a group, these policy activists had a coherent, and shared set of beliefs and ideals. This set of beliefs, and the shared value system that accompanied them, formed the basis of this informal networking, as well as the basis of the specific policy critiques that they developed in the course of their interaction with one another. The analysis in which they engaged led to the development of specific policy agendas, and fuelled a shared vision and goals for policy reform, which both drove their activism, and provided further basis for their connection to one another. The connection and interaction between people also reinforced commitment and created the type of supportive environment to enable action to occur. As the network grew and consolidated over the mid-1980s, the numbers of community activists with direct access to the policy process increased, as many of them moved into the bureaucracy, and as they were joined in the policy network by policy advisers to the new Minister for Housing.

The activist identity

One of the important features of the policy activists in this study is that, over time, most of them moved the location of their activism from the community sector into the housing bureaucracy. Although this came to constitute a political coup with regard to the Housing Commission, this was not a planned outcome. The policy activists who entered the bureaucracy from the community sector never thought that they could take on the bureaucracy in the way that they did. They still thought of themselves as community activists, and as 'irritants on the side' rather than as the potential new order.

Most of them entered the bureaucracy to implement and protect programmes for which they had successfully negotiated approval. A number of those interviewed conveyed a sense of 'going in' to the bureaucracy, as if on a secret mission. This move fitted well with the agenda of the new Minister, and his support allowed a process of infiltration to occur through the selection of people with the 'right ideas' that would assist the process of changing the culture of the Housing Commission.

The experience of the policy activists in this study, and that of femocrats before them, indicates that a move of institutional location, from the community to the public sector, is invested with particular meanings and significance. People undertaking this move had cause to consider their roles and identities, and to worry about losing a particular type of identity as an activist. For many, this move represented becoming 'the enemy' because of community sector workers' mistrust of both bureaucrats and the bureaucracy (Dowse 1984).

They not only moved into an environment that they distrusted, but one that was hostile to them and their agenda. Initially, many of them coped with this shift by clinging to their community sector activist identity, and developing a strong subculture within the Housing Commission. The staff in this area were recognised as being culturally different by the old guard of the commission, and were known disparagingly as the 'sandshoe brigade', in reference to their tendency to dress a little more casually than the traditional public service grey suit.

They also worked to retain their links with the community sector, by remaining involved with lobby groups, and by building close and interdependent relationships with the organisations that they funded. Because they had an understanding of the community sector perspective and experience, they were able to develop the programmes in a way that fitted the expectations of those groups. They could offer some translation of the bureaucracy to their community sector colleagues. As one respondent put it, 'someone who's been in both places can maybe see where people are coming from' (interview). The level of credibility and trust that they initially established meant that they received very little criticism in the early days from community sector people.

The role of the network in this move was crucial, as it gave people links to trusted bureaucrats prior to moving into the bureaucracy. The first few to go in provided a safety net for those who followed. They were able to encourage others to follow them by offering them a picture of the possibilities of activism within the Housing Commission. They also created a relatively protected area within the Community Programmes Division which sustained them in the early phases of their bureaucratic life.

Through the policy activism looking glass

Actors, strategies and the policy process

I have used the concept of policy activism to look at particular aspects of policy reform that I believe are not easily visible to the analyst because they occur informally, and in private arenas. These are aspects of the policy reform process that are not documented, or captured in formal structures or negotiations. Because they belong to the aspirations of individuals and their discussions with one another, they do not appear in the public realm. Policy activism throws the spotlight on aspects such as the goals and strategies of policy actors, the interaction between them and their relationship to the policy process.

The housing policy activists had a clear policy agenda and specific goals for reform in public housing policy which they pursued vigorously. They sought to influence and change this policy area from an explicit and articulated normative base which gave impetus to their mission. Strategically, they joined the forces of three powerful groupings, 'covering all the bases' of community, bureaucracy and political arenas. They used the bureaucracy to increase their collective access to policy formulation, political connections to access decision-making processes, and the community sector organisations and groups to ensure support and credibility for the reforms.

By joining together across a traditional divide between the community and governmental sections, the policy activists not only created a powerful strategic base, but they also moved beyond being a simple policy 'opposition', and expanded their policy thinking into planning specific feasible policy responses. These links between the activists provided a fertile ground for the development of policy agendas, and for the planning of policy responses to the problems that the activists believed existed. This gave the activists the opportunity to intervene in policy-making at the point of the setting of the policy agenda, rather than at the later phase of debating specific policy decisions. The policy activist network engaged with policy reform at the point of shaping the way in which the policy problem, and thus its solution, was being constructed (Schulman 1988, pp. 264–9).

Although many of the policy activists were active in lobby groups, and therefore in direct campaigns against the Housing Commission, they also had access either directly, or indirectly to the policy process. Initially, those with direct access were the bureaucrats already working in other areas of the state bureaucracy. The community activists had a form of indirect access through the various close, networked relationships with those within the bureaucracy. Collectively they forged access to the policy process at an informal level of policy-making which preceded the formal, public policy-making process. Non-state parties operating in this informal zone are no longer 'outside' the formal policy process, but neither are they fully incorporated and included. The policy activists later institutionalised this access, and brought the community sector within the formal policy process, with a series of committees and advisory bodies that gave community sector organisations a seat at the policy table.

Activism on the quiet—informal policy networks

The focus on policy activists also highlights the informal policy network that was created between them. This network is one of the most significant features of this case study as it provided a link between those policy actors who are traditionally the carriers of 'top-down' policy action and those who are usually associated with 'bottom-up' forces. In joining and developing a network of policy activists, policy actors stepped outside the confinement of the roles usually associated with 'bureaucrat' and 'community activist'. In this case study, I emphasise the importance of the normative commitments of bureaucrats and politicians as policy actors, and the impact of their links with outside activists. Likewise, I emphasise the access that the community activists had to the policy process as collaborators with bureaucrats and politicians.

This approach provides a view of policy reform processes that is similar to other syntheses of top-down and bottom-up such as Sabatier's (1986), but pays more attention to the location of activism as being in either the community or public sector. Although housing policy activists operated *across* the public and community sectors, their identification with the community sector, and their mistrust of the public sector is significant in terms of how they constructed their own identities as activists.

The development of structures typical of formal policy networks in the housing reform process (the Ministerial Advisory Committees) indicates that both formal and informal policy networks may operate in tandem. The formal policy network operated according to the rules of positional bargaining, with individuals acting as representatives of government and non-government stakeholders. Even though they were often the same set of actors as in the formal networks, the informal network operated on collaborative interaction, and individuals acted only for themselves and their cause. Again, formal policy network structures are often documented, while the informal policy networks require specific research to discover.

Key to the collaborative nature of the informal network is the shared activism that underlies it, and the connection of all the policy activists to a common set of beliefs and reform goals. For such activism to occur, seeking significant reform in a policy area, it must be attached to a reform movement of some sort. Using the housing reform case study, it is possible to argue that there are identifiable links between a social movement, as conceptualised by Melucci (1988), and an informal policy network. Indeed, that an informal policy network is one of the ways that the goals of social movements are pursued.

Melucci (1988, 1989) is critical of discussing social movements only in terms of visible mobilisation. He argues that a social movement remains alive in 'networks submerged in everyday life', by which he means the connections between people that are related to their shared values and identities (1988, p. 248). The activity of the policy activists' network shows an alternative form of collective action to the mobilisation usually associated with social movements. Unlike interest group activity, or massed demonstrations, it takes place in stealth, and with little obvious mobilisation. People do not gather in noticeable groups, but, linked across the network, activate collective responses 'on the quiet'.

Out of the woodwork

As noted earlier, there are two features which I believe differentiate policy activists from other types of policy reformers. The first is their activism, in which they are driven by their values and critique of existing policy to engage in reform activities. By definition they work against a dominant agenda. The second feature is their engagement in the policy process at an informal level, but within the process rather than operating from the outside. If a policy activist is a bureaucrat they will be a subversive, which will differentiate them from other bureaucrats. If they are involved in the community sector, they will have a form of access to the policy process which will differentiate them from other community sector activists. Given their focus on the reform goals, rather than the sector for which they work, they will work across sectors, and be linked to one another through networks.

The network formed by policy activists in the housing policy case study linked community sector activists with 'woodwork' activists within the bureaucracy. As the reform movement proceeded, increasing numbers of activists moved into the bureaucracy to join them. The network of activists lay beneath the surface of the bureaucracy, invisible but nibbling away at the structure that supported the old policy agenda. When this structure finally gave way, they moved out of the woodwork, took command of the bureaucracy, and opened it up to further reform. As members of a reform movement, the housing policy activists successfully challenged the dominant policy agenda and replaced it with their own policy agenda.

As they became the dominant policy force, there were certain consequences for their identities as activists. Actors both shape, and are shaped by, their organisations. In this case, as they were busy shaping programmes, policies, and increasingly, the institution of the Housing Commission, they worked within the confines of a bureaucracy and found themselves becoming increasingly conformist with regard to the requirements of public sector management. Although these policy activists operated within democratic principles of participation, and even introduced formal structures for the participation of non-State parties, once authority over the policy process was established, they risked becoming a form of policy elite. A number of those in the bureaucracy found it necessary to 'manage' the participation of other parties as they implemented their reform agenda, rather than allowing any significant contestability of the new policy agenda to occur. Once out of the woodwork, it was not long before they ceased to be policy activists, and became the guardians of the new dominant agenda.

Notes

Chapter 1

1 The National Schools Network originated out of an earlier National Project for Quality Teaching and Learning established in 1991, and which had a tripartite structure of inclusion of the (Labor-led) Commonwealth government, the State and Territory governments and non-government school authorities, the teacher unions and the Australian Council of Trade Unions. The 1993 Teaching Accord, signed between the Commonwealth government and the education unions, opened up this Labor style corporatism to include the teacher education faculties in universities (Yeatman and Sachs 1995, pp. 15–16). In 1997 the Commonwealth government stopped funding the network and thereby withdrew support.

2 Heclo (1978, pp. 102–3, p. 105, p. 108) uses the term policy activist, and is one of the few analysts of policy to do so. However, his reference is to those who participate in a highly professionalised and relatively sequestered world of policy-oriented issue networks in the American capital, Washington.

Chapter 2

1 'The test of a "good" policy is typically that various analysts find themselves agreeing on a policy (without their agreeing that it is the most appropriate means to an agreed objective)' (Lindblom 1959, p. 81). In making this claim, Lindblom has in mind the policy world—politicians, senior officials, ministerial advisers—rather than a general claim

234

about the democratic process. A successful policy is one which commands consensus among policy makers and interest groups. His discussion of how this policy world operates is expanded in Lindblom (1965).

Chapter 3

1 Our initial contact with the National Office of Overseas Skills Recognition arose from the fact that some of their senior officials reacted positively to some of our publications on topics relevant to their work.
2 The overarching concern of Australia's national training reform agenda is to improve the nation's skill formation processes. Major features of this reform include: training which integrates industry, enterprise and individual needs and which supports lifelong learning; competency-based training, achieving national industry and enterprise standards; more flexible pathways and delivery; increased access and improved outcomes for groups of people who have missed out on training opportunities in the past; complementary roles for on and off-the-job training; nationally recognised qualifications which are portable across industries and States and Territories; and a broader range of providers who co-operate and compete to meet national and international training demands.
3 For details of a typical standards development process see Ash, Gonczi and Hager 1992.
4 NOOSR surveyed 242 people involved in the competency standards projects for twenty professions. The response rate was 55 per cent. For each use of competency standards, respondents selected from 'no', 'don't know', 'probably' and 'yes'. The figures in Table 3.1 represent only the 'yes' responses.

Chapter 4

1 The Labor Women's Committee was an official part of the structure of the ALP. Originally known as the Labor Women's Central Organising Committee, it was formed in 1904 and abolished in 1986.

Chapter 6

1 I developed this notion in discussion with Anna Yeatman during the preparation of this chapter. It derives in part from Ted Marmor's analysis of the 'imbalanced political markets' (Marmor and Marone 1980, p. 127) and Palmer and Short's (1994, p. 47) notion of the 'imbalanced market for health care policies'.
2 Interest groups, or stakeholders, have a stake in the outcome of a policy; that is, they stand to gain or lose in some way from implementation of the policy.

3 This term derives from Sidney Sax's (1984) excellent book, *A Strife of Interests: Politics and Policies in Australian Health Services.*

4 In the period after 1987, fiscal policy was tightened, and the public policy agenda shifted to the notion of 'restraint with equity'. During this period, the real power in government was with the Expenditure Review Committee, and the emphasis in social policy shifted from the notion of the 'social wage' to 'social justice' (Howe 1996).

5 For example, Ann Kern, the Deputy Secretary of Health, and a prominent women's health activist, was a member of the Steering Committee which oversaw establishment of the CHF.

6 Congress was originally funded with less than $20 000 from the Department of Aboriginal Affairs in 1973. It was not started as a health service, but as a political advocacy organisation. In 1974–75 Trevor Cutter arrived in Alice Springs, and was employed by Congress to develop a health service. One of the earliest programs was a shelter program, within which tents were allocated to people for a nominal rental.

7 See Short (1997) for a closer examination of this review.

8 I am grateful to Paul Dugdale, who contributed this insight during a workshop convened by the editor to assist with the preparation of this edited collection

9 In suggesting these conclusions I am drawing on Hester Eisenstein's (1996) gripping analysis of the rise of the contemporary women's liberation movement in Australia and its remarkable political alliance with the Whitlam Labor government, an historical conjuncture which produced the 'femocrats'.

10 Glyn Davis' (1996b, p. 16) useful report on consultation and public participation, prepared for the OECD, indicates, '. . . Decisions on when to seek public participation in decisions are likely to emerge from dialogue between the technical requirements of officials and the political needs of elected officials'. This government-based perspective contrasts somewhat with Hilary Wainwright's (1994) New Left argument that social movements, not governments, seek democratisation and access. I think this case study provides evidence of an alliance of interests between the Hawke government, a reformist Minister, progressive public servants and community activists.

Chapter 7

1 The formation of the Unified National System involved the creation of a number of new universities. These were formed from amalgamations of former Colleges of Advanced Education and Institutes of Technology. Both the University of Western Sydney and the University of Technology, Sydney were formed in this way. As well as the creation of new universities, the Unified National System involved a significant expansion of many of the existing universities, as they incorporated former Colleges and Institutes. The new universities are sometimes collectively referred to as the post-1987 universities, that is, post the announcement of the Commonwealth government's plans for the Unified National System.

Chapter 8

1   The term 'gay lobby' has been invoked since the earliest days of the epidemic to characterise the success of the gay community, particularly when other interest groups failed to get their way at State and Commonwealth policy levels. The mass media also find the term useful, particularly when debates on other diseases, for example breast cancer, are used to question HIV/AIDS funding levels. The term is clearly pejorative, and is always intended to involve 'improper' influence, unexplainable success, or to suggest unfair advantage.

2   As of 31 December 1996, 5943 (84 per cent) of Australian AIDS cases cumulatively are attributed to male-to-male sexual transmission of HIV, and this category of transmission accounts for 4343 (85 per cent) of deaths. In all, 10 932 (80 per cent) of cumulative diagnoses of HIV infection in Australia are attributed to male-to-male sexual transmission of HIV (NCHECR 1997).

3   See King (1993) for an excellent account of the British gay communities and HIV/AIDS politics.

4   It should also be noted that Australia is (now) one of the few places where people living with HIV or AIDS are able to be open about their infection and can readily access available treatments (something that the gay communities were central to achieving).

5   Note that the overall number of infections to date attributed directly or indirectly to drug injection is 1093 or 8 per cent of HIV infections. Furthermore, it is likely that some of these, especially those reported in the tense atmosphere surrounding HIV/AIDS in the late 1980s, might actually be cases of (homo)sexual transmission, self-attributed to drug injection because of the stigma attached to homosexuality. Indeed, it must also be noted that there are 4347 and 142 cases of HIV infection in men and women respectively that have never been categorised (NCHECR 1997).

6   Before the reader rushes to declaim about the 'most' in this sentence not being 'all' in the face of a such a threat to health, think about drink-driving and tobacco-smoking, and note that this 'most' is a remarkable achievement. However, recent research reports have shown for the first time in Australia a worrying rise in unprotected anal intercourse with casual partners (*Sydney Star Observer* 1997b). It is too early to assess the causes or the net effect of these findings on potential new HIV transmissions.

Chapter 9

1   I acknowledge with thanks the contributions of housing co-operative members and other 'activists' who have made time for interviews and for speaking with me on this subject. In particular I wish to thank Jyotsana Hill for her support and contribution in finding and introducing me to a wide range of Bowden–Brompton community members. Where

    particular activists are named in this chapter, pseudonyms rather than real names have been used.

2   The term may be somewhat confusing since there are currently two forms of community housing in Australia: housing co-operatives and housing associations. The Hindmarsh Housing Co-operative which started life as the Hindmarsh Housing Association was, and is, what is currently defined as a housing co-operative.

3   Mick (not his real name) is recognised by all those I interviewed as the primary strategist, organiser and petitioner. He articulated the issues clearly, publicly and often had little respect for the professionals who came into the area as students/workers and who were not living in the area. He is universally acknowledged as being key to the successful changes that were brought about to the Bowden–Brompton area, particularly as I have described here for stage one. However, he did continue to be active in the ASC site development. He did not wish to be interviewed and his privacy is respected. Suffice to say that all of those who have to do with this renewal process see him as the original and key driver.

4   In 1996 CHASSA undertook a study of good practices in SA Housing Cooperatives. It became clear that the difficulty in using private sector based models for defining and describing 'best practice' was based in the limited model inherent to a provider/customer relationship. Because of the joint responsibility for asset maintenance and financial management a more appropriate description for the relationship between governments and housing co-operative members was the term coproduction.

Chapter 10

1   Interview material referred to in this chapter was collected as part of research for a doctoral thesis, 'Policy Activists and the Housing Reform Movement in New South Wales', submitted in Sociology at Macquarie University, 1998.

Bibliography

Alaba, R. 1994, *Inside Bureaucratic Power: The Wilenski Review of NSW Government*, Hale & Iremonger, New South Wales

Alford, R. R. 1975, *Health Care Politics: Ideological and Interest Group Barriers to Reform*, The University of Chicago Press, Chicago

Alford, R. R. and Friedland, R. 1985, *Powers of Theory: Capitalism, the State and Democracy*, Cambridge University Press, Cambridge

Altman, D. 1992, 'The most political of diseases', *AIDS in Australia*, eds E. Timewell, V. Minichiello and D. Plummer, Prentice Hall, Sydney

Anderson, D., Johnson, R. and Milligan, B. 1996, 'Performance-Based Funding of Universities', Commissioned Report No. 51, Australian Government Publishing Service, Canberra

Anderson, P. 1984, *Give Them a House and They Take a Street,* video

Anstie, R., Gregory, R.G., Dowrick, S. and Pincus, J.J. 1988, *Government Spending on Work-Related Child Care: Some Economic Issues*, Centre for Economic Policy Research, Australian National University, Canberra

Arendt, H. 1958, *The Human Condition*, Chicago University Press, Chicago

Ariss, R.M. 1998, *Against Death: The Practice of Living with HIV/AIDS*, Gordon and Breach, Newark NJ

Ariss, R., Carrigan, T. and Dowsett, G. 1992, 'Sexual identities of HIV positive men: Some implications for AIDS service organisations', *National AIDS Bulletin*, vol. 6, no. 7, pp. 20–4

Armytage, L., Roper, C. and Vignaendra, S. 1995, *A Review of Aspects of the Specialist Accreditation Programme of the Law Society of New South Wales*, Centre for Legal Education, Sydney

Ash, S., Gonczi, A. and Hager, P. 1992, 'Combining Research Methodologies to Develop Competency-Based Standards for Dietitians: A Case Study for the Professions', Research Paper No. 6, National Office of Overseas Skills Recognition, Department of Education, Employment and Training, Australian Government Publishing Service, Canberra

239

Association of Child Care Centres of NSW 1981, 'Discrimination and mismanagement of existing child care funding', *National Journal of Child Care*, vol. 3, no. 3, pp. 7–9

Atkinson, M.M. and Coleman, W.D. 1992, 'Policy networks, policy communities and the problems of governance', *Governance: An International Journal of Policy and Administration*, vol. 5, no. 2, pp. 154–80

Australian Broadcasting Corporation 1996, 'Submission: Review of the Role and Functions of the ABC', ABC, Sydney, September

Australian Bureau of Statistics 1993, 'Australian Standard Research Classification', Catalogue No. 1297.0, Australian Government Publishing Service, Canberra

——1996, 'Research and Experimental Development, All-Sector Summary 1994–1995', Catalogue No. 8112.0, Australian Government Publishing Service, Canberra

Australian Federation of Child Care Associations 1981, 'Submission to Senator F. M. Chaney', reprinted in *National Journal of Child Care*, vol. 3, no. 2, pp. 25–7

Australian Labor Party 1988, *Platform, Resolutions and Rules 1988*, ALP, Canberra

Australian Law Reform Commission 1994, *Child Care for Kids*, ALRC, Canberra

Australian Market Research 1986, *A Study to Identify the Information Needs and Networks of Low Income Families*, AMR, Canberra

Ball, S. 1993, 'What is policy? Texts, trajectories and toolboxes', *Discourse*, vol. 13, no. 2, pp. 10–18

Ball, S.J. 1994, *Education Reform: A Critical and Post-Structural Approach*, Open University Press, Buckingham

Ballard, J. 1989, 'The politics of AIDS', in *The Politics of Health: The Australian Experience*, ed. H. Gardner, Churchill Livingstone, Melbourne

——1998, 'The constitution of AIDS in Australia: Taking government at a distance seriously', in *Governing Australia*, eds B. Hindess and M. Dean, Cambridge University Press, Melbourne

Banks, G., Owens, H. and Hall, P. 1995, 'Research and Development, Volume 1: The Report', Industry Commission Report No. 44, Australian Government Publishing Service, Canberra

Bersani, L. 1988, 'Is the rectum a grave?', in *AIDS: Cultural Analysis/Cultural Activism*, ed. D. Crimp, MIT Press, Cambridge MA

Better Health Commission 1986, 'Looking Forward to Better Health', Vol. 1, Final Report, Australian Government Publishing Service, Canberra

Boreham, P. 1990, 'Corporatism', in *Hawke and Australian Public Policy: Consensus and Restructuring*, eds C. Jennett and R. Stewart, Macmillan, Melbourne

Boston, J. (ed.) 1995, *The State Under Contract*, Bridget Williams Books, Wellington

Brennan, D. 1994, *The Politics of Australian Child Care: From Philanthropy to Feminism*, Cambridge University Press, Cambridge

Brennan, M. 1993, 'Excellence and relevance—Two sides of the same coin', in *Research Grant Management and Funding, Symposium Proceedings*, eds F.Q. Wood and V.L. Meek, Australian Government Publishing Service, Canberra

Burke, P. 1991, 'Tacitism, scepticism and reason of state', in *The Cambridge History of Political Thought*, ed. J.H. Burns, Cambridge University Press, Cambridge

Callen, M. 1983, *How to Have Sex in an Epidemic*, News from the Front Publications, New York

Candy, P.C., Crebert, G. and O'Leary, J. 1994, *Developing Lifelong Learners Through Undergraduate Education*, National Board of Employment, Education and Training, Canberra

Cawson, A. 1985, 'Varieties of corporatism: The importance of the meso level of interest mediation', in *Organised Interests and the State: Studies in Meso-Corporatism*, ed. A. Cawson, Sage, London

Central Sydney Health Service 1991, *Strategic Plan. Working Together: Better Services For Better Health*, Central Sydney Health Service, Sydney

Clarke, T. 1997, *Silent Coup: Confronting the Big Business Takeover of Canada*, Canadian Centre for Policy Alternatives, Ontario

Collins, M. 1991, *Adult Education as Vocation*, Routledge, London

Commonwealth of Australia 1989, 'National HIV/AIDS Strategy. A Policy Information Paper', Australian Government Publishing Service, Canberra

——1993, 'The National HIV/AIDS Strategy, 1993–94 to 1995–96', Australian Government Publishing Service, Canberra

——1996, 'Partnership in Practice: National HIV/AIDS Strategy 1996–97 to 1998–99', Australian Government Publishing Service, Canberra

Commonwealth Department of Community Services and Health 1989, 'Management Plan 1988–89', CDCSH, Canberra

Commonwealth Department of Health 1985, 'The Review of Community Participation in the Commonwealth Department of Health: The Swinging Door', Australian Government Publishing Service, Canberra

Commonwealth Department of Health, Housing and Community Services 1991, 'Annual Report, 1990–1991', Australian Government Publishing Service, Canberra

Commonwealth Department of Human Services and Health 1994, 'Annual Report 1993–94', Australian Government Publishing Service, Canberra

Community Housing Assistance Service of South Australia 1996, *The Chicken or the Egg: Good Practices in South Australian Housing Cooperatives*, Community Housing Assistance Service of South Australia, Adelaide

Conigrave, T. 1995, *Holding the Man*, McPhee Gribble, Ringwood Vic.

Conley, M. 1992, 'Participation and advocacy by consumer and advocacy groups in the arena of national health policy and decision-making, and the impact of that activity on health promotion', Background paper prepared for the National Health Strategy, Commonwealth Department of Health, Housing and Community Services

Consumers' Health Forum of Australia 1992, 'Constitution of the Consumers' Health Forum of Australia Incorporated', CHFA, Canberra

——1996, 'Annual Report 1995–1996', CHFA, Canberra

Cox, E. 1995, *A Truly Civil Society*, Australian Broadcasting Corporation, Sydney

Davis, G. 1988, *Breaking Up the ABC*, Allen & Unwin, Sydney

——1990, 'Policy from the margins', *Culture and Policy*, vol. 1, no. 2, pp. 13-19

——1991, *Different Strokes: Public Broadcasting in America and Australia*, Joan Shorenstein Barone Center for Press, Politics and Public Policy, Kennedy School of Government, Harvard University

——1996a, 'Which agenda for the ABC?', *Communications Update*, September, no. 124, pp. 10–12

——1996b, 'Consultation, Public Participation, and the Integration of Multiple Interests into Policy-Making', Report prepared for the Organisation for Economic Co-operation and Development, Paris, May

Davis, G. and Gardner, M. 1995, 'Who signs the contract? Applying agency theory to politicians', in *The State Under Contract*, ed. J. Boston, Bridget Williams Books, Wellington

Dawkins, J. 1988, *Higher Education, A Policy Statement*, Australian Government Publishing Service, Canberra

——1989, *Research for Australia: Higher Education's Contribution*, Australian Government Publishing Service, Canberra

Deane, E., Johnson, L., Jones, G. and Lengkeek, N. 1996, *Women, Research and Research Productivity in the Post-1987 Universities: Opportunities and Constraints*, Australian Government Publishing Service, Canberra

Deleuze, G. 1988, *Spinoza: Practical Philosophy*, City Light Books, San Francisco

Department of Employment, Education and Training 1993, 'National Report on Australia's Higher Education Sector', Australian Government Publishing Service, Canberra

Department of Employment, Education, Training and Youth Affairs 1995, 'Research Income and Higher Degree Research', Higher Education Division, Australian Government Publishing Service, Canberra

——1996a, '1997 Key Competencies: For Work, Education and Life', Report on the Outcomes of the Key Competencies Pilot Phase, DEETYA, Canberra, December

——1996b, '1997 Higher Education Financial and Publications Research Data Collection Guidelines', Higher Education Division, DEETYA, Canberra, December

——1997, 'The Composite Index: Allocation of the Research Quantum of Australian Universities', email communication from the Research Branch, Canberra

Department of Environment and Planning 1984, *Bowden, Brompton, Ridleyton: A Draft Strategy Plan*, Department of Environment and Planning, Adelaide

Department of Health and Family Services 1993, *Census of Child Care Services*, DHFS, Canberra

Dowse, S. 1984, 'The bureaucrat as usurer', in *Unfinished Business,* ed. D. Broom, George Allen & Unwin, North Sydney

——1988, 'The women's movement's fandango with the state: The movement's role in public policy since 1972', in *Women, Social Welfare and the State,* 2nd edn, eds C.V. Baldock and B. Cass, Allen & Unwin, Sydney

Dowsett, G. W. 1992, 'Reaching men who have sex with men in Australia. An overview of AIDS education: community intervention and community attachment strategies', *Australian Journal of Social Issues*, vol. 25, no. 3, pp. 186–98

——1996a, 'Perspectives in Australian HIV/AIDS health promotion', in *NSW HIV/AIDS Health Promotion Conference: Keynote Addresses, Selected Papers and Future Directions*, comp. NSW AIDS/Infectious Diseases Branch, NSW Health Publication (AIDS) 96–0067, Sydney

——1996b, *Practicing Desire: Homosexual Sex in the Era of AIDS*, Stanford University Press, Stanford CA

——1998, 'Governing Queens: Gay communities and the state in contemporary Australia', in *Governing Australia*, eds M. Dean and B. Hindess, Cambridge University Press, Melbourne

Duckett, S. 1984, 'Structural interests and Australian health policy', *Social Science and Medicine*, vol. 18, no. 11, pp. 959–66

Duffin, R. 1997, 'Don't mourn, agitate', *Sydney Star Observer*, no. 346, March 20, pp. 6–7

Dugdale, P. 1991, 'The management of consumer consultation', *Australian Journal of Public Administration*, vol. 50, no. 1, pp. 17–22

——1992, 'Public management in the welfare state: Managerialism and consumer advocacy in Australia during the 1980s', MA thesis, Australian National University, Canberra

Durkheim, E. 1961, *Moral Education: A Study in the Theory and Application of the Sociology of Education*, Free Press, New York

——1965, *The Division of Labor in Society*, Free Press, New York

Economic Planning and Advisory Council 1996, *Future Child Care Provision in Australia*, EPAC, Canberra

Eisenstein, H. 1996, *Inside Agitators: Australian Femocrats and the State*, Allen & Unwin, Sydney

Elliott, G. 1982, 'The social policy of the New Right', in *Australia and the New Right*, ed. M. Sawer, Allen & Unwin, Sydney

Fairclough, N. 1996a, 'Forword', in *Language, Bureaucracy and Social Control*, eds S. Sarangi and S. Slembrouck, Longman, London

——1996b, 'Technologisation of discourse', in *Texts and Practices: Readings in Critical Discourse Analysis,* eds C.R. Caldas-Coulthard and M. Coulthard, Routledge, London

Feachem, R.G.A. 1995, *Valuing the past . . . investing in the future. Evaluation of the National HIV/AIDS Strategy 1993–94 to 1995–96*, Australian Government Publishing Service, Canberra

Federal Women's Labor Conference 1973, Minutes, Federal Women's Labor Conference, Canberra, personal papers of Elizabeth Reid

Ferrer, E. 1993, 'Resource allocation models in health: Implications for the provision of services to people from non-English speaking backgrounds', paper delivered at the Health for Multicultural Australia National Conference, Sydney

Flynn, R. 1992, *Structures of Control in Health Management*, Routledge, London

Foucault, M. 1972, *The Archaeology of Knowledge and the Discourse on Language*, Pantheon, New York

——1977, *The Archaeology of Knowledge*, Tavistock, London
——1978, *The History of Sexuality, Volume 1—An Introduction*, trans. R. Hurley, Penguin, Harmondsworth
——1983, 'Preface', in *Anti-Oedipus: Capitalism and Schizophrenia*, eds G. Deleuze and F. Guattari, University of Minnesota Press, Minneapolis
——1994, 'Pour une morale de l'inconfort', in *Dits et ecrits*, Vol. 3, Gallimard, Paris
Franzway, S., Court, D. and Connell, R. W. 1989, *Staking a Claim: Feminism, Bureaucracy and the State*, Allen & Unwin, Sydney
Freeman, J. 1975, *The Politics of Women's Liberation*, David McKay Company, New York
French, R. and Duffin, R. 1986, *Mossies Could Spread AIDS: An Annotated List of Media References to AIDS 1981–1985*, Gay History Project, Sydney
Frey, D. 1986, *Survey of Sole Parent Pensioners' Workforce Barriers*, Social Security Review, Canberra
Gillespie, J. 1991, *The Price of Health: Australian Governments and Medical Politics 1910–1960*, Cambridge University Press, Melbourne
Golden, O. 1990, 'Innovation in public sector programmes: The implications of innovation by "groping along"', *Journal of Policy Analysis and Management*, vol. 9, no. 2, pp. 219–48
Gonczi, A., Hager, P. and Athanasou, J. 1993, 'The Development of Competency-Based Assessment Strategies for the Professions', Research Paper No. 8, National Office of Overseas Skills Recognition, Department of Employment, Education and Training, Australian Government Publishing Service, Canberra
Gonczi, A., Hager, P. and Oliver, L. 1990, 'Establishing Competency-Based Standards in the Professions', Research Paper No. 1, National Office of Overseas Skills Recognition, Department of Employment, Education and Training, Australian Government Publishing Service, Canberra
Gonczi, A., Hager, P. and Palmer, C. 1994, 'Performance-based assessment and the NSW Law Society Specialist Accreditation Programme', *Journal of Professional Legal Education*, vol. 12, no. 2, pp. 135–48
Gott, T. (ed.) 1994, *Don't Leave Me This Way: Art in the Age of AIDS*, National Gallery of Australia, Canberra
Gray, G. 1996, 'Reform and reaction in Australian health policy', *Journal of Health Politics, Policy and Law*, vol. 21, no. 3, pp. 587–615
Green, N.E., Herndon, J.H. and Farmer, J.A. 1990, 'A clinical curriculum for orthapaedic surgery residency programmes', mimeo available from the authors at University of Technology, Sydney
Hacking, I. 1982, 'Biopower and the avalanche of printed numbers', *Humanities in Society*, vol. 5, nos. 3–4, pp. 279–95
Hager, P. 1994, 'Is there a cogent philosophical argument against competency standards?', *Australian Journal of Education*, vol. 38, no. 1, pp. 3–18
Hager, P. and Butler, J. 1996, 'Two models of educational assessment', *Assessment and Evaluation in Higher Education*, vol. 21, no. 4, pp. 367–78
Hager, P. and Gonczi, A. 1991, 'Competency-based standards: A boon for

continuing professional education?', *Studies in Continuing Education*, vol. 13, no. 1, pp. 24–40

Halperin, D. 1990, *One Hundred Years of Homosexuality, and Other Essays on Greek Love*, Routledge, New York and London

Heclo, H. 1978, 'Issue networks and the executive establishment', in *The New American Political System*, ed. A. King, American Enterprise Institute, Washington

Heywood, L., Gonczi, A. and Hager, P. 1992, 'A Guide to Development of Competency Standards for Professions', Research Paper No. 7, National Office of Overseas Skills Recognition, Department of Employment, Education and Training, Australian Government Publishing Service, Canberra

Home and Community Care Review Working Group 1989, 'First Triennial Review of the Home and Community Care Programme', Final report, Australian Government Publishing Services, Canberra, December

Horne, D. 1997, 'Learning curbs', *The Australian*, 19–20 April, p. 28

Horton, M. 1993, 'Homosexually active men and the evolving global epidemic of HIV', plenary presentation to IX International Conference on AIDS, Berlin, 6–11 June

Horton, M. and Aggleton, P. 1989, 'Perverts, inverts and experts: The cultural production of an AIDS research paradigm', in *AIDS: Social Representations, Social Practices*, eds P. Aggleton, G. Hart and P. Davies, Falmer Press, London

House of Representatives Standing Committee on Community Affairs 1991, *You Have Your Moments: A Report on Funding of Peak Health and Community Organisations*, Australian Government Publishing Service, Canberra

Howe, B. 1996, 'Citizens in the Republic', paper presented to Religion and Society conference, University of Sydney, November

Hughes, R. 1987, *The Fatal Shore*, Collins Harvill, London

Hunter, I. 1994, *Rethinking the School*, Allen & Unwin, St Leonards

Inglis, K. S. 1983, *This is the ABC*, Melbourne University Press, Melbourne

Jackson, T. 1990, 'Review of *Health Care and Public Policy: An Australian Analysis* by G. R. Palmer and S.D. Short', *Journal of Health Politics, Policy and Law*, vol. 15, no. 3, pp. 677–9

Jacobs, M. 1994, 'Sustainability and community', paper presented to the Hobart Convention

Johns, B. 1997, 'ABC response to the Mansfield Report', ABC press release, Sydney, 24 January

Johnston, B. 1997, 'Number and value', paper presented at What Counts as Research Seminar, Faculty of Education, University of Technology, Sydney, 14 March

Keating, M. 1988, 'Managing for results: The challenge for Finance and agencies', *Canberra Bulletin of Public Administration*, May, No. 54, pp. 73–80

King, E. 1993, *Safety in Numbers*, Cassell, London

Kingdom, J. 1995, *Agendas, Alternatives, and Public Policies*, 2nd edn, Harper Collins, New York

Kinsey, A.C., Pomeroy, W. D. and Martin, C.E. 1948, *Sexual Behavior in the Human Male*, W.B. Saunders, Philadelphia

Kippax, S., Connell, R.W., Dowsett, G.W. and Crawford, J. 1993, *Sustaining Safe Sex: Gay Communities Respond to AIDS*, Falmer Press, London

Kippax, S., Crawford, J., Davis, M., Rodden, P. and Dowsett, G.W. 1993, 'Sustaining safe sex: A longitudinal study of a sample of homosexual men', *AIDS*, vol. 7, pp. 257–63

Kippax, S., Crawford, J., Rodden, P. and Benton, K. 1994, *Report on Project Male-Call: National Telephone Survey of Men Who Have Sex With Men*, Australian Government Publishing Service, Canberra

Klein, R. 1990, 'Looking after consumers in the new NHS', *British Medical Journal*, 300, 26 May, pp. 1351–2

——1995, 'Big bang health care reform—does it work?: The case of Britain's 1991 National Health Service reforms', *The Milbank Quarterly*, vol. 73, no. 3, pp. 299–337

Knoke, D. 1990, *Organizing for Collective Action*, Walter de Gruyter, New York

Lather, P. 1991, *Getting Smart: Feminist Research and Pedagogy With/in the Postmodern*, Routledge, New York

Lin, V. and Duckett, S. 1997, 'Structural interests and organisational dimensions of health system reform', in *Health Policy in Australia*, ed. H. Gardner, Oxford University Press, Melbourne

Lindblom, C. E. 1959, 'The science of "muddling through"', *Public Administration Review*, vol. 19, no. 2, pp. 79–88

——1965, *The Intelligence of Democracy*, Free Press, New York

——1990, *Inquiry and Change: The Troubled Attempt to Understand and Shape Society*, Yale University Press, New Haven

Lindblom, C. and Cohen, D. 1979, *Usable Knowledge: Social Science and Social Problem Solving*, Yale University Press, New Haven

Lingard, B. 1996, 'Educational policy making in a postmodern state: On Stephen J. Ball's "Education Reform: A critical and post-structural approach"', *Australian Educational Researcher*, vol. 23, no. 1, pp. 65–91

Machiavelli, N. 1940, *The Prince and the Discourses*, Modern Library, New York

Macklin, J. 1991a, *The Australian Health Jigsaw: Integration of Health Care Delivery*, Commonwealth Department of Health, Housing and Community Services, Canberra

——1991b, *Hospital Services in Australia*, Commonwealth Department of Health, Housing and Community Services, Canberra

Majone, G. 1991, 'Analyzing the public sector: Shortcomings of policy science and political analysis', in *The Public Sector—Challenge for Coordination and Learning*, ed. F-X. Kaufman, de Gruyter, Berlin and New York

Mansfield, B. 1997, *The Challenge of a Better ABC: A Review of the Role and Functions*, Vol. 1, Australian Government Publishing Services, January

Marmor, T.R. and Morone, J.A. 1980, 'Representing consumer interests:

Imbalanced markets, health planning and the HSA's', *Milbank Memorial Fund Quarterly/Health and Society*, vol. 58, no. 1, pp. 125–62

Marris, P. 1996, *The Politics of Uncertainty*, Routledge, London and New York

Masters, G. and McCurry, D. 1990, 'Competency-Based Assessment in the Professions', Research Paper No. 2, National Office of Overseas Skills Recognition, Department of Employment, Education and Training, Australian Government Publishing Service, Canberra

Matrice, D. 1990, *Fair-Play Guidelines for Consumer Researchers*, Australian Government Publishing Service, Canberra

McCaughey, W. 1972, 'Day care—liberating who for what', *Dissent*, 28, Winter, pp. 3–8

McCaughey, W. and Sebastian, P. 1977, *Community Child Care: A Resource Book for Parents and Those Planning Children's Services*, Greenhouse, Carlton, Vic.

McCormack, R. 1991, 'Framing the field: Adult literacies and the future', in *Teaching Critical Social Literacy*, ed. F. Christie, Department of Employment, Education and Training, Canberra

Melucci, A. 1988, 'Social movements and the democratization of everyday life', *Civil Society and the State*, ed. J. Keane, London, Verso

——1989, *Nomads of the Present: Social Movements and Individual Needs in Contemporary Society*, Hutchinson Radius, London

Michaels, E. 1990, *Unbecoming: An AIDS Diary*, EMPress, Sydney

Milio, N. 1988, *Making Policy: A Mozaic of Australian Community Health Policy Development*, Department of Community Services and Health, Australian Government Publishing Service, Canberra

Mintzberg, H. 1987, 'Crafting strategy', *Harvard Business Review*, Jul–Aug., pp. 66–75

Moorhouse, F. 1980, *The Everlasting Secret Family*, Angus & Robertson, Sydney

National Audit Commission 1996, *Report of the National Audit Commission*, chaired by Bob Officer, Australian Government Publishing Service, Canberra, June

National Board of Employment, Education and Training (NBEET) 1992, *Achieving Quality, Higher Education*, Higher Education Council, Canberra

National Centre in HIV Epidemiology and Clinical Research 1997, 'Australian HIV Surveillance Report', vol. 13, no. 2

National Office of Overseas Skills Recognition 1995, 'The Implications of the Implementation of National Competency Standards in the Professions', Final Report, Research Paper No. 9, NOOSR, Department of Employment, Education and Training, Australian Government Publishing Service, Canberra

Nettleton, S. and Harding, G. 1994, 'Protesting patients: A study of complaints submitted to a Family Health Service Authority', *Sociology of Health and Illness*, vol. 16, no. 1, pp. 38–61

New South Wales Government 1995, *Economic Statement for Health*, NSW Health Department, Sydney

New South Wales Health Department 1993, *Leading the way. A Framework* for NSW Mental Health Services 1991–2001, NSW Health Department, Sydney

——1996, Implementation of the Economic Statement for Health, NSW Health Department, Sydney

Nyland, J. 1998, 'Policy activists and the housing reform movement in New South Wales', PhD thesis, submitted in Sociology to Macquarie University

Offe, C. 1984, Contradictions of the Welfare State, Hutchinson, London

Opit, L.J. 1984, 'The cost of health care and health insurance in Australia: Some problems associated with the fee for service system', Social Science and Medicine, vol. 18, no. 11, pp. 967–72

Palmer, G.R. 1978, 'Social and political determinants of changes in health care financing and delivery', in Perspectives in Australian Social Policy, ed. A. Graycar, Macmillan, Melbourne

Palmer, G.R. and Short, S.D. 1994, Health Care and Public Policy: An Australian Analysis, 2nd edn, Macmillan, Melbourne

Papadakis, E. 1984, The Green Movement in West Germany, Croom Helm, London

Parnell, B. 1992, 'Changing behaviour', in AIDS in Australia, eds E. Timewell, V. Minichiello and D. Plummer, Prentice Hall, Sydney

Parnell, B. 1997, Certain Movement Forward into Something We're Not Sure of: Avoiding Further HIV Transmission Amongst Gay Men in Australia, Australian Federation of AIDS Organisations, Sydney

Paton, C. 1992, Competition and Planning in the NHS: The Danger of Unplanned Markets, Chapman Hall, London

Pearse, J. 1996, 'The NSW economic statement for health: using casemix within an equity framework', paper presented to the Eighth National Casemix Conference, Sydney

Phillips, D. 1997, 'The current of change lapping at our ankles', Campus Review, vol. 7, no. 22, p. 12

Plummer D. 1992, 'The medical establishment', in AIDS in Australia, eds E. Timewell, V. Minichiello and D. Plummer, Prentice Hall, Sydney

Plummer, D. 1996, 'The glass ceiling for gay men in Australia's "mainstream" AIDS movement', Proceedings of a Workshop on Prioritising Gay and Homosexually Active Men: HIV/AIDS Social Research, Homophobia, and the Third National HIV/AIDS Strategy, comps. A. Malcolm and G. Dowsett, National Centre in HIV Social Research, Macquarie University, Sydney

Poulson, L. 1996, 'Accountability: A key-word in the discourse of educational reform', Journal of Education Policy, vol. 11, no. 5, pp. 579–92

Pratt, J. and Zeckhauser, R. (eds) 1985, Principals and Agents: The Structure of Business, Harvard Business School Press, Cambridge, Mass

Pusey, M. 1991, Economic Rationalism in Canberra: A Nation-Building State Changes its Mind, Cambridge University Press, Cambridge

Rabinow, P. 1997, 'The history of systems of thought', Ethics, Subjectivity and Truth, M. Foucault New Press, New York

Raymond, J. 1987, Bringing up Children Alone: Policies for Sole Parents, Social Security Review, Canberra

'Review of the Children's Services Programme 1981', unpublished Commonwealth Government Report

Richters, J., Van de Ven, P., Campbell, D., Prestage, G., Crawford, J. and Kippax, S. 1996, 'Sydney Gay Community Surveillance Report No. 3: Update to June 1996', HIV/AIDS and Society Publications, National Centre in HIV Social Research, Macquarie University, Sydney

Roberts, N. and King, P. 1991, 'Policy entrepreneurs: Their activity structure and function in the policy process,' *Journal of Public Administration Research and Theory*, vol. 1, no. 2, pp. 147–75

Rogers, A. and Pilgrim, D. 1991, 'Pulling down churches: Accounting for the British mental health users' movement', *Sociology of Health and Illness*, vol. 13, no. 2, pp. 129–48

Ronalds, C. 1989, 'Residents' Rights in Nursing Homes and Hostels', Final Report, Australian Government Publishing Service, Canberra

Rowse, T. 1985, 'Doing away with ordinary people', *Meanjin*, vol. 44, no. 2, pp. 161–9

Ryan, L. 1990, 'Women and the federal bureaucracy 1972–1983', in *Playing the State: Australian Feminist Interventions*, ed. S. Watson, Allen & Unwin, Sydney

Sabatier, P. 1986, 'Top-down and bottom-up approaches to implementation research: A critical analysis and suggested synthesis', *Journal of Public Policy*, vol. 6, no. 1, pp. 21–48

Sartre, J-P. 1979, 'A plea for intellectuals', *Between Existentialism and Marxism*, Morrow Quill Paperbacks, New York

Sawyer, M. 1990, *Sisters in Suits: Women and Public Policy in Australia*, Allen & Unwin, Australia

Sax, S. 1984, *A Strife of Interests: Politics and Policies in Australian Health Services*, Allen & Unwin, Sydney

Schulman, P.R. 1988, 'The politics of "ideational policy"', *Journal of Politics*, vol. 50, no. 2, pp. 263–91

Scotton R. and Macdonald, C. R. 1993, *The Making of Medibank,* School of Health Services Management, University of NSW, Sydney

Sedgwick, E.K. 1990, *Epistemology of the Closet*, University of California Press, Berkeley CA

Shadish, W., Cook, T. and Levitan, L. 1995, *Foundations of Program Evaluation*, Sage, Newbury Park, London & Delhi

Short, S. D. 1984, 'The medical profession and the shaping of the health care systems in Britain and Australia', Master of Science dissertation, Bedford College, The University of London

——1989, 'Community participation or manipulation? A case study of the Illawarra Cancer Appeal-a-thon', *Community Health Studies*, vol. 8, no. 1, pp. 34–8

——1997, 'Elective affinities: Research and health policy', in *Health Policy in Australia*, ed. H. Gardner, Oxford University Press, Melbourne

Smith, A. 1937, *An Inquiry into the Nature and Causes of the Wealth of Nations*, Modern Library, New York

Spearritt, P. 1974, 'The kindergarten movement: Tradition and change', in *Social Change in Australia: Readings in Sociology*, ed. D. Edgar, Cheshire, Melbourne

Stilwell, F. 1986, *The Accord . . . And Beyond: The Political Economy of the Labor Government*, Pluto Press, Sydney and London

Sydney Star Observer 27 Mar. 1997a, no. 347, Letters to Editor
Sydney Star Observer 17 Apr. 1997b, no. 350, p. 1
Tang, A. 1997, 'The changing role of government in community services: Issues of access and equity to administrative review', *Australian Journal of Public Administration*, vol. 56, no, 2, pp. 95–107
Tenner, E. 1994, 'Learning from the Net', WQ, Summer, pp. 18–28
Thompson, D. 1987, 'Coalitions and conflict in the National Health Service: Some implications for general managers', *Sociology of Health and Illness*, vol. 9, no. 2, pp. 127–53
Treichler, P. A. 1988, 'AIDS, homophobia, and biomedical discourse: An epidemic of signification', in *AIDS: Cultural Analysis, Cultural Activism*, ed. D. Crimp, MIT Press, Cambridge MA
United Kingdom Department of Health 1991, *The Patient's Charter. Raising the Standard,* Her Majesty's Stationery Office, London
Van Maanen, J. 1988, *Tales of the Field: On Writing Ethnography*, University of Chicago Press, Chicago
Van Waarden, F. 1992, 'Dimensions and types of policy networks', *European Journal of Political Research*, vol. 21, nos 1–2, pp. 29–52
Wadsworth, Y. 1984, *Do It Yourself Social Research*, Victorian Council of Social Service and Melbourne Family Care Organisation, Melbourne
——1989, 'Consumers' Health Forum Grants Programme: First Triennium, 1987–1989', Report of Internal Review, Consumers' Health Forum of Australia, Canberra
Wainwright, H. 1994, *Arguments for a New Left: Answering the Free-Market Right,* Blackwell, Oxford
Wanna, J., Forster, J. and Graham, P. (eds) 1996, *Entrepreneurial Management in the Public Sector*, Macmillan, Australia
Watney, S. 1987, *Policing Desire: Pornography, AIDS and the Media*, Methuen, London
Watson, S. (ed.) 1990, *Playing the State: Australian Feminist Interventions*, Allen & Unwin, Sydney
Weber, M. 1948, 'Science as a Vocation', in *From Max Weber*, eds H.H. Gerth and C.W. Mills, Routledge & Kegan Paul, London
Weber, M. 1978, 'Politics as a vocation', in *Max Weber Selections in Translation,* ed. W. G. Runciman, Cambridge University Press, Cambridge
Weeks, J. 1985, *Sexuality and its Discontents: Meanings, Myths and Modern Sexualities*, Routledge & Kegan Paul, London
Weir, M. 1992, 'Ideas and the politics of bounded innovation', in *Structuring Politics: Historical Institutionalism in Comparative Analysis*, eds S. Steinmo, K. Thelen and F. Longstreth, Cambridge University Press, New York
Whitlam, G. 1985, *The Whitlam Government 1972–1975*, Penguin Books, Australia
Wilenski, P. 1977, *Directions for Change*, Government Printer, NSW
——1986, *Public Power and Public Administration*, Hale & Iremonger, New South Wales
——1988, 'Social change as a source of competing values in public

administration', *Australian Journal of Public Administration*, vol. 47, no. 3, pp. 213–22

Williamson, O. 1975, *Markets and Hierarchies*, The Free Press, New York
——1985, *The Economic Institutions of Capitalism: Firms, Markets, Relational Contracting*, The Free Press, New York

Wooldridge, M., 1991, *Health Policy in the Fraser Years 1975–1983*, Department of Administrative Studies, Monash University, Melbourne

Woolgar, S. 1991, *Knowledge and Reflexivity*, Sage, London

World Health Organisation 1986, 'Ottawa Charter for health promotion', *Canadian Journal of Public Health*, vol. 77, no. 6, pp. 425–30

Yeatman, A. 1990, *Bureaucrats, Technocrats, Femocrats: Essays on the Contemporary Australian State*, Allen & Unwin, Sydney
——1994a, *Postmodern Revisionings of the Political*, Routledge, New York and London
——1994b, 'The reform of public management: An overview', *Australian Journal of Public Administration*, vol. 53, no. 3, pp. 287–96
——1995, 'Interpreting contemporary contractualism', in *The State Under Contract*, ed. J. Boston, Bridget Williams Books, Wellington
——1996a, 'The new contractualism: Management reform or a new approach to governance?', in *New Ideas, Better Government*, Australian Fulbright Series, eds P. Weller and G. Davis, Allen & Unwin, Sydney
——1996b, *Getting Real. The Final Report of the Review of the Commonwealth/State Disability Agreement*, Australian Government Publishing Service, Canberra

Yeatman, A. and Sachs, J. 1995, *Making the Links: A Formative Evaluation of the First Year of the Innovative Links Project between Universities and Schools for Teacher Professional Development*, School of Education, Murdoch University, Murdoch, WA

Index

INDEX

National Health Service 134
national health system 112, 114, 115,
178
National HIV/AIDS Strategy 174
National Labor Women's Conference 88
National Office of Overseas Skills
Recognition 11, 58, 59, 64, 69, 70,
71, 72, 73, 74, 76, 77, 235
National Project for Quality Teaching
and Learning 234
national research policy 148, see also
university research policy
National Schools Network 4, 12, 28,
29, 234
national training reform agenda 59,
67, 69, 70, 72, 235
needs 13, 15, 29, 41, 47, 86, 87, 223;
consumer 132, 133, 226; individual
13, 133
needs-based planning 3, 114, 128
neo-classical economics 7, 8, 25, 133
neo-classical economist 26
neo-Keynesian 6
neo-liberal 4, 7; contractualism 4;
rationalist 7
Netherlands 154
network(s) 5, 7, 15, 22, 37, 39, 45,
52, 106, 176, 177, 197, 208, 211,
217, 218, 227, 233 see also issue
networks; enterprise 45; informal
policy 220–1, 227–8, 229, 231–2
networking 3
new contractualism 117
new institutional economics 8
new left 26, 126, 127, 236, see also
participatory democracy
new managerialism 114, 143, 144
new public administration 127, 128;
movement 26
new public health 178; movement 108,
118
new public sector management 124,
139
New South Wales 5, 64, 87, 88, 92,
214, 216, 217
New South Wales Housing
Commission 218, 221, 222, 223,
224, 225, 226, 228, 229, 231, 233
New South Wales Law Society 59, 63,
66, 75
New South Wales Legislative Assembly
173
New South Wales Resource
Distribution Formula 114, 116, 117,
118

New South Wales Royal Commission
172
New Zealand 7, 8, 45, 48, 49
New Zealand on Air 49
News Sheet 94
NHMRC, see National Health and
Medical Research Council
non-government 234; agencies 9, 20;
providers 22; stakeholders 226
non-government organisation(s) 4, 8, 9,
18, 111, 126, 124, 127, 130, 185
non-state organisations 20
NOOSR 12, see National Office of
Overseas Skills Recognition
North America 61, 177
Northern Suburbs Aged Housing
Association 203
Norway 133
NSW, see New South Wales
NSW Labor Women's Committee, see
Labor Women's Committee
nursing 59, 64, 65
Nyland, Julie 5, 7, 10

occupational therapy 64
Office of Child Care 90
Office of the Status of Women 84
officialdom 23
officials 11, 15, 20, 21, 69, 70, 72, 88;
Commonwealth 15; state 15
Old Boys Clubs 172
Older Women's Network 137
ombudsmen 18
operational; formulation 34; statements
116
operational policy 18, 23, 29, 225
opthamologists 65
optometrists 65
Organisation of Economic
Co-operation and Development 133,
151, 154, 162, 163, 236
Ottawa Charter 178
outsource 50
Overseas Aid 127
overseas professional qualifications 11,
12; recognition 57, 70, 71, 72
overseas trained professionals 60, 77

paraprofessional 72
paraprofessions 71, 77
parents 84, 89, 91, 92, 94, 95;
involvement 92; rights 86
Paris Flat Housing Co-operative 206,
210
parliament 85, 125

261